DESIGNS AND FACTIONS

Designs and Factions

Politics, Religion and Ceramics on the Hopi Third Mesa

Lydia L. Wyckoff

UNIVERSITY OF NEW MEXICO PRESS
ALBUQUERQUE

Library of Congress Cataloging-in-Publication Data

Wyckoff, Lydia L.
Designs and factions: politics, religion,
and ceramics on the Hopi Third Mesa / Lydia L. Wyckoff.
p.   cm.
Text originally formed part of author's dissertation
submitted to Yale University for Ph.D. in anthropology.
Includes bibliographical references.
ISBN 0-8263-1178-4
1. Hopi Indians—Pottery.   2. Pottery—Arizona—Third Mesa—Themes, motives.
3. Hopi Indians—Politics and government.   4. Hopi Indians—Social life and customs.
5. Third Mesa (Ariz.)—Social life and customs.   I. Title.
E99.H7W93   1990
979.1'35—dc20   89-22687
CIP

TO DAVID, CHRISTOPHER AND BARBARA
WITH LOVE

CONTENTS

PREFACE

This text originally formed part of my dissertation which was submitted to the Graduate School of Yale University in partial fulfillment of the requirements for a Ph.D. degree in anthropology. I conducted the research in Arizona from March 1979 through September 1980. Research was undertaken as a participant observer and included interviewing Hopis, both potters and non-potters. I also examined collections at the Museum of Northern Arizona in Flagstaff and at the School of American Research in Santa Fe.

After returning to Connecticut in 1980 I spent the following four years preparing this text. As I still lacked important historical and comparative data, I filled this void with material from the National Archives, the Bureau of Census, the Beinecke Library at Yale University, and the Indian Law Resource Center which kindly provided me with exhibits from its *Report to the Hopi Kikmongwis and Other Traditional Hopi Leaders on Docket 196*. I also examined the Hopi ceramic collections at Wesleyan University, the Peabody Museum at Harvard University, the Museum of Natural History, and the Museum of the American Indian.

In the following study I have used the Hopi orthography in Voegelin and Voegelin (1957); when ceramic container terms have been transcribed differently from their usage, this has been indicated, as has the number of informants who provided the information on which my folk classification of ceramics is based. Hopi words within quotation marks remain as written by these authors. The names of villages, ceremonies and deities, and the term for village chief, kikmongwi, are given in their most commonly written form, as are bahana and sipapu. The glossary at the back of the book also includes Hopi ceramic terms.

Apart from well-known potters and persons already deceased, the names of individual Third Mesa potters who appear in the present work are my own invention.

Fairfield, CT
1989

ACKNOWLEDGMENTS

The research for this work was supported by the Yale Center for American Art and Material Culture and the Yale Committee on Archaeology. I express my sincere gratitude to Professor Michael D. Coe of the Department of Anthropology, Yale University, who supervised all phases of my work.

I would like to extend my thanks to the members of my dissertation committee— Professor Michael D. Coe, Professor Frank Hole and Professor Keith Basso. I would also like to recognize the following members and former members of the department for their help in various phases of my work: Professor Irving Rouse, Ellen Messer, Harry Merrick, Elizabeth Kyburg, and Kristine Rodriguez. Members of the Peabody Museum staff likewise assisted me, specifically Barbara L. Narendra; David Kiputh, who drew some of the illustrations (Map 1, Figs. 1 and 6); and William K. Sacco who photographed the plates, excluding Plates 1–4. Anne F. Wilde, formerly of the Yale University Press, edited the first draft of this manuscript.

I relied on the help of innumerable individuals and institutions both in the Northeast and the Southwest. My special thanks are due Barbara and Michael Stanislawski, then of the School of American Research; Willard Walker of the Department of Anthropology, Wesleyan University; Lea S. McChesney and Barbara Isaac of the Peabody Museum, Harvard University; and the staffs of the Museum of Northern Arizona; The American Museum of Natural History; the Museum of the American Indian; the Tuba City Indian Hospital, Public Health Service; the Hopi Tribal Council and Northland Pioneer College.

I also wish to express my gratitude to my family whose love and support was unerring.

Finally, I will forever be in debt to the Hopis who endured my stay and whose friendship made it possible for this study to be as complete as it is. It is my sincere wish that peace and harmony will come to you all.

CHAPTER ONE

INTRODUCTION

The official Hopi attitude toward Anglo-Americans was made clear to me on a cold March day in 1979 when I first read the sign at the entrance to Oraibi:

WARNING   WARNING

NO OUTSIDE WHITE VISITORS ALLOWED BECAUSE OF YOUR FAILURE TO OBEY THE LAWS OF OUR TRIBE AS WELL AS THE LAWS OF YOUR OWN. THIS VILLAGE IS HEREBY CLOSED.

On that day I also met for the first time an Oraibi potter who was to become a close friend.

Hopis, like other pueblo peoples, have become extremely wary of outsiders. This is hardly surprising in view of the Hopi experience of Spanish, Mexican, and Anglo-American dominance. Continued theft of their religious artifacts, the insensitivity of tourists, and the fact that outsiders, including anthropologists, who work on the reservation have no lasting commitments, have all served to reinforce the Hopis' suspicions.

I was at Oraibi that day in 1979 to begin research for this study. My first trip to the Southwest had been made the year before at the suggestion of Michael Coe, my

dissertation advisor at Yale. My research aimed to determine if my proposed area of inquiry, the relationship between ceramic decoration and world view, was valid and if so applicable to cultures in the Southwest. I remained there from April until August 1978, on grants from the Yale Center for American Art and Material Culture and the Yale Committee on Archaeology. During this time I worked for the Zuni Tribe for more than two months, visited the Eastern pueblos, and examined ceramic collections, specifically that of the School of American Research in Santa Fe. While in Santa Fe I spoke with Michael Stanislawski, whose studies of contemporary First Mesa Hopi and Tewa ceramics are well known (1969a, b, 1978), and he recommended that I work with the Hopi of Third Mesa.

Third Mesa is the westernmost mesa within the Hopi Reservation in northeastern Arizona. It is here that Oraibi, occupied since the thirteenth century, is located (Map 1). Although the pottery of First Mesa has been well documented, it is commonly believed by Anglo-Americans that the women who occupy the villages on or below Third Mesa do not make pottery.

The popular belief that ceramics are not made on Third Mesa exists because most Third Mesa pottery is either sold to Anglo-Americans as coming from First Mesa or bartered with other Hopis or pueblo peoples. Potters who sell their wares as

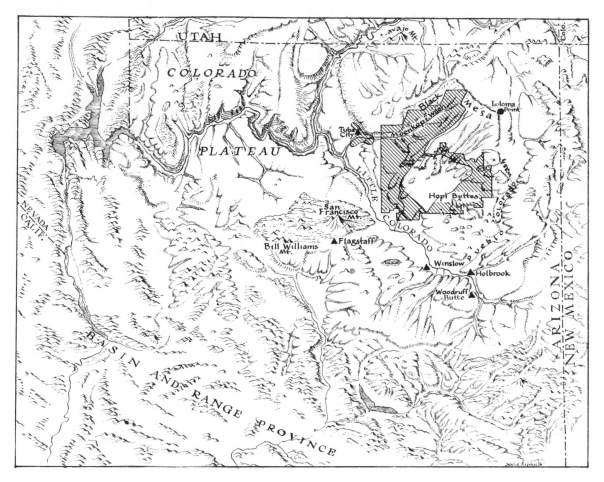

Map 1. The Southwest, showing the location of Hopi lands.

First Mesa pottery are permitted to do so by the residents of First Mesa who vigorously maintain control of the Anglo-American pottery market. First Mesa potters only permit access to this market to Third Mesa potters who have kin on First Mesa. Although some potters who do not have kin on First Mesa may sell some unpainted pottery as coming from Third Mesa, most of the pottery made by these potters is for local use or inter-pueblo barter.

Ceramics on Third Mesa are not of singular economic importance. In fact, this study sample of 115 ceramics by Third Mesa potters represents the entire year-long production of over half of these potters. As a cultural product, however, ceramics function in a multitude of ways, and my aim was to understand what those ways were, to examine what I have termed the "ceramic domain," which lies within the web of culture. Culture, as Clifford Geertz writes, is a web of "significance [man] himself has spun" (1973: 5), and material culture, whether in the form of pottery, blankets or automobiles, is a component of culture. As a component of culture, it occurred to me, stylistic attributes of ceramic decoration might reflect "world view."

Third Mesa embodies in miniature the history of the Hopi people and the conflicts that face them today. People are torn between past and present and divided according to their response to Anglo-American dominance. These conflicts affect how Hopis view the world around them and are expressed in the styles of pottery decoration Third Mesa women produce.

After my brief investigation of Third Mesa pottery in March of 1979 it was apparent that Third Mesa begged further study. I also realized, however, that the presence of Anglo-Americans was a source of deep conflict, as the sign at Oraibi had illustrated. Nevertheless, in June 1979 my husband and I and our eleven-year-old son moved to Tuba City, an agency town, and remained for sixteen months. The presence of my family turned out to add immeasurably to my research. My husband, a psychiatrist, worked in the Indian Health Service Hospital, our son attended the Tuba City public school, and our daughter, who arrived later, taught in the Bureau of Indian Affairs (B.I.A.) school. Adding to our intense involvement in Hopi life was my driving at least once a week between Tuba City and Third Mesa. On those days my car became the Hopi bus. All of these activities brought us into contact with Hopis and provided for us a privileged view of their world.

During this period I also spent four days in Flagstaff examining and photographing the Hopi pottery collection at the Museum of Northern Arizona, accompanied by the daughter of a Hopi potter from Oraibi. I wished to share my research with her, for I

had informed the potters of Third Mesa and my Hopi friends about the study I was undertaking. They not only gave me permission to examine, measure, and photograph their pottery, but also spent hours helping me acquire a working knowledge of the Hopi language.

Although I knew the Hopi were divided into Progressives and Traditionalists before our arrival in June of 1979, it was only after several months that I began to realize the depth of this division. The political-religious division between Traditionalists and Progressives is all-pervasive on Third Mesa. It determines where one lives and how, in that Traditionalists shun such modern conveniences as electricity and running water. It also influences where one works, since Traditionalists will not work for the Tribal Council but will work for the Indian Health Service and the B.I.A. In Tuba City and the adjacent Hopi village of Moencopi it even affects what school Hopi children attend. It also determines the style in which a potter works.

The differences between Progressives and Traditionalists lie in the relationship between Hopis and the modern world of the white man. Although Hopi myths indicate that factionalism has long been a part of Hopi culture it has centered around the presence of dominant foreign cultures since the arrival of the Spanish in the sixteenth century. It was because of the division among Hopis about whether or not to accept Catholic missions that Hopis destroyed the village of Awatovi in the eighteenth century. Later, with the arrival of Anglo-Americans, dissension between Hopis friendly and hostile to United States policies forced the division of Oraibi in 1906.

The division between "Friendlies" and

"Hostiles," as they were called by Anglo-Americans, concerned whether or not to accept the forced education policy of the United States government. The larger difference was whether or not to comply with or accept Anglo-American rules and values or to reject them and actively resist Anglo-American pressure. Although the line between Hopi and Anglo-American values is constantly shifting, this acceptance or rejection remains the fundamental difference between Progressives and Traditionalists.

Today Hopis have accepted the value Anglo-Americans place on their own educational system. Likewise, to a greater or lesser extent, all Hopis have been drawn into the American political system and cash economy. Progressives and Traditionalists differ, however, in what they believe should be the role of cash and the American government. Progressives support the Tribal Council as an organization which functions within the Anglo-American political system and serves to bring to the Hopi Reservation the material benefits of the dominant culture. Thus, the Tribal Council supports the construction of power lines and water mains and grants leases for strip mining. Traditionalists, on the other hand, reject the Tribal Council as contrary to the indigenous Hopi religious-political system. They consider the introduction of modern conveniences as but another means to force Hopis to become part of the Anglo-American economy, in which cash income is a necessity. They argue that this makes the Hopi less self-sufficient and fosters a decline in subsistence farming.

The recent division of the Hopi-Navajo Joint Use Area has further divided Hopis because the Traditionalists see the land division as another way for the United States Government to erode their aboriginal land base. Our residence in Tuba City was most fortunate because it permitted us neutrality in the face of these factional pressures. In order to conduct unbiased research as a participating observer I had to be extremely careful not to alienate members of either the Traditionalist or Progressive factions.

Neutrality required constant vigilance and even-handed allocation of my time. One or two nights a week I lodged with a family in Hotevilla, a stronghold of traditionalism. During the day I participated in household activities: cleaning, planting, collecting wild foods and craft materials, and making pottery. Weekends as well we usually spent with Traditionalist friends because it was a time of religious activity.

But I also taught at the New Oraibi branch of Northland Pioneer College, then located across from the office of the Progressive Hopi Tribal Council. The college is not directly affiliated with the Council but is part of the Arizona State college system. My work at Northland Pioneer College brought me into contact with Progressives whose potters likewise welcomed me into their homes and shared their lives with me.

My husband worked with both Progressive and Traditionalist Hopis. Our son attended the Tuba City public school where he made friends with his classmates, some of whom came from the adjacent Traditionalist village of Lower Moencopi. When our daughter joined us in December she accepted a teaching position at Moencopi Day School, where Progressives from Upper Moencopi send their children. This was extremely helpful. I had become good friends with a Traditionalist family in the lower village and had consequently been unable to establish rapport with many Progressives of the upper village. Our daughter's presence at the day school further alleviated my isolation from Hopi Progressives.

The differences between Traditionalists and Progressives, I discovered, were not mere social preference, party politics or economic policies but were so fundamental that each group conceived of the world around them differently. Traditionalists believe, in contrast to Progressives, that social distance must be maintained between them and the surrounding dominant society. Traditionalists, for instance, are clearly aware of the relationship between subsistence farming and their religion, and of the way religious organization intermeshes with social organization. Progressives, on the other hand, actively pursue the capitalist ethic, are frequently willing to leave their villages and kin in pursuit of wage labor; many have even become Christians and Mormons. It is these differences that are expressed in the different styles of decoration Traditionalist and Progressive potters apply to their pottery.

The concept of "world view" is a useful one in anthropology. Geertz defines a culture's world view as

> their picture of the way things in sheer ac-
> tuality are, their concept of nature, of self,
> of society. It contains their most compre-
> hensive idea of order. Religious belief and
> ritual confront and mutually confirm one
> another; the ethos [the moral, subjective
> aspect of culture] is made intellectually rea-
> sonable by being shown to represent a way
> of life implied by the actual state of affairs
> which the world-view describes, and the
> world-view is made emotionally acceptable

by being presented as an image of an actual state of affairs of which such a life is an authentic expression (1958: 421–22).

A given group's world view will therefore include their concept of natural and social space. Although world view provides a conscious ordering system, it also becomes internalized and therefore subconscious. As Arnheim concluded from his psychological studies of Anglo-American society:

> Every act of seeing is a visual judg-
> ment. . . . Visual judgments are not con-
> tributions of the intellect, added after the
> seeing is done. They are immediate and in-
> dispensable ingredients of the act of seeing
> itself (1954: 2).

These judgments are culturally determined and are part of a given culture's view of the world.

I argue that the different styles of decoration used by Progressive and Traditionalist potters are a material expression of their world views, their beliefs about the way things ought to be and "in sheer actuality are." Throughout the manufacturing process, potters make decisions based on lineage affiliation, place of residence and the vessel's use. Although function determines the general shape and size of a vessel whether made by Traditionalists or Progressives, it does not determine ceramic decoration. It is in ceramic decoration that a potter unconsciously expresses concepts of natural and social order. So, even though pots, at least by Progressives, are made and painted to be sold, the decoration is consonant with the potter's own aesthetic sense. In fact, it was through conversations about what potters consider and classify in Hopi as a "beautiful vessel" that I became aware of the significance of spatial relationships on the painted surface of the pot. The different design structures used by Progressives and Traditionalists parallel their differing concepts of the nature of Hopi/Anglo-American relations and consequently parallel their view of the world around them. These different structural styles are also found in furniture placement and in children's drawings. Thus, things as seemingly insignificant and unconscious as the arrangement of chairs in a room reiterate and reinforce cultural or subcultural differences. This use of space is critically important to our understanding of the relationship between material culture and the culture that produces it.

Material culture can no longer be considered a mere reflection of cultural values but as an active cultural component (Munn 1973). As an active component of culture, material objects have been manipulated to reinforce ethnic boundaries or subgroup variation (Hodder 1982). The styles of Third Mesa ceramic decoration do reinforce subgroup differences, and not just as symbolic expressions of subgroup identity but as material expressions of world views.

Stylistic differences have also been examined as they serve to communicate information (Wobst 1977). Contemporary examples include the nurse's dress, wedding rings, and military insignia. Since much of the information conveyed by these objects would be known without them by relatives and friends, the importance of this form of communication increases with social distance between the sender and the receiver, providing the receiver knows how to read the code. Since the Traditionalist ceramic style is seldom recognized as even being Hopi beyond the boundaries of Third Mesa proper where everyone knows who is Traditionalist and Progressive, communication does not appear to be chiefly important.

It seems to me, therefore, that if stylistic differences are a reiteration of differences in world view, then the communication of cultural differences is a by-product of the primary function of style which is to reiterate and reinforce cultural or subcultural values. This study of the ceramic domain, then, adds to our knowledge of Hopi culture by revealing the depth of the division between Progressives and Traditionalists. As one Hopi potter said, "We are two different people now."

And as the two different styles of painted decoration reinforce and communicate different world views, a new analogy for the construction of models for the interpretation of ceramic variation in the archaeological record emerges. It is hoped that this study, therefore, may contribute to what Renfrew (1983) has termed "cognitive archaeology."

CHAPTER TWO

THE HOPI AND THEIR SETTING

INTRODUCTION

The Hopi people among whom I lived inhabit the high barren desert of northeast Arizona, a land of harsh beauty and limitless vistas. They are a sedentary group, living in permanent villages located below or at the tops of mesas. Oraibi, the village that posted the sign excluding white people, is said to be the oldest continuously inhabited town on the North American continent. Archaeological evidence indicates that it has been occupied since the thirteenth century. The Hopi are quite different from their neighboring tribe, the Navajo, who are pasturalists. The Hopi lifestyle is similar to that of the Pueblo people of the Rio Grande who are also farmers and village-dwellers.

While pueblo peoples further East were dominated by the white man at an early date, the Hopi managed to keep much of their culture intact. This continuity and the beauty of their crafts and the complexity of their cosmology have long exerted a fascination over Anglo-Americans.

The Hopi have inspired ethnographic writings since Thomas Keam established the first trading post in the area in 1875. Fortunately, from the very beginning the bearers of Anglo-American culture have either been accompanied by ethnographers or have themselves become ethnographers. The first two studies of the Hopi made at the end of the nineteenth century were by interested amateurs, as was commonly the case when anthropology was but a developing discipline.

Alexander Stephen, a friend of trader Thomas Keam, worked among the Hopi through the 1890s and helped Keam collect pots for sale through the trading post. Stephen's study, not published until 1936, primarily concerns the Hopi who occupied the eastern villages of First Mesa, although Stephen did visit Second and Third Mesa to the west. Stephen's keen observation and participation in Hopi daily life make his accounts invaluable. In 1893 the second of the amateurs, Mennonite missionary Henry R. Voth, came to Third Mesa; his detailed accounts of Hopi ceremonies (1901, 1903a, b, 1905, 1912) are still some of the best ones available.

In the 1920s, the Hopi were studied for the first time by trained anthropologists when students of this new science showed an interest in them. These researchers focused on symbolism and individual expression in ceramic decoration (Bunzel 1929) and religion (Parsons 1939). In the early 1930s, what was to be an extremely important field party in ethnology was organized under the leadership of Professor Leslie A. White. The graduate students in this party were Fred Eggan, Ed Kennard, Jess Spirer, and Mischa Titiev. This and later follow-up fieldwork on Third Mesa led to important studies of Hopi kinship and social organization (Eggan 1950) and of social and ceremonial life and cultural change (Titiev 1944). The work of this group along with the earlier work of Stephen, Voth and Parsons form the foundation of our knowledge of the Hopi people. The extent to which these anthropologists became involved with the Hopi is shown by the fact that the Bureau of Indian Affairs asked Eggan to evaluate the feasibility of Hopi self-government in the 1930s. Tragically, Eggan's support of independent village government went unheeded and the Tribal Council, countering tradition by placing one government over all the villages, was established. The division between the Traditionalists and Progressives dates from this time and is based on support for or opposition to the Tribal Council.

Shortly after the fieldwork conducted by Eggan and others, Hack (1942) studied Hopi physical environment and farming practices, and in 1938 Leo Simmons (1942) recorded the autobiography of Don Talayesva, a Hopi from Third Mesa.[1] Thus, the period that Traditionalists consider a time when "things were the way they ought to be"—the period before the establishment of the Tribal Council—has been recorded.

Since the period of intense research in the 1930s, Hopi studies have been primarily concerned with religion (Bradfield 1973; Hieb 1972; Waters 1963), myth and folklore (Courlander 1971, 1982; Malotki and Lomatuway'ma 1984), cultural change (Nagata 1970; Thompson 1950), and material culture.[2] All of these studies, including my own, have built upon the excellent work conducted in the 1930s, and the writings of Stephen and Voth.[3]

My interest is in the different world views that Traditionalists and Progressives express in their pottery. In order to understand the division between Progressives and Traditionalists it is important to understand their shared cultural heritage. Their relationship to that cultural heritage is what defines them as either Progressive or Traditionalist. For example, the social organization described by Eggan in the 1930s is the Traditionalists' ideal of village autonomy under a hereditary chief-priest. Progressives, on the other hand, reject this political-religious system in favor of the Tribal Council and, in some instances, village councils. All Traditionalists, in contrast to Progressives, practice the traditional Hopi religion and reject Christianity, and are acutely aware of the intermeshing of social organization, religion and agriculture.

For the Traditionalists, the Hopi ceremonial cycle, albeit not as complete as it was at the turn of the century, parallels their agricultural cycle. It is also an enactment of their concepts of time and space, which are quite different from those held by the dominant Anglo-American society. Many Progressives, on the other hand, have fallen away from this traditional religion and have even converted to Christianity or Mormonism.

Traditionalists and Progressives have diverged so far that they view the reservation itself quite differently. All Hopis consider the three reservation areas recognized by the federal government—District 6, Hopi Partitioned Land and Moencopi Wash—as only a fraction of their land (Map 1). They also lay claim to the Colorado Plateau from Navajo Mountain in the north to Bill Williams Mountain in the west and to Loloma Point in the east. They also claim the Tusayan washes area, including the Little Colorado River and the Pueblo Colorado Wash to Woodruff Butte. Included in this area are the Grand Canyon and the San Francisco Peaks. The Hopi's claim is based on their traditional religious beliefs, oral history, and aboriginal land use. Hopis recognize that it is unrealistic to hope for the return of all of the land but attitudes toward the land held by Traditionalists and Progressives are very different.

Progressives conceive of the three areas recognized by the United States Government as a political unit that should be developed by Hopis for the economic benefit of all. Traditionalists, by contrast, do not recognize these areas as a political unit but rather as part of the sacred area defined by the four mountains. Traditionalists believe this land may be used but not individually owned or harmed, since it belongs to Masaw, the god of fire and death.

The following descriptions of this land, the agricultural cycle that takes place upon it and the gods who rule it summarize the foundations upon which traditional Hopis have constructed their lives.

PHYSICAL ENVIRONMENT

The Hopi Reservation is located in northeastern Arizona on the high, dry Colorado Plateau. The land there has been eroded into buttes and flat-topped mesas cut by deep canyons, the most famous of which is the Grand Canyon. This cutting has been done by rivers and streams which, except for the Colorado and San Juan Rivers, flow only during spring snowmelt or after a rainstorm. Most Hopis live in fifteen settlements on top of or just below three mesas, called First, Second, and Third Mesas.

In this harsh desert region, inland from the Atlantic Ocean and the Gulf of Mexico and cut off from the Pacific coast by a mountain barrier, moisture is scant and is governed by altitude. The northern Hopi lands rise to 7,500 feet above sea level and annually receive between fourteen and sixteen inches of precipitation as snow or rain, the most of any part of the reservation. The mean average temperature in this northern area is approximately 48°F (Hack 1942: 6). As the land gradually slopes toward the south, precipitation decreases with the elevation, and temperatures increase. The lowest part of the reservation is the Moencopi Area to the west of the high mesas. It lies at 4,500 feet above sea level and has an average mean temperature of 55°F (Whiting 1939: 5, 9) but only six to seven inches (annual mean) of precipitation.

In addition to the scant rains which feed the intermittently running streams, there are also small seepage springs located along the edges of the mesas. These create oases where large cottonwoods and willows grow. The experience of crossing this arid region and descending a sand dune, to be greeted by the honking of waterfowl bursting from between cattails in the shade of a cottonwood, is not easily forgotten. The availability of this underground water supply has always been critical for Hopi sedentary village life because springs have always supplied drinking water. It is not surprising that the annual ceremonies performed by the Hopi are directed toward rain and that one is for the continuation of these important springs, for water is precious in this arid land.

Southwest of the mesas the San Francisco

Peaks, the result of comparatively recent volcanic activity, rise dramatically more than 12,000 feet above the high semidesert plateau. Snow usually remains on these peaks throughout the summer in marked contrast to the hot, arid lands below. The cool, moist upper regions of the San Francisco Peaks support thick stands of fir, spruce, and aspen as well as a variety of grasses and ferns. On the lower slopes are stands of yellow pine and Douglas fir.

On the mesa tops where many Hopis live are scattered piñon trees, juniper, and sagebrush. In the still lower Tusayan washes area, and up the wash valleys, blue grama grass and drop seed grow, as well as such shrubs as Mormon tea, greasewood, saltbush, snakeweed, and rabbitbrush.

All of these microenvironments are utilized by traditional Hopis. Men undertake the long-distance collection of herbs and aspen for ceremonies from the San Francisco Peaks. Before the introduction of concrete building blocks, yellow pine and Douglas fir from here or the northern slopes of Black Mesa were used for house construction. Women collected wild vegetables, seasonings, and herbs found closer to the villages.

SUBSISTENCE

Collected Plants

Although the Hopi are farmers, collected plants provided an important means of sustenance as recently as the 1930s (Whiting 1939: 18). Even today, wild vegetables are still important to Traditionalist residents of Third Mesa who have neither irrigation to grow vegetables nor much cash with which to buy them.

Beeweed (*Cleome serrulata*) is a primary Third Mesa green vegetable. Other important greens include pigweed, once critical if crops failed (Whiting 1939: 20–21, 74), wormwood (*Artemisia dracunculoides*), and two types of beebalm (*Monarda menthaefolia* and *Poliomintha incana*). Many Hopis eagerly collect a wild lettuce (*Pectis angustifolia*) along the lower washes. At the Niman ceremony children still commonly chew cattails, although such natural snacks have largely been replaced by corn chips and candy.

Hopis still make "lemonade" from sumac (*Rhus trilobata*) and "tea" from *Tetradymia canescens* and *Thelesperma gracile*. The latter is so popular that I saw no commercial tea in a traditional Hopi household. By contrast, coffee, sugar, and bread are found in all Hopi households.

Other collected plants which are still of great importance include rabbitbrush (*Chrysothamnus*), *Parryella filifolia* for making wicker plaques, yucca for coiled plaques and sifters, and juniper for firewood and roof repair. Cottonwood is used for the manufacture of Kachina dolls; rabbitbrush (*Thelesperma gracile*) flowers, and sunflower seeds are used for dyes. Sunflower seeds are also used to oil the stones on which piki bread is cooked. Medicine men and women collect a variety of herbs including *Onosmodium* which is mixed with wild tobacco and ceremonially smoked.

Traditionalists tend to collect more plants since many Progressives reject the Hopi religion and are part of the cash economy. Most Third Mesa Hopis over the age of fifty, however, collect herbs from time to time whether they are Traditionalist or Progressive.

Livestock and Wage Labor

Livestock and wage labor have become more and more important for Hopi subsistence. With the coming of the Spaniards and the introduction of sheep, livestock gradually replaced hunting as a source of meat. As will be discussed later, cattle and wage labor have become a primary source of cash income in recent years, although agriculture continues to be important, particularly for Traditionalists.

Agriculture

At the time of Spanish contact corn, beans, squash, and cotton grew on the mesas and in the Tusayan washes area. Men were and still are responsible for the agriculture, although today they are frequently joined by women during planting and harvesting. Hopi farming remains subsistence farming in that production and consumption are geared to the survival of local groups. Hopis do not grow produce for outside markets nor is their production controlled either by the Anglo-American economy or the United States government.

This does not mean that people eat only what they grow. Farm produce is extensively exchanged as gifts, especially in ceremonial contexts. Hopi parents may give as much as fifty pounds of blue cornmeal as a "gift" in exchange for a basketry plaque given their child at his Kachina initiation ceremony (Nagata 1970: 149). Since a child will receive six to eight plaques on such an occasion, the amount of corn involved becomes considerable. Fruit and melons are also widely exchanged, usually between kin, but with the clear understanding that the gift-giving will be reciprocated. Hopi still barter produce with the Navajo for mutton and occasionally for jewelry, and sometimes sell produce to the Navajo for cash.

Agriculture in the Hopi area is difficult and insecure. At the high altitudes where there is reliable precipitation there are too few frost-free days to permit crops to ripen. Hopi agricultural techniques, therefore, must exploit the available moisture within the limited area that is sufficiently warm. For this reason corn, the staple Hopi crop, is planted between eight and ten inches deep for its roots to reach the underground water, necessitating a minimum of 120 to 150 frost-free days for the corn to ripen.

According to Hack (1942: 8), District 6 and the more southerly portions of the Hopi Partitioned Land have just enough frost-free days. Moencopi enjoys more, and so has been an important Third Mesa farming colony supplying food to Oraibi on the mesa top.

Hopi agriculture today is very similar to that described by Hack (1942) in the 1940s. Most corn is still planted in two-to-four-acre fields at the mouth of a wash where the stream spreads and the flow ceases. After a heavy rain, usually in July and August when the land is dry and the moisture from the winter snows has dissipated, flash floods wet the fields.

Dry farming is practiced most extensively on Third Mesa. The sand dunes on top of and along the slopes of the mesa are used as fields. This windswept sand is called "Hopi gold" by the people of Third Mesa, and they take great care to protect it by constructing rock and rabbitbrush windbreaks. Although corn and beans are grown in these sandy fields, the favorite crops are peaches and melons, which were introduced by the Spanish.

Forde (1931) has provided a detailed description of Hopi farming techniques; they have changed little since the late 1920s when he made his observations. However, a number of Hopis now use chemical fertilizer, mixing a handful with the damp sand at the base of the seed hole. Another innovation in Hopi farming is the tractor. On Third Mesa large cornfields are now usually plowed in the spring before planting so that the previous year's cornstalks may be mixed into the soil and left to fertilize dry fields.

The agricultural cycle begins in late February or March when fields are cleared of any growth that might decrease the available moisture and windbreaks are repaired or built. The first corn is planted toward the end of April to provide corn for the Niman ceremony in July. The main planting season is in May, when corn, beans, squash, melons, and other vegetables are planted. Occasionally, a planting stick of the type illustrated by Forde (1931: 389) is used to make the seed hole, but more commonly a metal pipe or pick is used. Planting is sometimes delayed because of cold or strong spring winds.

Throughout the growing season, Hopis carefully weed their fields. Sweet corn is harvested from August to September and eaten immediately. The main harvest of flour corn begins in late September and extends through October. Flour corn is commonly classified according to its color—yellow, blue, red, white, black, and speckled—and after harvest is sorted and stored and stacked like wood according to color. These different colored corns are associated with the cardinal directions and the nadir and zenith. Likewise, varieties of the Tepary bean and lima bean are known by their colors. Seeds for the "Indian triad" (corn, beans, and squash) to be used ceremonially or sown the following year are chosen from the best produce harvested, then carefully packed in tins or hung from the ceiling in bags or pottery jars.

The agricultural cycle not only provides food to eat but gives shape to the Hopi year. The repeating cycle of planting-growth-harvesting parallels the Hopi ceremonial cycle.

RELIGION AND MYTH

Ritual

All Hopi Traditionalists adhere to the traditional religion. Since the early descriptions of Hopi religious ceremonies and the first accounts of their mythology, there have been changes. New myths have emerged and some ceremonies are now seldom held. Today the most complete ceremonial cycles are maintained at the Traditionalist villages of Shongopavi and Mishongovi on Second Mesa and Hotevilla on Third Mesa, although originally, it is believed, each village held its own complete cycle. Today increased mobility made possible by the pickup truck and automobile has made it possible for people from other villages to attend ceremonies at another location. On Third Mesa the decline in the population of Oraibi, the sole village there until 1906, and the increased population of Moencopi, which was only a small farming colony in 1906, have encouraged the creation of a ceremonial cycle shared between them, although Oraibi remains the traditional religious center. Similarly, many residents of Bacavi belong to religious organizations in Hotevilla, and the ceremonial cycle has all but disappeared from villages that are Progressive.

The ceremonial cycle (Fig. 1) is a preparation for the agricultural cycle and tries to guarantee its success. The ceremonial cycle also enacts the emergence and maturation of the Hopi people, thus

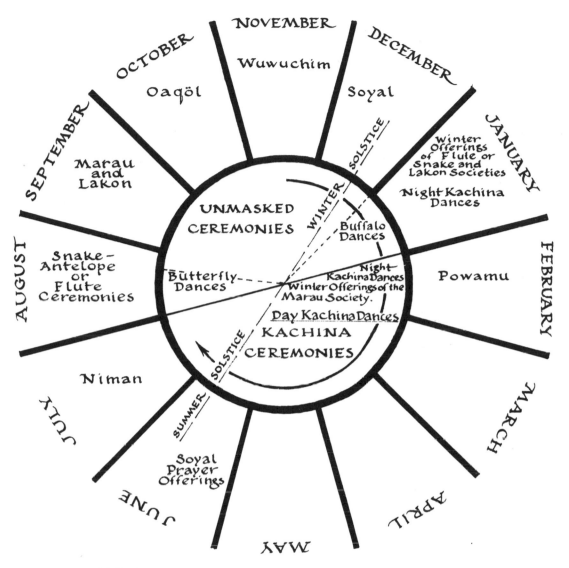

Figure 1. Ceremonial Cycle.

reinforcing their traditional identification with agriculture.

The first of the great winter ceremonies is Wuwuchim, which marks the beginning of the Hopi ritual cycle and the Hopi beginning in this, the Fourth World. It is held in November and begins with the "new fire" ceremony dedicated to Masaw, the god of death and fire who owns this world. Periodically Wuwuchim is extended to include the initiation ceremony. Initiation into manhood involves a reenactment of the emergence of the Hopi people.

The second great winter ceremony is Soyal, held at the winter solstice. Throughout the Soyal ceremony the reciprocity between male and female is emphasized. On Third Mesa two men impersonate two important Kachinas (*monqácina*) or spirits, the Soyal and the Mastop Kachinas. The Soyal Kachina appears briefly and walks like a child, "signifying that new life is being born" (Waters 1963: 155). The Mastop Kachina represents "the male power of fertility" and simulates copulation with Hopi women before leaving the village. The female earth has now been fertilized by the male sun.

Powamu in February is the third important winter ceremony. At it the god Muingwa brings about germination. As part of this ritual, beans are planted in the kivas eight days before the ceremony. The sprouted bean plants are then distributed to all households in the village by the men impersonating the Kachinas. With this ceremony, the agricultural cycle has been symbolically completed and the Kachinas have symbolically fed the Hopi.

The Kachinas are deeply revered and are central to the Hopi ceremonial cycle. Among the Hopi the Kachinas are as easily recognized as pictures of Jesus or the Virgin are among devout Catholics. They are the "breath" of the deceased, of past ancestors, animals, birds, and plants. Kachinas can take on cloud form or become cloud people, and as such they bring to the Hopi the gift of rain, so critical in their agriculturally marginal area. Because the dead can become Kachinas, who in turn can become clouds and bring rain, death maintains life and is a necessary phase of one recurrent cycle.

To the Hopi, death, like birth and initiation, is a transition from one stage to another. Traditional burial rites include giving a new name to the deceased and washing his or her hair in yucca suds. These two acts, significantly, are also part of the Naming and Initiation ceremonies.

Hopi burial rites also used to include placing a cotton "cloud mask" on the face of the deceased (Stephen 1936, 2:825). This reference to the Kachinas through the depiction of rain clouds further stresses the interrelationship of death and life made possible by rain. Hieb (1979: 577) has called rain the "spiritual essence of *navala*" of the Kachina as cloud people.

Although cause for deep family sorrow, the death of someone advanced in years (sixty or more) is considered appropriate and is usually met with quick acceptance.

Traditional Hopis believe that on the fourth morning after the burial, the $hík^{w}i$, or breath of the dead person, leaves his grave and, nourished by the food left at the grave site, journeys to the underworld where it may take on the attributes of the Kachinas. This land of the dead to which the soul travels is the place in which a soul's "genius" lived before it was embodied. Although the dead may become Kachinas or Cloud People, they also continue to exist in the underworld very much as they did on earth. They live in villages, farm their fields, and maintain the ceremonial cycle. The ceremonial cycle in the underworld, however, is reversed, with its seasons reflecting a mirror image of this world.

To illustrate: The yearly ceremonial cycle of the Hopi is divided into two parts. From Soyal, held at the winter solstice, to Niman, held at the first moon following the summer solstice, the Kachinas are present in Hopi land. Therefore, they appear at dances impersonated by men—as the Mastop Kachina at Soyal or as the bean-plant-distributing Kachinas at Powamu.

From Niman to Soyal, however, the Kachinas reside in the underworld and do not appear at Hopi ceremonies. Because the Kachinas' ceremonial cycle is enacted below in reverse, the Hopi hold a shortened form of the Kachinas' ceremonies six months before their own actual ceremony. This shortened ceremony refers to the main ceremony the Kachinas are holding below at the same time (Titiev 1944: 175). There are exceptions to this: neither Wuwuchim nor Powamu are given in their shortened form when these ceremonies are supposedly being held in the underworld because these two ceremonies are believed to involve the inhabitants of both worlds.

With the Niman ceremony or "Home Dance" in July the Kachinas depart for the underworld. By this time, Hopi farmers have planted their crops and the Kachinas, again impersonated by male dancers, receive gifts of green corn and melons, the "first fruits" of the Hopi fields. In this ceremony Hopis symbolically "pay back" the Kachina who fed them at Powamu, thereby enacting the recriprocal relationship Hopis believe exists between them and the spirit world. The Kachinas, who have lived at the Hopi villages since Soyal, now leave the villages to return to the San Francisco Peaks, their sipapu or place of emergence from the underworld. From here the Kachinas maintain their reciprocal relationship with the Hopi. They are the rain clouds that form on the Peaks in the summer and, carried by the prevailing winds, drift toward the Hopi mesas.

The Snake-Antelope ceremony of August attracted the attention of early Anglo-American visitors (Bourke 1884; Donaldson 1893; Dorsey and Voth 1902; Fewkes 1894; Stephen 1936; Voth 1903a), because the priests dance with snakes. The Snake Society is primarily concerned with the rain, whereas the Antelope Society is concerned with the maturing of the crops, which depends upon rain. The Snake Dance is shaped by the Hopi belief that the snakes released after the ceremony will carry the prayers of the Hopi to the underworld spirits.

The Flute ceremony, which alternates yearly with the Snake-Antelope ceremony, is concerned with the relationship of the springs and the villages. The crops depend upon rain for survival, but the villages depend upon the springs for drinking water.

The last three ceremonies within the cycle are Marau, Lakon, and Oaqöl. They have been described as "harvest festivals" (Bradfield 1973: 169) and are conducted by the women's societies with the aid of male priests. In these ceremonies reciprocity is enacted between men and women because, traditionally, the men harvested the fields while the women returned the produce to them in the form of food. This exchange is acted out symbolically by women who present baskets to the men at the conclusion of the ceremony.

Reciprocity between kin is at the center of both the Buffalo and Butterfly Dances, traditionally held in January and at the beginning of August. These are the only dances in which social organization is directly enacted in Hopi ritual. The boys usually dance with their "aunts" so that the girls' partners are their brother's sons or their father's brother, or ceremonial mother's brothers or their sons. Since clan membership is matrilineal, the partners are always from a different clan than the principal dancers. The partners, however, are all considered kin to the principal dancers. The primary importance of the dances is that they enact kin allegiance based on reciprocity, for gifts are presented to the Buffalo and Butterfly dancers by the

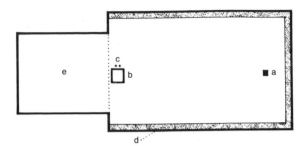

Figure 2. Kiva ground plan. (a) sipapu, (b) stove, (c) ladder, (d) ledges used as benches, (e) elevated section.

partner's clan lineage. The gifts in turn are "paid back" by the Buffalo or Butterfly dancers' lineage. Today a gift of pottery is expected from the Butterfly dancers' lineage.

Hopi ceremonies are elaborate prayer presentations. They usually comprise two sets of four days each plus a preliminary day, nine days in all. The three major winter ceremonies—Wuwuchim, Soyal, and Powamu—span twenty days in the years of Wuwuchim and Powamu initiation; otherwise these three ceremonies last sixteen days. Although there are variations, all ceremonies employ the same ritual elements: the making of prayer sticks, construction of altars, consecration of medicine water, ritual smoking, offerings of corn meal, and prayer and songs.[4]

The first eight days of a ceremony are devoted to prayer, conducted in the kiva, or underground ceremonial chamber (Fig. 2). Each kiva is constructed and "owned" by a particular clan or clans. The Hopi kiva is usually rectangular, with primary access by means of a ladder passing through a trap door in the roof. Symbolically, the kiva occupies an intermediary place between the upper world of the living and the lower world of the spirits. The floor is divided

into an elevated platform for the public and a larger lower level with benches along three walls for the participants. Where the lower level abuts the platform there is a "firepit," and an adjacent ladder to a smoke hole entrance in the ceiling. A hole symbolizing the sipapu, or place of emergence, is at the other end of the lower level. Ordinarily covered with a wooden plug, the sipapu is uncovered during ceremonies so that the spirits in the underworld can hear the prayers, songs, and dances. Ritual smoking is an important part of activities in the kiva evidently because smoke is linked to clouds (Stephen 1936: 106) and clouds to Kachinas.

One of the most important objects in the kiva is the "six-directional altar" (Fewkes 1927, pl. 3; Stephen 1936: 286, 512–13, 526) consisting of six lines drawn with sacred cornmeal. On these lines are six ears of colored corn, one each of yellow, blue, red, white, black, and speckled. The colors are associated with the four cardinal directions: yellow is north, blue is west, red is south, and white is east. The directions of above and below are portrayed by a diagonal line of sacred cornmeal. Above is black, and below is all colors (sometimes gray). Quartz crystals and other minerals may also be placed on the six directional lines, and other religious objects associated with specific ceremonies may be added.

On the ground in front of or around an altar are placed *tipóni*, fetishes of the chiefs (Stephen 1936: 1305), and carved wooden figures of deities. A *nahíkiypi*, or medicine bowl containing consecrated spring water, is placed in the center of the six-directional altar from consecration until the ninth day.

In addition to prayers in the kiva, a public dance held in the plaza is an integral part of most ceremonies. Each village has one or more plazas that are little more than wide streets. The most important one contains a sanctuary under which the fetish of the village is buried; this sanctuary is considered the center of the village. The public dances held there are the only parts of the Hopi ceremonies that outsiders may see.

Ceremonial dancers commonly carry gourd rattles in their hands and wear tortoise-shell rattles on their legs. When the dancers are Kachina impersonators, they may also wear a white ceremonial kilt embroidered with representations of rain clouds (see Fig. 18 in Chapter 6) and falling rain. Around their waists they wear either a white sash with a long fringe symbolizing rain or a sash embroidered with cloud symbols. Their limbs are frequently painted with the colors of the four cardinal directions. Stephen has referred to this painting as "chromatic prayer, as it is definitely regarded as a direct appeal to the four directions to hasten with rain to Hopi land" (Bradfield 1973: 50). Kachina impersonators also wear masks which are cleaned and repainted before each ceremony to renew the power of the Kachina within it. Before they undertake this deep religious responsibility the dancers purify themselves through prayer and abstinence.

Each ceremony is considered to "belong" to one or another of the villages' several matrilineal clans, although the participants come from a number of clans. According to myth, the relationship between each clan and its ceremony was established during the migration of the clans and their arrival at the Hopi mesas.

As this survey shows, maintenance of the ceremonial cycle makes enormous demands on every member of a Traditionalist village.

The men spend considerable time in the kiva praying, preparing costumes and practicing. For the women it is a time of incessant cooking. They must feed not only their families at home but also the men in the kiva. And, they must prepare food to be given as gifts.

Myth

While the Hopi ceremonial cycle stresses the relationship between religion and agriculture, and by extension, the interrelatedness of life and death, the Hopi emergence myth defines the relationship between the Hopi and Tawa, the Creator. It describes the Hopi's passage through three worlds which are successively destroyed before they arrive in this one, the Fourth World. The myth means that the Hopi may choose to follow the Creator's plan, or choose to ignore it. If they follow it, life will be sustained, but if they fail, if they are *qahópi* (not Hopi/not good), life will be destroyed.

In the traditional Hopi religion there are numerous gods; H. S. Colton (1947) has suggested that there may be as many as thirty-six. The most important are: Muingwa (god of germination); Masaw (god of death); Tuwavonytumsi (Sand young woman—the earth); Kogyengwuti (Spider Woman); Talatimsi (Daylight young woman/Dawn Woman); Sotuknangwu (god of the stars); Poqanhoya and Palongawhoya (the Twin Wargods).

It was Tawa the sungod, however, who was instrumental in bringing Hopi people into existence. He is the Creator and Father of the Hopi. In the beginning Tawa existed in endless space. He apprehended the concept of life, planned the proper order of things, and created the first world the Hopi were to inhabit.[5]

In the First World, Spider Woman created man "to understand the meaning of things" (Courlander 1971: 18) and "to give thanks to the Creator" (Waters 1963: 7) who wanted them to live in harmony. In this world, man was not yet human. At first the people were happy, but then Lavayihoya (the Talker) came. As a result, the people started gossiping and fighting, so as punishment Tawa destroyed their world by fire. Some people, however, remained true to the Creator's plan of harmony and peace, so they were hidden in the Ant Kiva. According to Waters (ibid. 13), they were put into the Ant Kiva to learn a lesson from the Ant People.

The Second World created by Tawa was less perfect, although man was further separated from animals. Tawa destroyed the Second World by freezing it, for again the majority had failed to follow his plan. This time they had been greedy and had made war. The faithful were once more hidden with the Ant People.

Emerging into the Third World the people found themselves fully human. But now it was more difficult for them to listen to the Creator because, as adults, the soft spots on their heads had become too hard. Pride led to war, "husbands sought other women and wives sought other men" (Courlander 1971: 19), excrement was smeared on the old people (Wallis 1936: 2), and all was confusion. This world was destroyed by a flood. The faithful, however, escaped up a reed as the waters rose.

When they arrived in the Fourth World, whose protector was Masaw, the Hopi were divided into "tribes," including one of "white men," and were told that Bahana, the White Brother, would some day return and help them. The Hopi were further divided into clans and began their

migrations. At this time the relationship was established between each clan and the animal, plant, bird, or natural object from which it took its name.

WORLD VIEW

Traditionally, Hopi religion functions to organize and define the Hopi world. It establishes the beginning of time and the genesis of man. It structures time and space and it sanctifies social structure. For the devout Traditionalist today religion validates life and makes understandable the radical changes that have taken place as the result of Anglo-American dominance.

The principles of duality and reciprocity are central to traditional Hopi religion and thought. The traditional importance of duality can be seen in the myth of creation and emergence. If this myth is divided into a series of like episodes (Fig. 3) two sets of opposites emerge—Creation and Destruction, and Differentiation and Unification.

In this myth the binary opposites of Differentiation and Unification are not reconciled. Differentiation between men leads to inequity and conflict which in turn cause destruction and death. Unification and equality in the Creator's plan are emphasized by the sheltering of the chosen people in the Ant Kiva. The ant hill is the ideal, a place where there is peace, happiness, and harmony, where all Hopi activity is directed toward the single goal of sustaining and perpetuating life. This is the ideal, but it fails because of human desire and greed (column C). As creation itself leads to differentiation, the Creator's ideal is possible only through destruction and death.

This belief colors the Hopi approach to

Hopi Myth of the Four Worlds

A Creation	B Differentiation into Multiples	C Opposition (Conflict)	D Destruction	E Unification
I First World (Endless Space)	Solids/waters Air/living creatures	*Lavaihoya*—talker Arguments—conflict	World destroyed	
				People in Ant Kiva (hill)
II Second World (Dark Midnight)	Buyers/sellers People who have/ have not	Greed—fighting War	World frozen	
				People in Ant Kiva (hill)
III Third World	Creation/ destruction Man adult Human Men/women	War	World flooded	
				People in reed (bamboo)
IV Fourth World (World Complete)	Tribes/clans Mountains/valleys Grass/trees			

Figure 3. Episodic segments of the Hopi creation and emergence myths.

everyday life. Today, as Progressives strive for tribal unity under the council, Traditionalists affirm that the ideal of Hopi unity will take place only with the destruction of this world. Before the destruction, say Third Mesa Traditionalists, all the people, Hopi or not, who choose to follow the Creator's plan will gather at Oraibi. Presumably Tawa will remove them to a safe place while he destroys the earth.

If the duality of creation and destruction is equated with life and death, this duality, in contrast to differentiation and unification, is reconciled. These two opposites are reciprocal and mediated by time—creation leads to destruction, destruction leads to creation. In myth, therefore, duality is also sanctioned as a division within the cycle of time.

Traditionally, the Hopi also sees a dual division of time and space in the sun's daily movement. As recorded by Titiev (1944: 173) the Hopi traditionally believe that:

> The sun has two entrances, variously referred to as houses, homes or kivas, situated at each extremity of its course. In the morning the sun is supposed to emerge from its eastern house, and in the evening, it is said to descend into its western home. During the night the sun must travel underground from west to east in order to be ready to rise at its accustomed place the next day. Hence day and night are reversed in the upper and lower worlds, for while it is light above, it is dark below and vice versa. . . . The same principle that is used to account for the alternation of day and night is likewise employed to explain the annual alternation of winters and summers, for the Hopi believe that these two are caused by the sun's movements between the upper and lower realms.[6]

According to Waters (1963: 191) the

Road of Life coincides with the movement of the sun, and so "man travels west at death to re-enter the *sepapuni* and return to the world below. Here he is reborn." Life and death are then also mirror images. Death is birth in the underworld and, therefore, many Hopi burial practices parallel those of birth.

Creation and destruction, death and life, night and day, winter and summer, then, are not in "binary opposition" (Lévi-Strauss 1963) like the opposites of differentiation and unification, but alternate as part of the continuity of life, a principle acted out in the ceremonial cycle, which also dramatizes the reciprocity under which the continuity is maintained.

Reciprocity is essential to an understanding of Hopi religion and thought. Tawa created the Hopi because he wanted them "to sing his praises." In turn, he ensures that life will be maintained. Prayer and prayer offerings are understood to be presentations which require a reciprocal exchange. The gods and the Kachinas are obligated to "pay back" the giver.

Death makes life possible because the Kachinas are the breath of the deceased; Kachinas feed the Hopi, and the Hopi ritually feed the Kachinas. The dead living in the underworld require the day and the summer; hence, this world must experience night and winter. Again, reciprocity is necessary in order to maintain life.

Reciprocity is also critical for male/female division. The sun (Tawa) is "father" whereas the earth (Tuwavonytumsi) is "mother"; the village chief (kikmongwi) is father to the village, which is mother. Traditionally labor was also clearly divided as being for males or for females. This division, and the reciprocal nature of the interdependency of men and women, is ritually acted out in the Marau, Lakon, and Oaqöl ceremonies.

Although the Hopi concept of duality is important, it is but one aspect of a broader classification based on the principle of correspondence. Above corresponds with below and north with south. East (associated with birth in the world, sunrise, and the winter solstice) corresponds with west (associated with death, sunset, and the summer solstice). Colors and numbers also correspond to these directions which are ritually portrayed in the six-directional altar.

This sixfold space, color, and number paradigm governs virtually every ritual act the Hopi makes, from the order in which dances are performed to the way in which the masks and bodies of the Kachina dancers are painted. This classification system is, for the Hopi, a statement of the way the world is, and thus to use Geertz's terms (1966: 7), a "model for" the way things "ought" to be. Everything falls within it—clouds and butterflies (Stephen 1936: 779), corn (Voth 1912: 26–27), lightning (Voth 1901: 127–28), rains and winds (Stephen 1936: 638), birds (ibid. 517), animals (ibid. 1325), trees, shrubs, flowers (Whiting 1939: 45) and beans (Stephen 1936: 354). This six-directional color and number paradigm is the Hopi apprehension of "natural order" and it affects all but the most acculturated Hopis regardless of their religion.

SOCIAL ORGANIZATION

Kinship

The traditional Hopi religion also defines and sanctions Hopi social organization.

Central to this organization is the clan, which Eggan (1950: 62) has described as the outstanding feature of Hopi social life.

According to myth, at their emergence into this world the Hopi divided into clans and then set out on separate migrations, during which many of the events linking clans together took place. These events, such as one clan's encounter with a bear and another's use of his hide, joined clans to form phratries which are exogamous clan groupings. It was also during this time that clans acquired specific forms of ritual knowledge. Because of this knowledge, which was considered useful for the entire community, clans were admitted to the villages. Clan control of specific ceremonies is therefore given mythical sanction.

Today, Hopi clans are landholding units. Traditionally, all members of a matrilineal clan believed they were descended through the female line from a common ancestor who could be traced back to the time of their emergence. Clans are still usually exogamous in that the Hopi do not marry within their clan.

Within each village there are several matrilineal clans named after some object or aspect of nature. Each has one or more "partner" clans; although these are not considered to be genealogically related, they traditionally formed exogamous phratries. Phratries are unnamed per se and, when referred to, are usually called after the clan that holds the most important ceremonial position.[7]

Although some clans and their ceremonies are more important than others, each clan is considered part of the fabric of the village, for each ceremony is part of the ceremonial cycle.

Within a given village, a clan is represented by one of the matrilineages that make it up.[8] The matrilineage is, therefore, from the Hopi point of view, the clan segment of a village. Such lineages are given no name other than that of the clan. Although conceived of as continuing back to the emergence, in reality lineage members can be named only for the preceding four to six generations. The clan lineage, or the most important lineage of a clan within a village, maintains the clan house. The head woman of this lineage, who is therefore the head woman of the clan in the village, will usually occupy this house in which the ritual objects and paraphernalia of the clan are kept. Thus, within each traditional village the clan is both a landholding unit and the basic ritual unit.

Within the boundary of each village, floodwater farming areas and irrigated garden areas are usually divided among the clans, the best land being set aside for the most important one. Clan land is commonly inherited by the women and worked by their husbands, who are frequently assisted by their sons and brothers-in-law. Clan land disputes are settled, if possible, by the clan chief chosen from the older men in the clan. By contrast outlying fields are usually inherited along non-clan lines, passed from father to son.

From birth a child is a member of his or her mother's clan. Because of the clans' strength and importance, they have the potential to disrupt the social fabric of the village. However, most Hopis participate in two other memberships which link the children with clans outside their own or their father's; thus, individual clan strength is weakened and village unity promoted.

Shortly after birth the infant becomes a "child" of its father's clan and phratry through a form of adoption (Bradfield

1973: 11–30). For a twenty-day period after the birth, the infant is taken care of by paternal aunts and the paternal grandmother. During this time an ear of corn or "corn mother" is placed in the cradle with the infant. At the end of the twenty days the child is named by the paternal grandmother and aunts. Once adopted the child should neither marry into the father's clan nor into any of the clans within the father's phratry.

For Hopis who follow the traditional religion, the kinship network is further extended upon a child's initiation at prepubescence into either the Kachina or Powamu society, marking the child's introduction into Hopi society as a whole. For the initiation, the child's parents choose a ceremonial father for a boy and a ceremonial mother for a girl, traditionally from a clan outside the phratries of either the natural father or mother. According to Eggan (1950: 27), this method of selection is intended "to give [a boy or girl] another group of relatives for he [she] is adopted into the ceremonial father's [or mother's] clan and becomes related to the whole phratry group."

The ceremonial parent now guides and educates the child in ceremonial affairs. The girl may join the society of her ceremonial mother and the boy will be initiated into the society of the ceremonial father during the Wuwuchim ceremony. A boy may also belong to the society "owned" by his clan, but this usually occurs only if he is specifically chosen and trained by a maternal grandfather or uncle to be his replacement. Most men of a lineage belong to the society or societies of their ceremonial father. This membership, like that of the Kachina or Powamu societies, cuts across clan lines and weakens lineage

allegiance and, therefore, unites the village.

Although women may join the Marau, Lakon, or Oaqöl society, these societies do not provide them the ceremonial bonding that occurs among the men. The household and immediate family are instead the focal point of women's lives.

The Household

Traditionally, the Hopi household consisted of the extended family whose residence was in the mother's village. In Traditionalist villages today, related families still usually remain in the area of the village allotted to the clan, where they are in constant contact with one another. Labor is shared, and sisters' children move at will between their "mothers'" houses. If a sister should die, become emotionally unstable, or leave the Reservation, her children are automatically taken into the household of another sister. This system provides considerable stability for the women and children and for the husband if he comes from the same village. The husband, however, frequently comes from another village, and thus his status and ceremonial obligations are associated with his lineage there rather than with the village of his wife and offspring.

Today, however, much of this has changed. Where once a newly married couple lived in the wife's mother's house, now the nuclear family single home has become so much a part of Hopi society that it is considered the husband's duty to provide a house for his wife.

Progressive nuclear families not only prefer to live independently but frequently choose to live near the place of the husband's employment rather than in the village of the wife's matrilineage. Although this is occasionally true for Traditionalists as well, matrilocality is preferred and remains the ideal.

The Village

Traditionally the Hopi could not be considered a "tribe," as there was no indigenous secular or religious authority that united the Hopi as a whole. Ethnic identity was based on a shared religion and language (a Shoshonean language within the Uto-Aztecan family) and a pueblo lifestyle. Each Hopi village was an autonomous landholding unit.

Today, of the fifteen named Hopi settlements, excluding the agency town of Keams Canyon, ten are landholding units. On First Mesa these are Walpi, Sichomovi, and Hano; on Second Mesa Shongopavi, Shipaulovi, and Mishongovi; on Third Mesa Oraibi, Lower Oraibi, Hotevilla and Bacavi.

All these villages, except for New Oraibi, Hotevilla and Bacavi, were founded between the thirteenth and eighteenth centuries. Some of the older mesa-top villages are among the most traditional of all the Hopi settlements; people there do things the old way without electricity or running water. The First Mesa village of Hano, however, is anomalous. According to Dozier (1966) Hano was created in 1700 when Tewa from the Rio Grande Valley were given their village site and agricultural land around it in return for their services as warriors for the Hopi. In Hano people speak Tewa, a language distinct from the Hopi tongue spoken only 100 yards away at Sichomovi.

New Oraibi, founded in the early 1900s, and Lower and Upper Moencopi are not located on the mesa tops. Until 1959 Lower and Upper Moencopi were a single village. The original Moencopi had been an Oraibi farming colony located on part of Oraibi's outlying land. Moencopi's position as an Oraibi colony may have been part of a pre-contact pattern.

The pre-contact pattern may actually have included three villages—the mother village, the colonial village and the guard village. At First Mesa, for instance, Walpi is the mother village and Sichomovi is the colonial village dependent on Walpi "for religious initiation" (Connelly 1979: 540). Hano is the guard village for Walpi. On Second Mesa, Shongopavi is the mother village, Shipaulovi the colonial village and Mishongovi the guard village, established according to legend to watch for the arrival of the white man (Nequatewa 1936: 39). In a similar way the original Moencopi was ceremonially dependent on the mother village of Oraibi on Third Mesa.

There are other more recent settlements founded as a result of Anglo-American contact. Most of these are located along Arizona State Road 264 and are politically Progressive. Most of the Hopi population growth is taking place in these new settlements because they provide electricity and running water and an easier way of life.

Below First and Second Mesa, "suburbs" have developed whose residents may retain the landholding rights (Forde 1931: 377) they have in the parent village on the mesa top. The oldest of these "suburbs" is Polacca, begun in the 1900s, which has now become the largest Hopi settlement in District 6. Polacca is largely a settlement of development-style houses stretching along Arizona State Road 264; many of its residents do retain First Mesa landholding rights and some even maintain a mesa-top residence for use during ceremonial occasions. Below Second Mesa, Torvera, a small settlement of converted Hopis, clusters around the Baptist Mission founded in 1901. Also below the mesa, along the paved road (Arizona Route 264), are a number of houses, a trailer park, and the Second Mesa Day School. This group of buildings is sometimes referred to as "downstairs" or ʔitá·ki·tpik, as opposed to the villages, which are ʔó:va, on top of the mesa.

In Traditionalist villages there still exists a hereditary group of priests or chiefs. The head chief is called a kikmongwi (kikmóŋʷi) or "village chief," whose position is hereditary but may rotate among chiefs (Eggan 1950: 106–7). The relative importance of the kikmongwi varies from village to village but in recent years their authority has been limited by the Tribal Council.

Although since the coming of the white man there has been factionalism within villages because of differences of opinion about how the villages should respond to the white newcomers—Oraibi split into traditional and progressive factions in 1906, for instance—some anthropologists believe that such factionalism has always been a part of Hopi village life.

The traditional lack of centralized tribal authority coupled with village factionalism, frequently along clan lines, led Titiev (1944: 68) to conclude:

> Never has any town been entirely free from strife, and never has a leader arisen to mold the autonomous villages into a coor- dinated unit worthy of being called a tribe. Whatever other talents they may possess, the Hopi do not have the gift of statecraft.

According to Titiev (65–68) village factionalism is the result of "the great emphasis on individual freedom, the lack of a political mechanism to enforce policy and, lastly, the lack of an authority to unify the divisions of clans, phratries and religious societies." For traditional Hopis it is irrational to have a "police force," for they believe that tradition has established "correct behavior" and it is incumbent upon the individual to act accordingly. Hopis can choose to plant their crops or not, join a religious society or not, participate in community activities or not. As Titiev (65) writes, "the phrase 'Piumi' ('It's up to you') may well be the motto of Hopi society."

Although harmonious unity is the Hopi ideal it has not always been maintained. In fact, Hopi social life is properly understood as an ongoing process of homogeneity and differentiation, the model for which is the Hopi creation myth.

The ideal of the harmonious village and the reality of Hopi factionalism parallel the binary opposites of unification and differentiation in the creation and emergence myth. The ideal village is like the mythological Ant Kiva where everyone works together for the good of the community, but differentiation within the village, such as occurred at Oraibi in 1906, has led to destruction and strife.

Today's division between Progressives and Traditionalists dates from the 1930s and the establishment of the Tribal Council. Traditionalists wish to maintain the cultural values, social organization and religious practices that existed before the Council was established and, for the most part, before the period of intensive Anglo- American contact in the 1880s.

But factionalism within villages and between villages has been a recurrent theme in Hopi history. It is only against the backdrop of this history that the contemporary factionalism between residents of one mesa and another and between Progressives and Traditionalists can be fully understood.

Although the individual is in many ways free to do what he wishes, each act is considered either *hópi* (Hopi/good) or *qahópi* (not Hopi/not good). Thus in a Hopi village, where privacy is out of the question, public opinion is the primary mechanism for behavioral conformity. In the past the war chief may have had some enforcement authority, and today, in Traditionalist villages, Kachinas as impersonated by Hopis can request that appropriate behavior be observed. The Kachina impersonators, however, cannot enforce their will. If a person's antisocial behavior becomes extreme, he or she is considered to be either a witch or bewitched. Accusations of witchcraft may have functioned in the past to control deviant behavior, particularly the excessive acquisition of goods or the hoarding of produce, both of which Hopis frown on.

Accusations of witchcraft are still common today. Several of the potters I talked to believed witchcraft was being used against them, and mental illness, physical problems, failure and even premature death are often attributed to it. Jealousy of another's success and a desire for personal gain are often given as reasons for the use of witchcraft.

The effects of witchcraft reach beyond the individual, however. Hopis believe witches cause a lack of harmony, and such social discord may prevent the rains from falling or cause the crops to fail.

NOTES

1. Two other Hopis from Third Mesa have more recently written or dictated their own biographies (Carlson 1964; Udall 1969) as has a Tewa from First Mesa (Yava 1982).

2. Anglo-American interest in Hopi material culture has a long history. Keam and Stephen made an extensive collection of artifacts in the late nineteenth century, the bulk of which are now at the Peabody Museum, Harvard University (Wade and McChesney 1980, 1981). Voth collected Hopi material for the Field Columbian Museum, Chicago, and for the Fred Harvey Company of Harvey House hotel and restaurant fame. The Harvey collections are now at the American Museum of Natural History and the Museum of the American Indian, Heye Foundation, New York, and at the Heard Museum, Phoenix (B. Wright 1979). During this early period of acquisition collections were also made for the Smithsonian Institution by Stevenson (1883) and later by Fewkes (1898, 1919) who excavated the ruins at Sikyatki. In the 1920s Bunzel worked with the potters of First Mesa and in 1935 the Peabody Museum (Harvard) began excavations at Awatovi (Montgomery, Smith, and Brew 1949; Smith 1952, 1971; Olsen and Wheeler 1978). In 1926 the Museum of Northern Arizona was established; as will be discussed in detail, the Museum played an important role in the development and specialization of Hopi crafts (McKenna 1983) but, enthralled by the beauty of First Mesa Sikyatki Revival ceramics, it ignored the ceramic production of Third Mesa. This played a significant role in fostering the popular belief that ceramics ceased to be produced on Third Mesa. During the 1960s the Stanislawskis (1969a, b, 1973, 1978) conducted ethnoarchaeological research on First Mesa.

3. For a comprehensive and annotated bibliography of Hopi research see Laird, 1977.

4. The most extensive descriptions are found in Bradfield (1973); Dorsey and Voth (1901); Stephen (1936); Titiev (1944); Voth (1901, 1903a, b, 1912); and Waters (1963).

5. There are many accounts of Hopi origin: Cushing 1923: 163–70; Hopi Hearings: 1955; Nequatewa 1936: 7–34; Stephen 1929: 3–13; Voth 1905: 1–16.

6. This concept determined the traditional naming of the months. At Oraibi the calendar was as follows (Titiev 1944: 174):

WINTER		SUMMER	
Kel-muya	November	Kel-muya	June
Kya-muya	December	Kya-muya	July
Pa-muya	January	Pa-muya	August
Powa-muya	February	Powa-muya	September
Isu-muya	March	Angok-muya	October
Kwiya-muya	April	Isu-muya	October
Hakiton-muya	May		

7. As the Kachinas are the spirits of deceased ancestors, the Kachina rituals should act as a model for clan relations. As previously stated, the *monqácina* are the most important Kachinas and they appear only singly. Most Kachinas are dressed and dance alike, and rain, upon which life depends, is brought by all the Kachinas. Thus, although some are more important than others, they are equally important in the maintenance of life. This is also true of Hopi clans and their social and ceremonial function. For a ceremony to be successful, everyone present must "open his head" to the Creator, thus the restriction against covering one's head during a ceremony. The ritual must be carried out in harmonious unity if it is to be successful and, traditionally, the ceremonial cycle, which demands the participation of everyone in the village, has to be completed in order to maintain life. Likewise, as the ceremonies within the cycle are owned by separate clans, all the clans must act together to maintain

life. It appears, therefore, that two opposites exist in Hopi social organization and Kachina presentations—equality and unification as opposed to inequality and differentiation.

8. Kinship terminology clearly indicates the importance of the matrilineage or clan segment in Hopi thought. The Hopi kinship system is "classificatory"; Eggan (1950: 19) has stated that "the Hopi have emphasized the *social recognition* at the expense of the *genealogical relations*." Genealogical distinction, in fact, is important only within the lineage, not for outsiders attached by marriage. In Ego's father's lineage, for example, all the women are "grandmothers" or "father's sisters," and all the men are "fathers." In the mother's father's lineage, which stands in a similar position to Ego as it is related through marriage, the women are "grandmothers" and the men "grandfathers," regardless of generation. Men marrying women of Ego's own generation and below are simply termed "male relatives-in-law." All women marrying into Ego's own lineage are, regardless of generation, classed as "female relatives-in-law" and are regarded with a degree of caution and suspicion. In contrast to these classifications is the lineage itself. Particularly important is the fact that children call their mother and mother's sisters "mother," and that sisters call one another's children "child" and grandchildren "grandchild." These terms indicate the importance of the matrilineage, made manifest in the extended family based on matrilocal residence and, traditionally, occupancy of a single household.

CHAPTER THREE

HOPI HISTORY AND THIRD MESA VILLAGES

INTRODUCTION

In 1540 when the Spanish conquistadors arrived in the Southwest a new chapter in Hopi life began. The 336 Spanish soldiers, of whom 250 were mounted, entered the Southwest under the command of Francisco Vásquez de Coronado. The first village encountered was the Zuni pueblo of Háwikuh which was quickly taken. From there a force was dispatched to the Hopi villages where a virtual repetition of the Háwikuh episode followed: Spanish calling for obedience to God and the king; Hopis demanding that they leave; Spaniards approaching; Hopis resisting; Spanish storming the village; Hopi surrender.

Coronado's expedition in 1540 set the tone for Hopi-White relations. Although very different in their approaches, Spanish and United States policies had in common military domination followed by a policy of assimilation to force Hopis to become civilized, productive citizens as defined by the dominant society. Both the Spanish and the Anglo-Americans were determined to stamp out the uncivilized behavior of Hopis through conversion and education.

For the Spanish, conversion meant conversion to the Catholicism brought by the missionary fathers and a willingness to labor for the benefit of the crown. For the Americans, conversion meant incorporation into the American cash economy, the

relinquishment of Hopi language and religion and attendance at one of the American-run boarding schools—in short, conversion meant becoming an American.

In either case, the result for the Hopi was the same. The most significant and long-lasting effect of white contact with the Hopi has been the fission of the Hopi people into two opposing and hostile camps.

The long-term existence of inter- and intrapueblo conflict is evident in the creation and migration myths. Central to the Hopi creation myth is the opposition between differentiation and unification. In this myth differences cause Hopis to attack one another and destroy each other's villages in a drastic falling away from the mythical ideal of the cooperative ant hill, a theme which is repeated in the clan migration myths and the reason why, Hopis explain, there are so many prehistoric ruins, each of which is claimed by a clan.

It is also possible that the exhaustion of locally limited natural resources created village fission long before the arrival of the Spanish. Some Hopis, in fact, say that this was why the village of Oraibi split in 1906.

In short, the extent to which village factionalism existed before the arrival of the Spanish will never be known. What is certain, however, is that after the Spanish and their missionaries arrived, Hopi society fractured along quite specific lines. There were Hopis who were friendly to the Spanish and who converted to Catholicism, and there were Hopis who resisted the Spanish and opposed Catholicism.

These two groups confronted one another in 1700 at Awatovi, where Hopis hostile to the Spanish killed village residents who had converted to the faith of their conquerors. But this was only a minor victory in a struggle that was eventually to be lost. With the arrival of the Americans in the 1840s, the rift dividing Hopis deepened.

While Spanish contact with Hopis was military and missionary with the goal of incorporating them into the Spanish political system, the American policy was initially one of isolation as expressed in the reservation system. The American policy, which had gradually developed since the 1850s, was based on the belief that Native Americans were barbarians who needed to be civilized. American policymakers thought that if Hopis became Christians, were educated, and became property owners they would be able to become productive capitalists.

Given United States governmental policy it is not surprising that the earliest force for change was the Indian trader and the basis for this contact was economic.

In 1875 Thomas Keam established the first trading post among the Hopi in the canyon named for him. This brought Hopis into increased contact with Anglo-American society and introduced them to a cash economy. Hopis bartered or sold crafts at the trading post, allowing the craftsmen to remain at home and, initially, to supplement their home-grown diet with cash purchases such as coffee and sugar. As "Indian-made" goods became popular with tourists, the total cash income from crafts for the Hopi, excluding trading-post barter, reached $10,000 in 1891 (Donaldson 1893: 46).

In the following decade an even more important event took place when the first boarding school was established on the reservation.

The Hopi boarding school was established in 1887 in some converted buildings at the trading post in Keams Canyon. The American government believed that if Hopi children were removed from their parents and families, they would abandon their heathen ways. Native American societies with their barbaric influences could then be broken apart (Spicer 1962: 348).

The forced removal of children from their families in order to attend school, frequently not to return home for one to four years, was one of the most divisive forces in Hopi history. Just as the Hopi had been divided on the issue of the re-establishment of Spanish missions after the Pueblo Revolt, so they were now divided in their attitude toward education.

American Indian educational policies were designed to encourage the Native American to become an American capitalist. In this manner the schools drew the Hopi further into the American economic system, a process begun by the establishment of the trading post.

Also central to American policy toward the Indian was the idea that the basis of civilization was in knowing how to manage individual property. Policymakers now argued that if Native Americans were given individual land instead of land assigned as a tribal reservation, they would become industrious Christians and desire to be like other civilized Anglo-Americans. This was the reasoning behind the allotment of land as prescribed by the Dawes Act of 1887.

Although the government's attempt to break up clan land into individual allotments was abandoned in the 1890s because of hostile resistance, the capitalist ethic had become an integral part of any exposure to Anglo-American society, be it at the trading post or in boarding school. Consequently, more and more Hopis began to join the cash economy, further dividing the Hopi by placing the educated wage earners, even if not Christian, in opposition to the agricultural Hopis, who almost always practiced the traditional religion.

Both the Hopi and the federal government recognized the division. American government officials called the group that supported federal programs like education and land allotment "Friendlies" and those opposed "Hostiles." The distinction still exists in the present division between Progressives and Traditionalists.

Throughout the Spanish and Mexican periods of Hopi history the Hopi considered themselves a separate power, an equal government willing and capable of defending their land. But the Hopi were forced to recognize they were no longer capable of defense when Oraibi, declaring war against the United States in 1891, was unable to oppose the cavalry when it arrived. From then on Hopis declared themselves pacifists and turned to passive resistance, hiding their children so they could not be taken to school and removing land allotment stakes.

For Traditionalist Hopis much of their history has taken on an aura of myth. Before the establishment of the boarding school and agency in 1887 "things were the way they ought to be," a time when there was harmony and peace and "everyone worked together"—the ant hill of myth.

According to Traditionalists, this life based on the traditional Hopi religion is the one they want to maintain. The Anglo-Americans, they believe, brought to Hopi evil things, like liquor, and evil ideas, like the notion that the land is not sacred and can therefore be sold. But the most destructive element now associated with Anglo-Americans is differentiation, the fact that Progressive Hopis have left the true way. Traditionalists see the United States federal government as an evil influence, and they see the factionalism it encourages as the enduring legacy of Anglo-American contact.

SPANISH AND MEXICAN PERIOD: 1540–1848

Hopi history as recorded by Europeans begins in 1540, when Coronado sent Lieutenant Pedro de Tovar northwest to explore the reported "seven cities" of the Hopi. De Tovar was accompanied by seventeen horsemen, three or four footmen and Juan de Padilla, a Franciscan friar (Winship 1896: 488). Arriving at either Kawaiokuh or Awatovi on Antelope Mesa, de Tovar was met by Hopis who told him not to cross a line drawn on the ground. After some discussion through interpreters brought from Zuni and a Hopi blow to a Spaniard, de Tovar decided to attack. The Hopi were quickly defeated and came "to give the submission of the whole province" (ibid. 488).

The next Spanish incursion into the Hopi area occurred in 1593 when Antonio de Espejo came to prospect for mines in the area. Espejo was initially warned by friendly Zunis that the two largest Hopi pueblos were "waiting to make war . . . and that the other pueblos had not decided either for war or peace" (Hammond and Rey 1966: 188). The Hopi's final decision was evidently for peace, because they greeted Espejo cordially and allowed him to visit Awatovi, Walpi, Shongopavi, Mishongovi, and Oraibi. After their initial resistance, the Hopi's response to the powerful Spanish force became limited acceptance. They probably had heard of the atrocities committed against the Tewa by Coronado at Tiguex and by Espejo at Puala, and of the Mexican slave-raiding expeditions.

In 1598 more Spaniards arrived, this time as colonists. The contract for the settlement of New Mexico had been awarded to Don Juan de Oñate, and in accordance with the law of 1573 he was instructed that his "main purpose shall be the service of God our Lord, the spreading of His holy Catholic faith, and the reduction and pacification of the natives of the said provinces." Oñate was to bend all of his "energies to this object, without any other human interest interfering with this aim" (Hammond and Rey 1953: 65).

Oñate, who had risked a fortune in order to equip this venture, was determined to protect his investment, since he had received no financial assistance from the Crown. Oñate wanted to secure allegiance from the Indians before launching missionary efforts among them so he visited the Hopi in November and found them willing to give formal submission to Spain. Later, with the help of Hopi guides he prospected in the area, finding some copper but not the silver he was looking for. Since the demands of establishing a new colony on the Rio Grande then prevented further contact, a mission program was not established at Hopi.

Mission and administrative programs had not been very successful other places, and some pueblo peoples were resisting forcibly. The troublesome pueblo of Acoma, for instance, had been attacked in January 1599 by a punitive Spanish force, the village destroyed, and most of its inhabitants killed. Some Hopi men were among the captured, and after a month's confinement they were brought to trial and sent back to Hopi with their right hands severed as a warning. But by and large the Hopi were spared the atrocities visited upon pueblos further east.

Oñate resigned in 1607 and was replaced by Don Pedro de Peralta as governor of New Mexico. During this period the Indians of the Rio Grande began to move toward Christianity. In 1607, only 400 had been baptized, whereas the friars counted 17,000 in 1620 (John 1975: 66). With these conversions accomplished the friars began to turn their attention to the Hopi who had remained outside the missionary enterprise. Thirty new friars arrived in New Mexico in 1629, doubling the existing number.

On August 20, 1629, three Franciscans—Francisco Porras, Andres Gutierrez, and Cristobal de la Concepcion—arrived to establish a mission at Awatovi. According to Father Estevan de Perea who accompanied them, they were "received with some coolness." (Perea 1633 [1945]: 217). Despite their reception, Porras gained the confidence of the people; he mastered the language in less than nine months and was apparently mourned by the Hopi of Awatovi at his death.

By the time of Porras's death, missions had also been established at both Shongopavi and Oraibi. The three mission villages were provided with schools and, possibly, village organization in the Spanish form. The lack of recorded history during the 1640s implies that there were no extreme excesses on the part of the friars nor overt resistance to their presence. That the Hopi were not unhappy is suggested by their refusal to join the people of Taos in a plan for revolt in 1650 (Spicer 1962: 191).

In contrast to the Hopi experience the eastern pueblo peoples were exploited by both civil and religious authorities. Furthermore, the presence of Spanish goods and livestock stimulated Apache and Navajo raids during which pueblo peoples lost their lives defending Spanish property. These conditions kept the fires of rebellion smoldering and, following a severe drought which lasted from 1666 to 1671, a general uprising erupted. The Pueblo Revolt of 1680 succeeded in driving out the Spanish entirely for twelve years.

The Hopi joined in this revolt because by that time they had seen how cruel the friars could be. In 1655, for instance, a group of Hopis from Shongopavi went to Santa Fe to complain about the excessive tribute demanded of the village by Fray Salvador de Guerra. When they returned the Franciscan friar covered them with turpentine and set fire to them (Hacket 1937: 141). Friars at other villages were equally harsh, but in some cases the Indians had their revenge. The two friars at Oraibi, the friar serving at Shongopavi, and the two friars at Awatovi were all murdered during the 1680 revolt.

Despite the presence of the friars, the effect of Christianity upon the Hopi pueblos at this time seems to have been minimal and to have faded entirely after the 1680 revolt. The remarkable exception is Awatovi. The memory of Francisco Porras, the original friar, may explain why, after the Spanish reconquest in 1692, Awatovi accepted a new Catholic mission.

After the 1692 reconquest of New Mexico engineered by General Diego de Vargas, and after an unsuccessful Rio Grande pueblo rebellion in 1693, increasing numbers of refugees from the Rio Grande began to find their way to the Hopi mesas. These refugees, primarily Tewa, Tiwa, and Keres, founded the pueblos of Hano and Payupki. More Tiwa refugees arrived after another revolt in 1696, and may have founded a community in the area of Five Houses on the Polacca-Winslow Road (Brew 1949a: 20). The presence of these "irreconcilables" from the Rio Grande reinforced the Hopi's anti-Spanish attitude (Siguenzo y Gongora 1693 (1932): 84).

True to the Spanish pattern, missionaries soon followed the military after the reconquest. In 1699, possibly because they opposed the reopening of the missions requested by the people of Awatovi, the leading chiefs of Oraibi went to see the Spanish governor in Santa Fe. They presented themselves "not as subjects and vassals of the Crown, but as delegates of a foreign power sent to conclude a treaty of peace and amnesty" (Bandelier 1892, Part II: 371–72). They proposed that each nation keep its own religion and not try to convert the other. This proposal was rejected and missionaries were sent to the Hopi mesas.

Except for Awatovi, which received the friars well, Hopis categorically rejected these missionary endeavors. The resistance seems to have been led by Oraibi, the pueblo not only most opposed to missionary activity, but also the largest. In 1776, Father Escalante reported that seventy-six percent of the population lived at Oraibi, with the remaining twenty-four percent split equally between First and Second Mesas.

Opposition at Oraibi was led by its chief,

a powerful Hopi named Don Francisco de Espeleta. Despite or perhaps because of having been given a Spanish name and having been brought up by the friars at Oraibi who taught him to read and write, Espeleta opposed missionary activity. As he is described as having "more than eight hundred Indians" (Valverde 1732 [1937]: 385) under his command, the other pueblos seem to have contributed warriors to his cause. When the friars sent from Santa Fe appeared at Hopi, Don Espeleta threatened them with his army, and the friars retreated to the capital. Soon forces from Oraibi, and probably from Shongopavi and Walpi, attacked Awatovi. They destroyed the village, killed all the men who resisted, and took the women and children to other villages.

Since the destruction of Awatovi in 1700 the acceptance or rejection of white values and Christianity has acted as a catalyst for Hopi intra- and inter-village conflict. This is most clearly seen at Oraibi, which has remained a Traditionalist village. Even today Oraibi residents will proudly recount how they led the resistance against Spain and show you where the Spanish mission once stood. Events at Awatovi are seen as evidence of the Hopi ability to overcome foreign dominance, the goal of all Traditionalists. In fact the Traditionalist position has remained much the same as that expressed by the leaders of Oraibi in 1699 when they presented themselves as a separate people proposing a treaty of peace and religious noninterference.

In 1701, the year following the destruction of Awatovi, Governor Pedro Rodriguez Cubero led an unsuccessful punitive expedition against the Hopi, and during the next thirty-odd years, all Spanish attempts at religious conversion and military control met with failure. The Hopi attitude toward their Spanish neighbors after the revolt was clearly aggressively hostile, as demonstrated by the Oraibi-led destruction of Awatovi and their 1706 attack on Christian Zunis (Spicer 1962: 193).

By 1776, however, the Spanish-Hopi relationship had changed to one of coexistence: neither culture dominated. This new relationship was due less to a change in Spanish policy than to the fact that their forces were engaged against the Apache and Comanche warriors. Missionaries came and left unharmed but unheeded. The total rejection of the Spanish religion cannot be more clearly seen than in the Hopi reception of Fray Francisco Garcés. Arriving at Oraibi from Sonora with Yavapi traders who acted as guides, he was refused entry to a house. Garcés spent the night on an Oraibi street, while gracious Hopis entertained his Native American guides (Coues 1900, vol. 2: 364).

Despite their failure to convert the Hopi to Christianity, the Spaniards had a profound impact on Hopi material culture. Horses, donkeys, and sheep became an integral part of Hopi life and new food plants, specifically chili peppers and peaches, were incorporated into their diet. Spanish contributions also included metal tools such as knives, axes, picks, saws, and chisels.

Livestock introduced by the Spanish replaced wild game as a source of meat. In 1776 the occupants of Oraibi are described as having "good horse herds, droves of sheep and some cattle"; along with other Hopis they raised "abundant crops of maize, beans, and chili," although they suffered from a scarcity of wood and good water (Thomas 1932: 152). The rise in the Hopi horse and cattle herds following the revolt of 1680 was probably effected through trade with the Navajo. Metal goods may also have been part of this commerce or acquired through interpueblo trade.

Toward the end of the eighteenth century Spain again focused attention on the Hopi. In 1778 Juan Bautista de Anza was made governor of New Mexico in the hope that he could establish communication between Santa Fe and Spanish settlements in Sonora and California (John 1975: 521–22). In order to achieve this goal Anza needed to control Comanche and Apache warfare and to pacify the Hopi. Because he had been instructed not to use force against the Hopi, Anza hoped to accomplish this by relocating the Hopi in the Rio Grande pueblos.

In all likelihood, when Anza arrived on the Hopi mesas in 1780 he thought his task would be simple since the Hopi were stricken by a three-year drought. But although he remained on the mesas for seven days talking to the village leaders, they all remained "inexorable in their purpose of remaining heathen, preserving their customs, and remaining in their desolated pueblos" (Thomas 1932: 109).

This was a desperate time for the Hopi. Anza estimated the population on the Mesas at 798, a fraction of Escalante's estimate of 7,499 in 1776. Many had died. Some had gone to live at Zuni with the Havasupai. Others had begun to wander, trying to subsist by hunting and gathering. There were also raids by the Navajo, who were likewise stricken by the drought, and

in 1781 suffered a severe smallpox epidemic. Nonetheless, most Hopi wanted to stay at their mesa-top pueblos. Anza's visit was not a total failure, however, as he had successfully traded with the Hopi and the chief of Walpi had accepted his gift of a pack horse and supplies. Anza also persuaded 200 Hopis to return with him to the Rio Grande. He had hoped for more, and might well have been more successful had not a party of forty Hopi families who had gone to meet him been murdered by the Navajo. In 1781, however, the rains returned and, for those who had survived, prosperity as well. According to Spicer (1962: 196) the Franciscans reported that by 1782 the Hopi, despite their independence from Spanish rule, were better off than the Indians in the Rio Grande pueblos.

Throughout the remainder of Spanish rule in New Mexico the Hopi were never under Spanish civil or religious control. Ironically, when the Hopi were forced into contact with civil authorities it was because of the Navajo.

During the 1700s some Navajo gradually moved westward as a result of pressure from Ute and Comanches who had moved into the Navajo area from the plateau region. By the end of the eighteenth century the Navajo were concentrated in an area from Zuni north to the San Juan River, and from the Rio Grande pueblos to the Hopi villages in the west.

During this period the Navajo acquired large herds of horses and flocks of sheep. Although the Navajo periodically raided Spanish and pueblo settlements to increase their livestock, Navajo-Pueblo and Navajo-Spanish relations could be generally considered friendly.

After 1800, with the death of Antonio el Pinto, a Navajo leader friendly with Spanish authorities, the situation changed. Navajo livestock raids brought Spanish reprisals and were used as an excuse to justify Spanish slave raids for laborers and household servants (Spicer 1962: 213). As a result, Navajo raids likewise escalated and were no longer merely to acquire sheep and horses but also captives, whom the Navajo either kept or traded. It was during this period that the Navajo increasingly raided Pueblo villages, including the Hopi. By 1819 the raids had reached such proportions that five Hopis traveled to Santa Fe to ask for Spanish protection against the Navajo (Bancroft 1889: 287). But the Spanish government, then in the throes of disintegration, was unable to respond.

Spanish rule in New Mexico finally came to an end two years later with the Mexican Revolution. The new Mexican government did not attempt to administer the Hopi area, nor did the church attempt to convert the people. The Mexican government in Santa Fe also remained unable to control Navajo raids.

Under Governor Facundo Melgares, however, the province of New Mexico invited commerce with the United States. Although not part of an established Anglo trade network, Hopis were in contact with parties of Anglo fur trappers who visited briefly from 1826 to 1828 and again in 1834.

Navajo raiding continued, and the outbreak of the United States-Mexican war in 1846 allowed the Navajo to raid at will. As Hopis struggled with this problem, Anglo-American traders, military forces, government officials, and a new group of missionaries waited in the wings.

THE AMERICAN PERIOD: 1848–1930

Introduction

With the end of the Mexican war in 1848, the United States became the third outside government with which the Hopi had direct contact. Hopeful that the new government would do something about the continuing Navajo attacks, a group of seven Hopis went to see John S. Calhoun, the Indian Agent, in October 1850. Calhoun assured the delegation that he would do his best to control Navajo incursions; the government established Fort Defiance toward this end in 1851.

Since the Americans were not antagonistic to the Hopi, and since their military presence brought about a decrease in Navajo attacks, the Hopi were at first inclined to regard the new government favorably.

Through the 1850s and 1860s, the Hopi came into contact with soldiers in pursuit of the Navajo and with other Anglos who seem to have conducted themselves well. Perhaps as a result of the Anglo contact, however, a smallpox epidemic broke out in 1853. This catastrophe was followed by drought, so that by 1863 the population was estimated at 4,000 (Sabin 1935: 874) in contrast to Ten Broeck's estimate of 8,000 in 1852 (Donaldson 1893: 26, 45).

During this time the United States government was not actively involved in Hopi affairs. Hence, the first sustained contact the Hopis had with Americans besides soldiers was with the Mormons.

Traders, Agents, and Missionaries: 1848–1906

The Mormon Connection. In 1858 Brigham Young appointed Jacob Hamblin as a

Mormon sub-Indian agent and instructed him to visit the Hopi. The Mormons' interest in the Hopi was both ideological and practical. Their ideological interest sprang from their belief according to the *Book of Mormon* that the American Indian originally came from Palestine, and could thus be considered "of the blood of Israel" (Little 1881: 62) and so could be converted.

The Mormon attitude toward Hopi religion differed dramatically from that of the Protestant missionaries of the same period. As Hamblin explained:

> Some people call the Indian supersti-tious. I admit the fact, but do not think that they are more so than many who call themselves civilized. There are few people who have not received superstitious tradi-tions from their fathers. The more intelli-gent part of the Indians believe in one Great Father of all; also in evil influences, and in revelation and prophecy; and they are quite as consistent as the Christian sects of today (Little 1881: 107).

The tolerance of the Mormons, who allowed converted Hopis to continue to engage in Hopi traditional ceremonies, enabled them to convert a number of Hopis to the Church of Jesus Christ of Latter-Day Saints. In marked contrast is the intolerance of the Methodist Church which supplied traveling evangelists to northern Arizona. According to H. R. Voth, a Mennonite missionary who came to Oraibi in 1893 (quoted in James 1974: 153), his predecessor, presumably a Methodist, mocked and sneered at the Hopi religion and kicked their sacred objects.[1] And Methodist Bishop Harwood complained,

> Why should we expect the Indian to be any better than any other heathen people? Why

should we expect him to be anything else than low in morals, selfish, clannish, thiev-ish, murderous, unkind to women when they have never been taught to the contrary (1910: vol. II: 118–19).

In view of the years of friendly Mormon contact, and the insensitivity of United States officials, it is not surprising that the people of Oraibi formed an alliance with the Mormons which led to the founding of a Mormon settlement near the Oraibi farming colony of Moencopi in 1875. The Oraibi leader Tuuvi was instrumental in achieving this alliance, and Tuba City, the Mormon settlement named for him, remained the dominant Anglo influence on Third Mesa for more than a decade.

On the practical level, Brigham Young was interested in the Hopi because he hoped that as converted "sons and daughters of Abraham," they would move north of the Colorado River and thus form a buffer between Mormon settlements in southern Utah and more hostile tribes.

The first contact between the Mormons and the Hopi took place in 1858, just eleven years after the first pioneers arrived at the Great Salt Lake in Utah. On October 28, 1858 twelve men, including Hamblin, left for Hopi, crossed the Colorado at Ute Ford, and a week later arrived at Oraibi. Hopis greeted them as the fulfillment of the bahana myth. Hamblin recounted:

> After our arrival in the village, the lead-ing men counseled together a few minutes, when we were separated and invited to dine with different families. A man beckoned to me to follow him. After traversing several streets, and climbing a ladder to the roof of the first story of a house, I was ushered into a room furnished with sheepskins, blan-kets, earthen cooking utensils, water urns,

and other useful articles. It seemed to me strangely furnished, yet it had an air of comfort; perhaps the more so, for the reason that the previous day had been spent in very laborious traveling, on rather low diet. . . .

A very aged man said that when he was a young man, his father told him that he would live to see white men come among them, who would bring them great blessings, such as their fathers had enjoyed, and that these men would come from the West. He believed that he had lived to see the prediction fulfilled in us (Little 1881: 61–62).

We do not know the source of this bahana myth, but it is not surprising that the myth telling of the arrival of the White Brother developed as the Hopi saw increasing Anglo expansion. From their point of view the prophecy gave the Hopi control over their circumstances. Moreover, since the arrival of Anglos was cloaked in theology, the myth was subject to interpretation.

After visiting all seven pueblos on the Hopi mesas Hamblin returned to Utah, leaving four members of his party at Oraibi "to study their language [and] offer them the gospel." The men's stay was brief, however. As one recounted, "a division arose among the people as to whether we were the men [bahana] prophesied by their fathers. . . . This dispute ran so high that . . . the chief men among [them] advised [the Mormons] to return" (Little 1881: 62–63).

But that autumn an undaunted Hamblin returned to Oraibi with $60 worth of trade goods, primarily wool, wool carders, spades, and shovels, intending once again to leave men to indoctrinate the Hopi. This time he wanted to encourage the Hopi to move north of the Colorado. The men who remained with the Hopi at Oraibi were Marion J. Shelton and Tales Haskell.

True to the directive of Brigham Young, Shelton and Haskell helped the people of Oraibi in every way they could— sharpening saws, carding wool, making powder horns and bullet molds, and repairing houses (Brooks 1944). Although they were evidently still considered to be the bahana, the Hopi now told them that the people of Oraibi could neither follow their gospel nor move north of the Colorado until "the re-appearance of the three prophets who had led their father to that land and told them to remain on those rocks" (Little 1881: 65). Thus, myth countered myth. The Hopi were willing to trade with the Mormons, feed them and befriend them, but they remained intransigent when it came to adopting their religion.

One event of lasting importance did take place, however. It was during this time that Shelton and Haskell became friends with Tuuvi, the Oraibi resident who later assisted the Mormons in establishing Tuba City near Moencopi.

When Hamblin returned to escort Shelton and Haskell back to Utah it appeared as if their mission had failed. But since the Hopi were again suffering from drought, the people of Oraibi asked Hamblin to pray with them in their ceremony before he departed. Nature succeeded where Shelton and Haskell had not. Rain fell the following night which convinced the Hopis of Hamblin's good intentions and three Hopis accepted an invitation to visit the Mormon settlements.

Hamblin subsequently made only two brief visits to the Hopi in 1863 and 1865, since the Mormons were engaged in a nagging war of attrition with Navajos and

Paiutes throughout the decade. The Mormon-Indian war, sometimes referred to as the Black Hawk war, prevented further missionary work.

The Hopi were also suffering at the hands of the Navajo. With the outbreak of the American Civil War the U.S. Army was withdrawn for service elsewhere and Navajo attacks on the Hopi villages increased markedly. In 1861 John Ward visited Oraibi and reported that the situation was desperate. Brigadier General James J. Carleton, assisted by Kit Carson, moved in force and in 1863 began a three-month scorched-earth campaign against the Navajo in the Hopi area. Carson's campaign brought hardships to the Hopi as well. Oraibi leaders were briefly taken prisoner in the belief that they had formed an alliance with the Navajo. Hopi fields thought to belong to the Navajo were burned, and Carson insisted that warriors from all the Hopi villages except Oraibi join his force.

With the imprisonment of the Navajo at Bosque Redondo in 1864 their raids largely ceased, although according to Nagata (1970: 32), sufficient numbers had escaped the Carson dragnet to remain a threat to the farming community of Moencopi during the four years that most Navajo were at Bosque Redondo.

The Hopi were also plagued by another of their periodic droughts at this time. By 1866 conditions had become so severe that a group of Hopis went to New Mexico to plead for government food supplies. Because the Hopi area was considered to lie within the new Arizona Territory no aid was forthcoming, but the government proposed that the Hopi move to better lands in the Tonto Basin in central Arizona. They rejected this proposal. Drought and starvation were again followed by a

smallpox epidemic. To escape the conditions on the mesas many Hopis fled to Zuni. After the drought and epidemic ended, they returned and brought back with them some knowledge of Spanish, Zuni Kachinas, and the Shalako ceremony, as well as a new style of pottery decoration later known as Polacca Polychrome. No sooner had conditions begun to improve, however, than the Navajo completed their Long Walk back to the Hopi area, and in 1868 once again began raiding Hopi villages.

When Hamblin returned to resume missionary work among the Hopi in 1869, he was for the first time received coolly, evidently because the Hopi feared Navajo reprisals if they befriended their enemies, the Mormons. But when Hamblin returned the following year with Major John Wesley Powell, all was well. Tuuvi and his wife Pulaskanimk returned to Utah with Hamblin and were treated as dignitaries. They visited Mormon communities, a flour mill, and a cotton mill which awed Tuuvi. As a result of this visit, Tuuvi not only agreed to the establishment of a Mormon community adjacent to Moencopi but also requested that it have a spinning mill.

Although the Mormons' ostensible motive for the establishment of the colony to be known as Tuba City was to provide protection for the Oraibi farming village at Moencopi, the Mormons had also been planning a southward movement into Arizona once they had colonized the Kaibito Plateau. The people of Oraibi may or may not have been aware of this, but the urgent situation at Oraibi was enough to force them into an allegiance with the Mormons. The size of the pueblo was so large in relation to the available arable land and water (Donaldson 1893: 30–31) that the Hopis of Oraibi needed the fertile Moencopi Wash for permanent use. The Mormon presence at Tuba City made this possible by providing the security necessary for a farming colony, so that people from Oraibi moved to Moencopi in increasing numbers.

While the Mormons developed Tuba City on the west, Keams Canyon developed to the east of First Mesa. In 1875, the year the Mormons settled at Tuba City, Thomas Keam was issued a trader's license (McNitt 1962: 161). This was a major turning point in Hopi history.

During the latter half of the nineteenth century in the more remote regions of the Southwest, the principal bearer of Anglo-American culture was the Indian trader. The trader provided and frequently introduced Native Americans to American foods and goods. In order to acquire these items Native Americans needed a source of cash income. Although they occasionally bartered crops for goods at the trading post, craft products became a primary cash source as Native Americans sold or traded their crafts for manufactured goods. The trader meanwhile sold the crafts to the tourists who were beginning to discover the Southwest. Under the direction of traders, Navajos began to weave rugs and Hopis to make a new variety of pottery—Sikyatki Revival ware.

By the 1890s, the Hopi trader Thomas Keam was one of the most successful and influential men in the region. Born in England, Keam arrived in this country via Australia and shortly thereafter enlisted in the cavalry. Although little is known of his private life, emotions, or motivations, Keam clearly felt a sense of responsibility, if not empathy, toward Native Americans. He married a Navajo woman, spoke the Navajo language fluently, and was eager to establish a school for the education of young Hopis.

His interests seem to have been wide-ranging. By 1880 Alexander M. Stephen, who became the principal researcher for the Second Hemenway Expedition under the direction of Jessie Walter Fewkes, came to live with him. In 1881 Captain John G. Bourke (1884: 82) described Keam's library. It contained, he wrote, "choice specimens of literature—Shakespeare, Thackeray, Dickens, Paine and other authors."

Multilingual, Keam served as a Spanish interpreter at the Fort Defiance Indian Agency and later became the Navajo sub-Agent. His sympathy for the plight of Native Americans earned him the respect of Navajos and the contempt of government agents. In fact it was because of Keam's conflict with W. F. M. Arny, the dishonest Navajo agent, that around 1873 he left the Navajo reservation and moved to Keams Canyon on the Navajo-Hopi boundary along the east-west trading route. Although Keam claimed (letter from Thomas V. Keam to Commissioner J. D. Atkins, February 11, 1886) that he had intended to establish a cattle ranch in this lush, well-watered canyon, it was also an ideal location for a trading post.

Keam's trading post gradually developed into the equivalent of a small village. In 1881 the trading post probably consisted of ten buildings; five years later there were eighteen (ibid.). During these formative years the presence of a post twelve miles from Walpi made more Anglo goods accessible, specifically sugar, coffee, flour, matches, and metal buckets and hoes.

An important aspect of the trading post at Keams Canyon was that it acted as the local inn. During Bourke's visit the number of "guests" at the trading post fluctuated between six and eight, including five members of the U.S. Geological Survey (Bourke 1884: 353).

By 1886 Keam had a separate building specifically for Hopi goods, probably of First and Second Mesa manufacture since Hopis from Oraibi traded mainly with the Mormons to the west.

The major difference between Tuba City, the western Mormon trading center, and Keams Canyon was that the United States Government became part of the eastern center. In fact, the first government building had been erected there between 1873 and 1874. By contrast, the western Mormon center was frequently in conflict with the government, which had implications for U.S.-Hopi relations. As Bourke observed, the Mormons were already exerting an influence upon the Hopi.

> The Moqui[2] Indians . . . care but little for the [Keams Canyon] Agency or anybody connected with it. Their nearest villages are fifteen miles away, across a plain of heavy sand, while their most populous community, Oraybe, is between thirty and forty miles by the shortest trail. . . .
>
> I mention these facts to emphasize the difference between our slouchy ill-judged methods and the clean-cut, business-like ideas predominating in the Mormon management. The Latter-Day Saints are busy among the Moquis, and have met with considerable success. Their emissaries live among the Indians, and not forty miles away, and are constantly improving their opportunities for adding to an influence already considerable and not always friendly to the "Washington Great Father" (1884: 79–80).

United States Government and Mormon relations had always been cold and at times flared into direct conflict. The Mormons had sought the Hopi as allies and had been successful at Oraibi. It is difficult to determine to what degree the Mormons may have fostered antigovernment sentiment, as Bourke claimed. But the Hopi certainly associated the government with the repression of their traditional religion, a religion the Mormons tolerated. Ever since the inception of Grant's Peace Policy in the 1860s Protestant missionaries had worked hand-in-hand with the government to stamp out native religion. This linking of church and state, based on the concept that Christianized Indians would become civilized Indians (and vice versa), could only have led to Hopi sympathy for the Mormons' anti-government stance.[3]

Soon, however, problems developed between Hopis of Third Mesa and the Mormons. According to Nagata (1970: 33), after the founding of Tuba City the Mormons began to appropriate Hopi land: "They soon began to invade the territory that the Hopi regarded as theirs. The Hopi farmers were relegated to the position of sharecroppers by the Mormons."

W. E. Traux, the Hopi Agent at Keams Canyon from 1875 to 1876, made a report to the Commissioner of Indian Affairs in 1876 in which he urged that a Hopi reservation be established to protect the Hopi from the Mormons. Traux's reaction to the founding of Tuba City and his fear of Mormon influence were perhaps extreme, but in 1879 Tuuvi himself wrote to Agent Mateer (letter from William R. Mateer to the Commissioner of Indian Affairs, May 1, 1879) requesting protection from Mormon expansion.

Unfortunately, the government did not

actively respond to this complaint, holding to its policy of Christianization and civilization. In fact it was at this time that the Protestant missionaries, Mr. and Mrs. Taylor, prepared to open a mission school at Keams Canyon.[4]

Then in 1882, in part because of Mormon incursions onto Hopi land, the government established the Hopi Reservation, ostensibly to protect the Indians near Tuba City from their Mormon neighbors. But the Hopi now faced another threat from Anglo-Americans, one that ultimately was to be even more devastating.

The acculturative pressure begun in 1875 with the establishment of the trading post at Keams Canyon increased in the 1880s. First a Protestant missionary made an aggressive attempt to establish a mission school at Oraibi. More importantly, the Hopi agent J. H. Fleming endorsed the establishment of an Indian School in Albuquerque. The question of schooling was to divide the Hopi as nothing else had previously.

Education and Schools. Between 1849, when the Bureau of Indian Affairs moved from the War Department to the Department of the Interior, and 1887, when the Dawes Act was passed, the United States Government gradually developed a policy designed to assimilate Native Americans into Anglo-American culture. With the passage of the Dawes Act in 1887, government policy definitely changed. Under its provisions schools were to be set up, native religions replaced by Christianity, and private land ownership substituted for communal tribal holdings. The act marked a major change in the way the government looked at the Indian. In the past the federal government had been

committed to no more than the maintenance of peaceful relations between white settlers and Native Americans.

That was the function of Indian agents. But apart from maintaining the peace, they had no consistent directives, and so their activities and impact varied widely. This created an unstable situation in which Native Americans were frequently dependent on the whims of an Indian Agent whose average tenure was usually less than three years (Spicer 1962: 350).

Between 1849 and 1887, however, some agents pushed for Hopi education, among them J. H. Fleming, the head of a separate Hopi Agency at Keams Canyon. Excluding the year in which the agency had been built, the Hopi had been until now administered from Fort Defiance, frequently jointly with the Navajo.[5] Agent Fleming believed that education was the tool of civilization, and if the Indian could be removed from his heathen environment and taught the value of white man's ways and religion he could become "Americanized." Such was Fleming's goal, but his tenure lasted only a year. Fleming departed as Hopi Agent in 1883, and the Hopi Reservation was again administered as part of a joint Hopi and Navajo Agency from headquarters in Fort Defiance (James 1974: 101).

Thomas Keam also believed in education for the Hopi, and proposed the establishment of a school at his trading post. Keam's intellectual bent and sympathy for Native Americans may well have motivated his support for a school, though more selfish motives may have accounted for part of his interest in Indian education. It is possible that he wanted to become the Hopi Agent. His visit to Washington to propose the use of his buildings for an Indian school in 1884 came just two years after his bid to become the Navajo Agent was rejected. Keam may have foreseen the reopening of a separate Hopi agency at Keams Canyon and now aimed at heading the agency.[6]

As the Hopi Indian trader Keam provided the most consistent Anglo-American presence on the reservation, and although we do not know his personal ambitions we do know that he was sympathetic to the Hopi and that he was an intellectual. It is possible, therefore, that he opposed the removal of Hopis to the Albuquerque boarding school as advocated by Fleming but supported Hopi education.

Whatever his ultimate intention, Keam was assisted in his push for Hopi education by Lololoma, kikmongwi or village chief of Oraibi, who would later become known as the leader of Third Mesa Hopis identified by United States government officials as "Friendlies." When Keam visited Washington in 1884 to propose the use of his Keams Canyon buildings as an Indian school, he may have been accompanied, presumably at his own expense, by some Navajos and Hopis, including Lololoma (Nequatewa 1936: 131, n.47).[7]

Although Lololoma later recalled that this trip to Washington was responsible for his support of "the system of education existing among the white people" (Donaldson 1893: 56), he had already abandoned the Oraibi antigovernment position. Lololoma's change in attitude is noted by Cushing (1922: 258–59), who visited Oraibi in 1882. Lololoma welcomed the white man against the wishes of another Oraibi leader who Cushing said traced "his descent from the mythic grandmothers of the human race—the Spider and the Bat." Thus, a leader of the Spider Clan was

already established as the Oraibi leader of Hopis soon to become known by government officials as "Hostiles."

The conflict between the Hostiles and the Friendlies ultimately led to the division of Oraibi in 1906 and the founding of the "hostile" village of Hotevilla. Antagonism, stimulated by differences in opinion about Anglo education, was increased in 1886 when twenty Hopis and Tewas asked the United States Government for doors, windows, and board floors for their houses and a school for their children. Unfortunately, this document is now missing from the National Archives but, according to McNitt (1962: 194), all seven Hopi pueblos were represented by the signees, who used their clan marks. The petition for a school was sent by Keam to the Commissioner of Indian Affairs, and in May of that year Keam leased all of his property to the government for $100 a month (ibid. 195) for the purpose of Hopi education.

The following year, 1887, Congress passed the Dawes Act, which had three features: the establishment of boarding schools, the establishment of a Code of Religious Offenses, and the allotment of Indian land. The Code of Religious Offenses was to be enforced by federal agents and missionaries funded by the government to establish local reservation schools. That same year James Gallagher, the school superintendent, arrived with supplies to convert the trading post into a boarding school. The school's opening on October first with fifty-two pupils (James 1974: 107) was a turning point in Hopi history.

The students who attended the boarding school at Keams Canyon were humiliated and degraded by school officials who attempted to force Hopis to abandon their culture. The students were not allowed to speak Hopi or wear Hopi clothing. They were given English names, required to attend Christian services, and were punished if they practiced the Hopi religion or customs. For the first time since the Pueblo Revolt, Hopis were exposed to massive forced acculturation.

Radical social change occurred with the establishment of the boarding school. The school divided families and disrupted traditional education and socialization. The Hopi child, as part of the government school program, was forcibly subjected to Protestant teachings and to the American capitalist system. These children soon came to consider cash a necessity; as a reward for maturity and development, educators allowed them to have cash-paying jobs. In contrast to their traditional value system, the children were taught to strive for individual achievement and to anticipate cash as the reward for their success.

When they completed their education Hopis were encouraged to work at either the Keams Canyon or the Tuba City Government Agencies. The Indian Agents had "the explicit aim of protecting them from reverting to the primitive ways of the Indians" (Nagata 1979: 179). By the early 1900s the Ladies Aid Society of the Presbyterian Church at Flagstaff had been contacted to find enough "good white homes" in which Hopi girls could work as maids. Thus, by the 1900s on First Mesa, and to a lesser extent on Second and Third Mesas, educators and missionaries were reaping the rewards of their labor as craft sales and opportunities for wage labor led the Hopi further into the white man's world.

The Dawes Act and the founding of the boarding school system during the 1880s and 1890s brought radical change to the Hopi. Economically for the first time the Hopi became part of the national economy as wage labor increased and more and more commercial goods and materials reached the mesas.

Reaction to the school varied. The more favorable response was from the pueblos of First Mesa, which had traded extensively with Keam while the villages of Second and Third Mesas had more commonly traded with the Mormons of Tuba City. Although not all the residents of the three First Mesa pueblos supported the school, they did not oppose it, apparently for a number of reasons. First, they had experienced greater exposure to the Anglo-American culture than other Hopis and employment at the school continued to bring even more First Mesa residents into the white sphere of influence. Further, Tewas occupying the First Mesa pueblo of Hano were far more willing to work with Anglos and to adopt Anglo "values." Dozier (1966) has argued that the Hano Tewa felt they had been ill-treated by the Hopi and consequently chose to align themselves with the Anglo-Americans. Such an alliance would place them in a more powerful position vis-a-vis the Hopi. By 1889 Fewkes (1922: 273) observed that "the people of the East [First] Mesa and especially of Hano . . . sent the majority of their children to school."

On Second and Third Mesas, the pueblos expressed their opposition to the school in the typical Hopi way. They boycotted it. At Oraibi the Hostiles, who were apparently the majority, simply did not send their children to school. But their passive resistance was shaken into active opposition in 1890 when, in order to balance and increase school attendance which had declined to thirty-five (Donaldson 1893: 57), the government established village quotas. Conflict between the mesas was inevitable.

The potentially explosive situation between the residents of the different mesas over education was exploited by government officials who used First Mesa men in the arrest of Oraibi Hostiles from Third Mesa. The incident took place in November 1890 when Keam, with a party of officials, went to Oraibi to explain the new quota system. He asked Lololoma to point out the Hostile leaders there. This Lololoma did and, as a result, "one of the principal 'medicine men'" was taken into custody. When Keam and the officials were leaving with their prisoner, they met another man from Oraibi. What happened next is described by Donaldson (1893: 58):

> The Oraibi then directed his conversation to Polaki [the Tewa interpreter], whose face grew stern as he listened, and he finally leaned forward suddenly and seized the Oraibi by the blanket at the shoulder, and calling to us, said: "This is the great medicine man of all the Moquis, and he threatens my life and the lives of all the others here; he is the brother of the prisoner, and the man most of all that we want." At this movement of Polaki, Mr. Collins [the government school superintendent] just as suddenly turned his horse and took hold of the man on the other side and forced him to go along. On his resisting this compulsory movement Mr. Collins dismounted, and with his lariat "took a hitch" around the man's wrist, remounted, and tied the other end to the pommel of his saddle, and then started off at a canter, the "great medicine man" taking long quick strides in order to keep from falling.

This incident clearly reveals the upheaval and division prevailing in 1890: the Tewas and Hopis of First Mesa in support of the government educational program, the division among the Hopis of Third Mesa, and the ever-increasing pressure of American policy. For nearly fifty years government officials and missionaries had worked to Christianize the Hopi. In 1887 the Code of Religious Offenses empowered government officials to forbid forcibly, if necessary, Hopi ceremonies considered offensive. What this suppression of native religion meant was made clear in 1923 when Commissioner Burke, giving reasons for government opposition to indigenous ceremonies, asserted the interdependence of Christianity and the individualistic capitalist ethic:

> You [Indians] must first of all try to make your own living, which you cannot do unless you work faithfully and take care of what comes from your labor, and go to dances and other meetings only when your home work will not suffer from it. I do not want to deprive you of decent amusements or occasional feast days, but you should not do evil or foolish things or take so much time for these occasions. No good comes from your "giveaway" custom at dances and it should be stopped. It is not right to torture your bodies or to handle poisonous snakes in your ceremonies. All such extreme things are wrong and should be put aside and forgotten (James 1974: 187–88).

The initial struggle to Christianize and educate the Hopi after the passage of the Dawes Act had an unexpected result, however. It crystallized anti-government opposition.

The Hostiles' strength was evident in 1891 when the Keams Canyon schoolteacher, the Indian agent, an interpreter, and six cavalry men went to

Oraibi to demand the return of some children who had run away from the Keams Canyon School. The delegation was met by Oraibi warriors whose numbers were enough to cause the American party to retreat (Fewkes 1922). The Americans were also treated to the startling appearance of two individuals dressed as Spider Woman and Masaw as part of the traditional Hopi declaration of war. Reinforcements were requested from Fort Wingate and about ten days later, four troops of armed cavalry arrived. They met no opposition and arested six "chiefs," one of whom escaped. (The events that took place at this time are described in detail by Keam in Donaldson 1893: 37–38). The remaining five were taken to Fort Wingate where they were jailed. Oraibi leaders of both factions were imprisoned. This may have had the effect of bringing even more support to the Hostile cause.

Land Allotment. More trouble began in the spring of 1891 when government surveyors entered the Hopi Reservation and the Moencopi Area in order to implement the allotment of land under the Dawes Act of 1887. Under its provisions, which were completely opposed to the traditional Hopi clan ownership of land, 160-acre parcels were allotted to individual Indians and "surplus" land was sold by the government. The purpose of the Dawes Act was to further "Americanize" the Indian by making him a private landowner and, thereby, part of the capitalist system. All Hopis opposed land allotment but at Oraibi Hostiles led the resistance and, when the surveyors had left, pulled up their survey stakes (Fewkes 1922: 274). As a consequence, land parcels were not distributed on the Hopi Reservation,

although in 1903, 20-acre irrigation plots along the Moencopi Wash were given to individual allottees (Nagata 1970: 34). The result of the land allotment, however, was that the total amount of Indian-held land was reduced by nearly two-thirds. Thompson (1950: 197) believes that the "disastrous consequences" of this act would have been even worse had not the Hopis resisted the division of clan land. Whatever the case, the attempted allotment of Hopi land probably reinforced the position of the Hostiles at Oraibi.

The Mennonites. In 1893 the divided Oraibi people were confronted with yet more Anglo-American intervention when the Mennonite missionary H. R. Voth arrived. One of the most important figures in Hopi history, Voth was a man whose own conflicts mirrored the conflicts of the Hopi.

As both a missionary and an ethnographer Voth was apparently "unable to choose one role or the other or to integrate the two in a meaningful way" (Eggan 1979: 7). He had come to Oraibi as a missionary at the suggestion of Peter Stauffer, the Keams Canyon Agency carpenter who was also a Mennonite, and his Oklahoma friend Ralph P. Collins, the school superintendent (Eggan 1979: 2; James 1974: 148). But beginning in 1897, Voth also worked with George A. Dorsey at the Field Museum in Chicago as an ethnologist. The Mennonite historian Kaufman stated later, "In many ways H. R. Voth was ahead of his time and entered sympathetically into the various religious practices and customs of the Hopis" (1931: 144).

Voth spent his first year at Oraibi building his home and studying the Hopi language. Voth explains that only when he could talk with the Hopis in their language and only when the Hopis

> found out, that we were willing to take care of their sick, could extract aching teeth better and quicker than their doctors, that their children, their poor, could get pieces of cloth as gifts and many favors, and especially that I did not mock and sneer at their religion . . . they more and more opened their kivas . . . and their knowledge and their hearts to us. (Voth *in* James 1974: 153).

At the same time, however, Voth was preaching in the streets of Oraibi knowing full well that once baptized, a converted Hopi would be forbidden to watch or take part in the very ceremonies that he was documenting and the federal government was trying to forbid.

In 1893 a government day school was established on the Oraibi Wash a mile downstream from Voth's mission. This school, like the one at Second Mesa, was established in the hope that since Hopi children could now attend a local day school their parents and relatives would willingly comply with obligatory school attendance. This did not prove to be the case.

On February 2, 1902, a roundup of children took place led by Hopi Agent Charles E. Burton and aided by agency employees and Navajo police. The Hopi children were forced at gunpoint, at night, to walk naked the mile to school. Ironically, the preceding year Voth had begun to construct a chapel on top of the mesa at Oraibi and had "more Hopi help with the project than he could use to advantage" (James 1974: 157).

The violence used to "round up" the school children must have appalled the Reverend Voth who, as a Mennonite, was a pacifist. Voth and two schoolteachers[8] stood in tacit opposition not to the government educational policies but to the ruthless manner in which these were carried out. And so it was to Voth that the Hostiles turned for advice (Carlson 1964: 40; Nequatewa 1936: 132, n.47) and in 1903, as a humanitarian and a member of the Indian Rights Association, he urged an investigation of Agent Burton and the Oraibi school principal John L. Ballinger. Voth left the Oraibi mission shortly after the infamous winter roundup.

The Division of Oraibi and the Aftermath

For many residents of Third Mesa the division of Oraibi in 1906 separates time. In 1906 there was one Third Mesa village, Oraibi, and its farming colony at Moencopi. By 1911 there were four separate communities besides the original farming colony, which had increasingly become a haven for those wishing to escape the bitter dissension at the mother village.

The government policy of education *per se* is not considered responsible for the division, but the people of Third Mesa point to the differing responses of Hopi people to "white ways" as clearly the cause of the split. Government interference was not the only factor in the division of Oraibi, however. Nequatewa (1936: 131–32, n.47) argues that the division was the result of the need to disperse the population, and that the leaders fomented hostilities to bring this about.[9] Informants today, including four elderly people who were children or teenagers when the division of Oraibi took place in 1906, agree that it was inevitable because of the acute water shortage and a need "to spread out." The factionalism and eventual fission of

Oraibi has also been studied by Titiev, who concludes that Lololoma's support of the government education program "provided a *casus belli,* but that the primary division of the village resulted from the splitting of the weak phratry tie that had held two strong clans together" (1944: 75).

Titiev states that in 1891 Lomahongyoma argued that he should be allowed to use Bear Clan land because he was the leader of Oraibi and in fact "went so far as to select a good field for himself on Bear Clan territory, and this he cultivated until his expulsion in 1906" (1944: 79).

Friction had existed between the Bear and Spider clans for some time, clearly indicated by the fact that by the 1890s the conflict had become part of Oraibi mythology (ibid. 73–74). Both the Bear and Spider clan members acknowledged the myth that portrayed the Spider Clan as dissenters and advocates of the belief that the bahana would return if there was conflict. But the Hostiles also believed that when the true bahana returned "he would be able to converse with his younger brother [the Hopis] in Hopi, and that he would produce a stone to match the one held by the Hopi. On both counts, Lololoma was accused of having made an erroneous identification of his American friends as Bahanas" (Titiev 1944: 74). This myth explains the conflict between the two clans and also explains the Anglo-American presence; and it allows for the Hopis' diverse responses to this presence.

Lololoma died in about 1901 (Nequatewa 1936: 130, n.41) and was succeeded as leader of the Friendlies by Tewaquaptiwa. Lomahongyoma meanwhile became less active in Hostile affairs, eventually turning over his leadership to a younger man, Yokioma. These two young and uncompromising leaders rapidly reached an impasse. It appears that after 1897 even though the majority of the people were still Hostiles their support was declining. In January 1906 they invited members of the Second Mesa Hostile faction to join them at Oraibi (Nequatewa 1936: 60–65). Since the water supply was extremely limited, the Second Mesa newcomers placed even greater pressure on Oraibi resources. During the following months Friendly leader Tewaquaptiwa attempted to evict the Second Mesa faction, and by September a violent confrontation seemed inevitable. Learning of the crisis, the Mennonite missionaries came up and "made the people on both sides give up their weapons" (Nequatewa 1936: 67). Hostile leader Yokioma then proposed a pushing match to decide the question, drawing a line on the ground as a challenge. Yokioma was pushed over the line by Tewaquaptiwa and the Oraibi Friendlies, evidently supported by the residents of Moencopi (Titiev 1944: 86–88). Yokioma and his Hostile followers then gathered up food and belongings and left Oraibi.

Although the precipitating factor of the split had been the presence of the Second Mesa Hostiles at Oraibi, the division of Oraibi residents into Hostiles and Friendlies had occurred much earlier, and had been furthered by Lololoma's support of government schooling. The final rift was simply the culmination of the village's inability to contain two opposing views concerning how the Hopi ought to respond to the white man.

As they moved north, the Hostiles paused at Hotevilla Spring, intending to stop only briefly on their way north, presumably either to the Kiet Siel-

Betatakin or the Four Corners area. Soon after their arrival, however, troops arrived from Keams Canyon. Yokioma and several Hostile leaders were arrested and taken to jail, and their supporters from Second Mesa either jailed, sent to the Carlyle School, or returned to their village (Nequatewa 1936: 74–76). The troops also collected all school-age children and transported them to the Keams Canyon boarding school. The remaining Hostiles, now consisting of women, pre-school children, and old men, unwilling and unable to return to Oraibi, were left virtually without food and shelter. It was finally agreed that the remaining Hostiles should remain at Hotevilla Spring, at least for the winter, and arrangements were made for them to collect their remaining belongings from Oraibi. The one hundred people who remained at Hotevilla Spring remember the first winter painfully; starvation and exposure took many lives. The spring brought more disagreement, but as the summer of 1907 progressed it became clear that the Hostiles would remain at Hotevilla Spring. That winter the first kiva was constructed, and the village of Hotevilla came into existence.

The expulsion of the Hostiles and the division at Oraibi had a profound effect. The elderly still remember vividly the events of September 6, 1906, and have passed down accounts to following generations. These tragic events divided families, clans, and phratries, and thus began the disintegration of Oraibi, which in 1891 had had a population of 905 (Donaldson 1893: 45) and twelve or thirteen kivas. At the time, however, the expulsion of the Hostiles was seen as a victory and was celebrated by a Butterfly Dance. But for even the most dedicated Friendlies this victory was short-lived: a

month later the Hopi Agent decided that Tewaquaptiwa should be "educated," and he was forcibly sent to Sherman Institute, a government Indian school in Riverside, California.

Third Mesa—Agents and Reformers: 1906–1934

Within six years of their departure from Oraibi, the residents of Hotevilla, under the traditional political-religious leadership of Yokioma (he was released from prison in April 1907), had built five kivas and established the most complete ceremonial cycle on Third Mesa.

Lomahongyoma, the original founder of the Hostile faction, had apparently never wished a complete break with Oraibi (Nequatewa 1936: 74), and shortly after his arrival at Hotevilla agreed to return with some sixty followers on the condition that he accept the government education program and "stay out of the flute ceremony." In spite of his agreement, Lomahongyoma and his followers were hounded out of Oraibi (Titiev 1944: 93–94). But since Lomahongyoma was now considered a Friendly by government officials he received government assistance, specifically building materials, to construct his new village of Bacavi, adjacent to Hotevilla. The people of Bacavi, like those at Hotevilla, quickly built a kiva but they never established anything more than the most fragmentary ceremonial cycle. With the founding of the Mennonite Mission at Bacavi some residents even became Christians.

The third community established at this time was New Oraibi which developed around the Mennonite Mission, the government day school, and the trading post established by Lorenzo Hubbel (McNitt 1962: 204). Some families had moved to New Oraibi from the mesa top before 1906, possibly to avoid the tensions in Oraibi proper. Eventually, because of the government's actions following the division of Oraibi, almost everyone, whether originally Hostile or Friendly, turned against the government. The only Third Mesa communities to remain friendly to the government were New Oraibi and Bacavi.

Government Policy.   The government strategy was clearly to reward Friendlies and isolate Hostiles. In line with this policy, after the initial roundup of school children, Hotevilla was left in comparative isolation and its jailed leaders slowly returned.

Problems were not long in coming, however, and once more the school was at their source. Children removed to Keams Canyon were not allowed to return to Hotevilla for summer holidays unless their parents promised to bring them back in September (Udall 1969: 99). But in 1910 the more lenient Superintendent Lawshe replaced Superintendent Miller and allowed Hotevilla children to go home for a holiday; in September the children did not return to the school. Lawshe was therefore replaced as school superintendent and head of the Hopi Agency by Leo Crane, who was harsh in enforcing government policies.

One of Crane's first acts as superintendent, before even talking with the Hotevilla residents, was to request troops to enforce school attendance. In November 1911, troops arrived and collected fifty-one girls and eighteen boys. These children were not allowed to return home until 1915, and then only after Keams Canyon School was closed for fear

the buildings would collapse. School-age children were ordered to complete their education at the Hotevilla-Bacavi Day School which had been built in 1913.

Yokioma, who had been arrested in connection with the 1911 roundup, spent four of the eight years of Crane's administration in jail. He had been jailed by Crane in 1912, for instance, when he appeared at the Agency to file damages for the forced clipping of his sheep (Crane 1925: 178–82), but Crane had clearly failed to undermine his power. Hotevilla still remained the stronghold of opposition to the government.

Moreover, Friendly leader Tewaquaptiwa had returned in 1910 an embittered man from his experience at Sherman Institute in California. He felt that government officials did not recognize that he had acted in their interest in expelling the Hostiles from Oraibi. While his rival Yokioma had returned to his people after little more than a year in jail, Tewaquaptiwa had been forced to suffer nearly a four-year exile. The importance of his change of heart made itself felt during the administration of Robert E. L. Daniel, who succeeded Leo Crane in 1919. Tewaquaptiwa had by that time concluded that if Hopi society was to be maintained, alien white forces along with Hopis who had become Christians could not be tolerated at Oraibi. Nor could missionaries be permitted either at Oraibi or Moencopi. When Tewaquaptiwa tried to removed the Mennonite missionaries he was arrested along with Frank Siemptewa, chief of Moencopi. In 1925 Siemptewa, with the support of the people of Moencopi, was able to banish the Reverend Frey, the Mennonite missionary, and in 1942 after the Mennonite church was struck by lightning for the second time, the mission at Oraibi no longer existed (Dockstader 1979).

Thus, in the 1920s, Agent/Superintendent Daniel had to contend with an increasingly negative attitude toward the government from Oraibi and Moencopi as well as from Hotevilla, which remained adamantly hostile. Daniel's reaction was to use force to make the Hostiles conform to Anglo-American values, even to cleanliness.

Daniel's most notorious and well-publicized move against Hotevilla came in June 1921, when, he recounts, he "went to Hotevilla with eight employees and seven policemen, all well armed with revolvers" (James 1974: 178) to dip the population in Black Leaf-40, a sheep delouser. The incident has been described by one of the victims:

> They drove us to a place where there is a clinic and there they forced us into a door and inside were many men who would grab us and throw us in a tub full of water. There were many Hopi people and some from Walpi. I do not know who they were but they were there and we women folks had these Hopi belts and they would grab our belts and pull our clothes off and throw us in the tub. When one falls in it and swallows it it burns your throat. It must be the same thing that they dip the sheep in. And when we were thrown in these vats the men folks would reach to a woman and grab every place and rub us all over (Hopi Hearings 1955: 72–73).

As a result of their resistance to their people being dipped, Yokioma and other men from Hotevilla were jailed.

Daniel, however, had failed to consider the outraged reactions of former Friendly Tewaquaptiwa, whom he also jailed, and the people of Oraibi. He had also made the mistake of arousing white sympathizers who supported the Hotevilla residents and decried the actions of the Keams Canyon Agency. Daniel's response was to recommend that "no permit to visit the Hopi Reservation be issued to artists and literary people for longer than ninety days" (James 1974: 181).

Anglo-American interests in Native American arts first began in the 1880s and had steadily increased as more and more tourists reached the Southwest. With the coming of the railroad and the opening in 1904 of the El Tovar Hotel on the south rim of the Grand Canyon, the albeit still isolated Hopi area began to attract visitors. Tourists visited the Hopi area for different reasons, but by 1915 their general attitude toward Native Americans seems to have been characterized by a vague romantic notion that in acquiring civilization Anglo-Americans had lost the innocence maintained by the Native Americans. This romantic view of Native Americans further stimulated collectors of Native American arts and was the basis for Indian Reform movements that were to have such a profound impact on the Hopi in the 1930s. Because of growing Anglo-American concern over the treatment of Indians, Tewaquaptiwa was soon released from jail after the sheep-dip incident, as was Yokioma somewhat later.

Thus by 1922 new alliances were forming. The government policy of educating Tewaquaptiwa in order to consolidate governmental control over Friendly Hopis had clearly backfired. Furthermore, the government strategy of discriminating against the Hostiles isolated within a single village had not only failed but had also spurred the creation of Hotevilla as a new religious center on Third Mesa. Because Oraibi leader Tewaquaptiwa, now hostile to the government, recognized the erosive effect of Christian government schooling on traditional Hopi culture, he encouraged the release of many ceremonies from Oraibi to Hotevilla.

The outcry of many Anglo-Americans, now organized as a result of the Hotevilla dipping incident, reached a higher pitch. The publicity given the sheep-dip episode brought so many protests against the Bureau of Indian Affairs that in 1924 Daniel was replaced as agent by Edgar K. Miller. In the same year, as a result of activities of the National Association to Help the Indian and the Indian Welfare League, Native Americans were declared U.S. citizens (Dockstader 1979: 530). As citizens, Hopis were theoretically entitled to the protection of the Constitution, which permits freedom of religion.

The Hopi had from the time of the Mormons frequently known Anglos and Anglo groups opposed to the government policy. Sometimes, unexpectedly, these were missionaries; at other times anthropologists or, as Crane called them, the "sentimentalists" and the "weak-minded." What is important is that not only was suppression of the Hopi religion stopped, but also that Hopis now understood the power of national publicity. Sadly, the immediate impact was increased hostility between Christianized capitalist Hopis supported by the B.I.A. and missionaries, and Hopis who wished to maintain their traditional religion.

By 1930 the villages most staunchly opposed to government programs were Hotevilla and Oraibi on Third Mesa, Shongopavi and Shipaulovi on Second Mesa and Walpi on First Mesa. In contrast, the majority of the residents of First Mesa, who frequently worked for the B.I.A., supported the government. Apart from converted Hopis who lived either at the Second Mesa Baptist Mission or in Mishongovi, the other center of government support was at New Oraibi on Third Mesa.

NOTES

1. Parsons (1939: 862) has claimed that a Moravian Mission was established at Oraibi in 1870. There is no record of this mission nor any attempt to establish a mission in the Moravian Archives, Bethlehem, Pennsylvania. Parsons may have assumed that this mission was Moravian because it was referred to as the "United Brethren." This name, however, was also used by both the Evangelical United Brethren and the Methodist Episcopal Church. In 1968 these churches united to become the United Methodist Church, and their archival material is now being acquisitioned in the archives of Drew University, North Carolina. It is, therefore, at present, inaccessible. It is critical that this material be examined.

2. Anglo-Americans referred to the Hopi as the Moqui until the early 1900s.

3. Given the anti-Mormon attitude of the period, the Mormon presence probably stimulated Protestant activity. As Nagata (1970: 33) states, "The Mormons were entangled in a competition with the Protestant missionaries and [by the late 1880s] the Indian Rights Association, both of which entered the area with the aim of wooing the Indian from their faiths and removing the Mormons."

4. One of the many areas that have been neglected by researchers is missionary activity among the Hopi. Nothing has been published on either the role of the missionary or of the United States during the 1880s. Government sources,

however, are at least readily available, whereas missionary sources, when they exist, may be found only in a central denominational library or in various churches. According to Bourke (1884: 94), Mr. Taylor sent out forty copies of his yearly reports in 1881. This number suggests that he was supported by various church agencies. The location of these reports and others is sorely needed to gain a clearer understanding of this period of Hopi history.

5. A list of Hopi agents can be found in Donaldson (1893: 36) and James (1974: 107–8).

6. The government, however, did not re-establish an independent Hopi Agency until 1899.

7. Whitely (1988: 75, 319, n. 1) has argued that Lololoma did not visit Washington until 1890.

8. The two schoolteachers known for their sympathetic attitude toward the people of Oraibi were a Mrs. Gates, who was apparently dismissed because of her sympathies (James 1974: 128) and who later funded a Mennonite mission to instruct Hopi farmers (Kaufman 1931: 141), and Belle Axtell Kolp. Mrs. Kolp's affidavit, which led to the investigation of Agent Burton, provides a detailed description of wretched conditions and cruel practices at Oraibi in January and February 1902.

9. Whitely (1988) concurs with this opinion and has argued that much of the apparent conflict between Hostile and Friendly leaders was to force the dispersal of the Oraibi population.

CHAPTER FOUR

TRIBAL FACTIONALISM: PROGRESSIVE AND TRADITIONALIST

INTRODUCTION

The United States government policy toward the Hopi from the time of the Mexican War until 1934 intended cultural extermination. Policymakers believed that if the Hopi were educated, converted to Christianity (specifically Protestantism) and transformed into land-owning capitalists, they could become civilized Americans. The government's goal was for the Hopi to cease to exist as a culturally distinct people.

By 1930, however, American social and anthropological thought had been profoundly influenced by Franz Boas. Boas, who came from Germany in 1884, is considered the founder of American anthropology. His fieldwork among Native Americans of the Pacific Coast region led him to reject the earlier idea that Native American languages were "primitive." Boas recognized each language and culture as unique. Because of the theories of Boas and his students, a shift to cultural relativism took place in this country that permitted and even encouraged the maintenance of Indian cultures as distinct from Anglo-American culture.

From increased awareness and a greater value placed on the uniqueness of other cultures, government policy changed. Policymakers now agreed that some aspects of Native American cultures should be perpetuated and regarded as part of the greater heterogeneous American culture, as immigrant groups were. With this in mind Native Americans were encouraged to develop a limited form of self-government. Nevertheless, the government never abandoned its original goal of "civilizing" and Americanizing the Indian, although it would carry out these processes more humanely. But once more white action divided the Hopi. This time, the Progressives would work hand in hand with Anglo-Americans to bring about what Traditionalists regard as a betrayal of what it means to be Hopi. They would work with whites to achieve their ends which, in this century, had to do with money. If what divided the Hopi in the nineteenth century was education, what divided them in the twentieth was cash.

This time the threat to the Hopi people was both from without and within. This threat was in the form of the Tribal Council established by the American government. The Council is intended to represent the Hopi themselves, as the Hopi tribal government. But it has provoked arguments between Hopi factions since its formation, dividing Hopi into Traditionalists and Progressives. In this century it has also served as the greatest agent for change in Hopi life.

Until the 1930s the American policy of "civilizing" the Native Americans had been coupled with a policy of political isolation.

In effect, the government kept the Hopi distinct from the rest of the country and even from the state within which their land was located. This isolation allowed the Hopi political systems to continue unchanged until the passage of the Hopi Constitution in 1936. From then on the traditional Hopi system of village government was radically limited. The Hopi would now be divided on the basis of their reaction to the Hopi Constitution and to the Tribal Council it created.

For Traditionalists, who follow the traditional religion with its religious-political village leadership, the Constitution was but one more foreign concept being forced upon them. For Progressives, who advocate further involvement in the American cash economy, the Constitution was good since it established the Tribal Council which provided employment and later allowed the development of strip mining and the acceptance of a federal cash settlement for lost lands.

Traditionalists do not accept the Tribal Council because it is contrary to the Hopi's centuries-old system of religious-political organization. Traditionally, each village was an autonomous unit governed by clan and religious leaders led by the kikmongwi or village chief. There was no organization at the tribal level, although village leaders might meet to discuss mutual concerns and might even agree to combined military action, as happened at Awatovi in 1700. Traditionalists are also opposed to the Tribal Council since it is a body of officials elected without regard to their religion, hereditary rights, or traditional training. These Tribal Councilors have usurped much of the authority of traditional clan and religious leaders.

Progressives, who are frequently Christians, support the Council because it remains the vehicle for federal programs, many of which are geared to raising the Hopi "standard of living" Progressives favor, even though such programs also make Hopis dependent on cash.

Traditionalists are acutely aware of the interrelationship between their religion and subsistence agriculture and oppose a dependency on cash for two reasons. The first is that the demand for cash will make wage labor a necessity and force the abandonment of subsistence farming. The other is that economic dependence will prevent Hopi independence as a self-sufficient nation. For this reason, Traditionalists oppose services which demand continuous cash payments, like electricity, but do not object to the use of a truck battery as a source of power for a television set.

The Progressives, on the other hand, feel that Hopis should become further involved in the American cash economy because of the benefit not only to the individual but to the tribe as a whole. With economic development as their goal, Progressives have supported the Tribal Council which, as the only Hopi government recognized by the United States government, has sole authority to permit mineral development on reservation land.

Since the 1950s mineral development, aside from the legitimacy of the Tribal Council itself, has divided the Hopi. Resentment toward the Council has been heightened because it is the agent of mineral development on the Hopi Reservation. Traditionalists are deeply opposed to mining on the grounds that since the earth is sacred, it should be neither mutilated by strip mining nor sold.

But for the Progressives the earth is a source of capital and capital helps develop tribal enterprises, increase employment, and create an Anglo-American lifestyle—all desirable goals.

Both Traditionalists and Progressives recognize the overwhelming dominance of Anglo-American culture but have developed different strategies to meet this threat. They both acknowledge the Tribal Council as a vehicle of assimilation. But their opposing attitudes toward the Tribal Council and their conflicts over other issues, such as the Navajo-Hopi Act, the Indian Claims Commission, the partition of the Joint-Use Area and the mining of Black Mesa exist because of their differing strategies in the face of Anglo-American domination.

Disagreement over the legitimacy of the Tribal Council and, therefore, the legality of its actions, is the thread that runs through twentieth-century Hopi factionalism. Even today Traditionalists are defined by their opposition to the Tribal Council.

TRIBAL FACTIONALISM: 1934–1979

The Indian Reorganization Act

The Indian Reorganization Act or Wheeler-Howard Act of 1934 provided for the establishment of a Hopi Constitution and Tribal Council and was the culmination of the efforts of several reform movements. This Act was an attempt to return self-government to the native tribes and to prevent their further exploitation by Anglo-Americans. Its proponents could not have anticipated the dissension their good intentions would cause. The act was implemented by John Collier, who assumed

the post of Commissioner of Indian Affairs in 1933. Collier was one of the new breed of reformers influenced by the theory of "cultural relativism" espoused by Boas and his students but unfortunately had a limited understanding of how the Hopi functioned as a people.

As one of the founders of the American Indian Defense Association, Collier had opposed Commissioner Burke's suppression of Indian ceremonies. The American Indian Defense Association was also one of several groups that had applied pressure for Yokioma's release from jail after the sheep-dip incident of 1921. The group's greatest achievement came in 1923 when it actively worked for the resignation of Secretary of the Interior Albert B. Fall. The association had helped to uncover evidence that much of Fall's suppression of Indian religion—carried out by Burke—was related to his attempted grab of pueblo land in New Mexico (James 1974: 186). The group was also instrumental in bringing to light Fall's involvement in the Teapot Dome oil scandal (Clemmer 1978: 58). As a result of these revelations Fall was imprisoned. Subsequent public opinion supported the reformers, who were able to demand that Fall's successor, Hubert Work, conduct an investigation of Indian affairs (James 1974: 174).

The Department of Interior inquiry conducted by the Brookings Institution concluded that federal policy aimed at "civilizing" the Indian had been too rapid and that pre-adolescent children should not be removed to boarding schools. When results of this study and of a concurrent Senate investigation became known, it was clear that changes suggested by the reformers had to be made.

But it was not until John Collier took

over as Commissioner of Indian Affairs and pushed through the Indian Reorganization Act of 1934 that the Senate and the Department of the Interior's recommendations for increased federal aid for health and housing were carried out.

The Indian Reorganization Act was designed to protect Native Americans from Anglo-American greed and oppression and to permit them a sense of ethnic identity within American culture. Toward this goal each Native American tribe, with the help of the B.I.A., was encouraged to establish a democratic constitutional government. The Indian Reorganization Act also attempted to strengthen the tribal land base by empowering the Secretary of the Interior to restore and purchase Indian land and by prohibiting the sale of Indian land without Indian consent. Since Native Americans were now encouraged to maintain their customs, religious suppression ceased for the most part.

Among some of the decimated and demoralized Plains tribes, the Indian Reorganization Act had a positive impact. It created a unifying system of tribal government which served as a catalyst for ethnic pride. This was not the case for the Hopi, however.

Collier requested that the anthropologist Fred Eggan inquire into the feasibility of a tribal government at Hopi. Collier had in mind a central government uniting all Hopis. Eggan, on the other hand, clearly assumed that the existing religious/political system at the village level would be maintained when he reported that each village was "entirely competent" to assume the responsibility of self-government (letter to Commissioner Collier, Jan. 11, 1934). But the fact was the Hopi considered that they had always had self-government. The

Kikmongwi of Shongopavi, Lomahaftewa, wrote Collier (March 4, 1934):

. . . regarding the matter as in forming or organizing a self-government, which we already have that has been handed down from generation to generation up to this time.

The Hopi Agent Ernest H. Hammond, sharing Eggan's view, felt that the village communities would be willing and eager to submit their constitutions for consideration (letter to Commissioner Collier, February 15, 1934).

Collier, however, was not thinking of Hopi government as being at the village level, as it had traditionally existed, but envisioned a "tribal" form of government. In 1936 Collier appointed Oliver La Farge, a well-known author and Indian sympathizer, as a special representative to guide the Hopi toward "political freedom"—as Collier conceived it in Anglo-American terms. La Farge composed the "Constitution and By-Laws of the Hopi Tribe, Arizona" on October 24 of that year. It was submitted to the Hopis and Tewas and was approved by a vote of 651 to 104. The validity of this election has been a source of bitter debate.

Opponents argue that the vote tallies did not reflect the opinion of the majority of Hopis because many voters expressed opposition by abstention, the traditional Hopi way of expressing disapproval while avoiding confrontation and conflict (*Notes for Hopi Administrators* as quoted in the Indian Law Resource Center report, 1979: 48).

Jorgensen and Clemmer argue (1978: 69–71) that because of abstentions, the 755 votes cast in 1936 did not represent forty-seven percent of the eligible voters as

Collier had argued, but rather, twenty-nine percent. Thus the 755 votes did not meet the requirement of thirty percent of the adult voting population established under the terms of the Indian Reorganization Act.

More than sixty-one percent of the eligible voters on First Mesa voted, and of these, 31.8 percent voted against the Constitution, indicating that abstention was not exercised there. But abstention seems to have been a factor on Second and Third Mesas. On Second Mesa only eleven people (5.3 percent of the voting population) voted against the Constitution. The only Second Mesa village overwhelmingly in favor of the Constitution was Mishongovi, whose votes probably reflected the influence of the adjacent Baptist Mission which had been established in 1901 (Means 1960: 45) and had converted a number of Mishongovi residents.

On Third Mesa, abstention reached boycott proportions in some villages. Except for New Oraibi, abstention was the method of opposition. In New Oraibi, which had been founded by "Friendlies," many of whom were Mennonites, and which had been electing its own village council since 1930, more than 70 percent of the eligible inhabitants voted. In view of its history and composition it is not surprising that New Oraibi supported the proposed Tribal Council, 116 to 9. But apart from the nine negative ballots in New Oraibi and one other negative vote cast in Hotevilla, probably an error, there were no negatives votes on Third Mesa, only abstention. A mere 5.2 percent of those eligible in Hotevilla and 10.9 percent in Oraibi cast their votes. In the more progressive village of Bacavi 59.8 percent of the eligible voters voted.

The correlation between voter abstention and villages known for their opposition to the Tribal Council clearly indicates that abstention was used to express opposition. Abstention had always been used in this manner because it allowed for individual expression while avoiding conflict, both traditional Hopi values. After the establishment of the Tribal Council the Traditionalists maintained their anti-ballot position until the late 1950s, when they proposed that a referendum be held and the negative vote be used to express opposition to the Council. The Tribal Council, however, did not respond to this request, perhaps because it feared the strength of the Traditionalists at that time.

The adoption of the Constitution in 1936 created the "Hopi Tribe" and established the Hopi Tribal Council. After the election the separation widened between the Traditionalists, who call themselves *hopívitsïkani* (those who observe the Hopi way), and Progressives, those Traditionalists call *kansïhoyam* (little council people). Traditional Hopis became increasingly aware of the corrosive effect of the Council because it represented a totally alien political concept. The election itself had further divided the Hopi villages and brought about the official recognition of Upper and Lower Moencopi as two political units. Although both the upper and lower villages were allotted one representative each to the Council, Lower Moencopi, like Hotevilla and Oraibi, has never participated in the Tribal Council. The Traditionalists have always refused to join the Tribal Council since they do not wish to be part of an institution they consider contrary to traditional religious beliefs and values.

The Hopi Constitution also served to

intensify, if not create, intermesa conflict. Since the Hopis and Tewas of First Mesa and the Progressives of Third Mesa embraced the Constitution, they now began to vie for control of the Council. New Oraibi became the administrative center for the Tribal Council, although its first chairman was from First Mesa.

This first incarnation of the Council in 1936, however, proved to be short-lived, lasting only seven years. The termination of the Council in 1943 was caused by a lack of support both from Traditionalists who had always opposed it, and from Progressives who objected to the Council's attempt to administer grazing permits in accord with the unpopular federal stock reduction program.

The federal stock reduction program was an attempt to improve the quality of grazing land. Ever since the increase in livestock toward the end of the nineteenth century, range land throughout the Southwest had become dangerously depleted, adversely affected by drought as well as by overgrazing. Some of the worst lands were those used by the Navajo, whose population had grown rapidly since their release from Bosque Redondo in 1868. The Navajo had exceeded the capability of their reservation land to support their pastoral economy. Consequently, increasing numbers of Navajo were encroaching upon the Hopi Reservation, where the grassland became so radically destroyed that the government decided to reduce the number of livestock allowed on it. Although the Navajo were more severely affected by the federal stock reduction program, similar reductions were demanded of the Hopi.

The founding of the Hopi Tribal Council in 1936 coincided with these land-management programs of the B.I.A. In an attempt to preserve the range land, cause the least hardship to the greatest number of Indians and, the B.I.A. hoped, prevent Navajo-Hopi friction, the Hopi Reservation was divided into land-use districts. Only one of these, District 6, was under the jurisdiction of the Hopi Agency. The others were under the Navajo Agency because most of the livestock belonged to Navajos even though the land the animals grazed on belonged to the Hopi Reservation. District 6 included only the Hopi and Tewa villages and surrounding land.

Under Article VII of the Hopi Constitution, the Tribal Council was now responsible for the execution of the range land policy and for issuing livestock permits. Although the Council had never approved either the division of the Hopi Reservation into grazing districts or the issuance of permits, it lost much of its original support because of its association with the unpopular federal program. The kikmongwis of all three Second Mesa villages withdrew their support of the Council, as did the traditional villages of Third Mesa. Although Collier visited Hopi in 1938 to try to assuage Hopi fears and bolster the Council, he had little success. By 1939 there were not enough certified representatives to constitute a quorum and the Council ceased to be recognized by the Bureau of Indian Affairs after 1943.

The Council, although not recognized by the B.I.A., continued to exist unofficially and to express its concern regarding the Hopi Reservation boundaries to John Collier (Indian Law Resource Center 1979: 60, 62). What the Hopis were afraid of was that District 6 would become a new, smaller reservation. That is exactly what happened and many blamed the Council for it.

The steps that led to the shrinking of the

reservation began in 1941 when Collier ordered that the boundaries of District 6 be studied. A report made in July 1942 recommended that approximately 100,000 acres be added to the 500,000 acres of the original District 6. This report was approved by the superintendent of the Hopi Agency and by Byron P. Adams, Chairman of the Hopi Tribal Council.

Evidently Adams felt obliged to accept District 6 as the sole area open to Hopi livestock, and he therefore assumed that an increase in the size of the District would lessen the impact on the Hopi of the proposed government stock reduction program. Most assuredly he had no idea that the report he had signed would be used to establish District 6 as the new exclusive Hopi Reservation. Nonetheless, these new boundaries were approved by Washington in April 1943.

With the redefinition of the Hopi Reservation as the expanded District 6, the Tribal Council lost the last lingering support it had among the Hopi people. Recognizing this fact, and also that the Council lacked the power to carry out the federal stock-reduction program, the United States government ordered the Council disbanded. From 1943 until 1951 the Hopis practiced their traditional village-based form of government. That did not mean, however, that Anglo acculturative pressures declined. With the coming of World War II, many Hopis left the Reservation either to join the armed forces or to work in nearby cities. Those who returned frequently brought with them new ideas and expectations.

The Indian Claims Commission

A further wedge was driven between Traditionalists and Progressives when the government established District 6 as the new Hopi Reservation. This time, the two factions disagreed over how the land should be reclaimed. The Progressives believed that the only way they could reclaim their land was through the Indian Claims Commission, an agency established by Congress in 1946. They were encouraged to do this both by the Bureau of Indian Affairs and by John S. Boyden. A devout Mormon, Boyden was the United States Attorney who had represented the government in all the Indian cases handled by the Utah office between 1933 and 1946.

Subsequently, in 1951 the newly reinstated Tribal Council, with the help of Boyden and the B.I.A., submitted Docket 196, a petition alleging that Hopi aboriginal land had been taken by the United States without just compensation to the Hopi people. The Indian Claims Commission authorized Indians to file claims like Docket 196, for a period of five years, against the United States for past injustices. Congress desired to put an end to the legal and moral issue of Indian land claims. In addition, some congressmen wanted to reward returning veterans for their service during World War II (Indian Law Resource Center 1979: 80).

Although the Bureau of Indian Affairs encouraged all Indians to file land claims, the filing was particularly important for the Hopi. In 1944 uranium and coal had been discovered on Hopi land and a number of companies were seeking leases. But because leases for mining could be obtained only "by authority of the Tribal Council or other authorized spokesmen for such Indians" (ibid. 74) and approved by the Secretary of the Interior, no leases had been authorized. Land rights first had to be established in accordance with United States law and "authorized spokesmen" for the "Hopi tribe" identified by the Bureau.

Since the Tribal Council had been dissolved in 1943 Hopi "self-government" had been effectively administered under the traditional leadership of the kikmongwis, except at New Oraibi and Upper Moencopi, which were governed by village councils. In June 1948, however, Acting Commissioner of Indian Affairs William Zimmerman, Jr. recommended that the Tribal Council be reconstituted for the specific purpose of authorizing mineral leases. This was done in 1951, although the Council was not officially recognized until 1955.

Naturally, the resurrection of the Tribal Council met resistance from Traditionalists. The same year a conference of Traditional kikmongwis and religious leaders was held at Shongopavi. The meeting lasted several days and witnessed the birth of what Clemmer (1978: 90) has termed the Hopi Resistance Movement. It was at this meeting that the Traditionalists formulated their resistance, on religious grounds, not only to the Lands Claims Commission and the Tribal Council but also to the proposed Navajo-Hopi Act.

The Navajo-Hopi Act

The Navajo-Hopi Act was designed to raise capital for reservation development and to this end authorized $88,570,000 for improvements on the reservations. On the Hopi Reservation these included wells, stock troughs, fences, flood-control dikes, and roads (Clemmer 1979: 534). Their construction provided wage labor to an increasing number of Hopis.

The Progressives supported the act. In addition to wanting to lease land to mineral companies, the Progressives also sought to raise their "standard of living," as defined by the dominant society, and become wage earners. Capital was necessary to create jobs and to provide cash for Anglo-American goods.

The Traditionalists, as could be expected, opposed the act. They realized that increased jobs and dependency on cash, as opposed to subsistence farming, would undermine traditional Hopi religion. Their resistance was most clearly stated in a five-page letter, signed by the kikmongwis of Shongopavi, Mishongovi, and Hotevilla and by twenty religious leaders, sent to President Truman on March 28, 1949. The letter was prompted not only by the Navajo-Hopi Act but more importantly by Boyden's proposal to submit Docket 196 to the Indian Claims Commission; in it the Traditionalists articulated their myths, prophecies, beliefs and goals.

The principal author of this letter was probably Thomas Banyacya, who acted as interpreter-spokesman for the Traditionalists. Although we must rely on Banyacya for much of our information, it was understood that he was only a spokesman for the unified Traditionalist religious leadership whose position set forth by the letter can be summarized as follows:

> It is part of the divine plan that the Hopis came to their land which was given to them by the Great Spirit Masaw. This land is sacred and the Hopis were given the task to guard this land not by force of arms, not by killing . . . but by humble prayers, by obedience to our traditional and religious instructions and by being faithful to our great Spirit. [They go on to state] that they must follow the divine plan until judgment day, when the Hopis' white brother, who went east, will return with his Stone Tablet to

the Hopis. The Stone Tablets when together, and if they agree, will prove to the whole world that this land truly belongs to the Hopi people and that they are true brothers. Then the white brother will restore order and judge all the people here who have been unfaithful to their traditional and religious principles and who have mistreated his people.[1]

This statement was the premise for Traditionalist opposition (1) to any land claim, for the land is already Hopi, (2) to any land lease, for the land is sacred, (3) to the Atlantic Treaty, for Hopis are forbidden to take up arms, (4) to Hopis becoming tax-paying citizens under state jurisdiction, for they are "a sovereign nation," (5) to the Navajo-Hopi Act which set aside funds for the "development" of these reservations, since the Hopis considered themselves a self-supporting people.

Despite such obvious opposition to the Land Claims Commission by a significant group of Hopis, Boyden and the Progressives submitted Docket 196 to Congress. Boyden's petition, entered in August 1951, surprisingly asked only for money damages. The concept of receiving money for land was not only against Traditionalist doctrine but would also be opposed by virtually all Hopis. The only explanation for the acquiescence of the Progressive leaders was that Boyden had convinced them that they had no hope of ever recovering all their lost land. And should their claim be won, Boyden must have told them, it would not result in "a full discharge of the United States of all claims and demands touching any of the matters involved in the controversy," as guaranteed in the Indian Claims Commission Act.

Although some people argue tht Boyden was primarily interested in his own material gain (Indian Law Resource Center 1979: 141–43, 149–55), he and Hopi Progressives were genuinely concerned with raising capital for Reservation development, although that goal was in conflict with that of the Traditionalists.

By 1950, and throughout the next decade, Hopi Traditionalists and Progressives were about equal in number (ibid. 100). The widespread support for the Traditionalist position was due to a number of factors, not the least of which was Dan Katchongva, Yokioma's son, a charismatic figure and a brilliant and forceful speaker.

Katchongva, with his friend Banyacya acting as his spokesman and interpreter, launched a protest campaign against Washington in the early 1950s. Katchongva made it clear that the Traditionalists were fully aware of the illegal nature of the newly re-established Tribal Council that the Progressives supported.

Because of this split within the Hopi, the Bureau of Indian Affairs did not recognize the Council as a legislative body but merely as an advisory one. In 1955 Senator Barry Goldwater urged that the Tribal Council not be officially recognized until the situation had been investigated. This was undertaken between July 15 and July 30, when a committee held meetings at the Hopi villages. The record of these Hopi Hearings is an invaluable document that reveals the diversity of Hopi opinion and the conflict between Progressives and Traditionalists, residents of First and Third Mesas, and residents of Upper and Lower Moencopi.

A few weeks later, official recognition of

the Hopi Tribal Council was recommended by the Commissioner of Indian Affairs Glenn L. Emmons in a letter dated December 1, 1955, but clearly the Hopis remained about equally divided in their support of this controversial body.

The Tribal Council and Mineral Rights Leases

Although the Council was officially recognized in 1955 as the Hopi government, according to its own constitution it lacked the power to grant mineral leases. The Solicitor's Office of the Department of the Interior had ruled in 1959 that the Tribal Council could not do so since the constitution specifically empowered the Council "to prevent the sale, disposition, lease or encumbrance of tribal lands." Nonetheless, the oil companies, the Bureau of Indian Affairs, the Progressives, and John S. Boyden all desired Hopi mineral exploration.

The Tribal Council preferred not to call for a referendum on the issue because it did not want to face the strength of the Traditionalists. Nor did it want the Traditionalists to discover that the most easily accessible surface mineral was coal. In the West, coal is most cheaply extracted through strip mining, the scale of which would be an anathema to the Traditionalist view of the land as sacred. Though unaware of the Council's plans, Dan Katchongva had written a letter to protest against mineral development on behalf of the traditional leaders of Mishongovi, Shongopavi, Oraibi, Hotevilla, and "the majority of the Hopi people" (Indian Law Resource Center 1979: 128).

Boyden and the Tribal Council decided to attack from another angle. They asked the Secretary of the Interior to delegate leasing authority to the Tribal Council under Article VI, Section 3 of the Hopi Constitution which permits the Council to exercise powers delegated to it by the Tribe or by the Secretary of the Interior. The Tribal Council was thus granted the power to lease mineral rights on May 29, 1961, and a few months later the Council signed a lease with the Fisher Contracting Company for coal exploitation within District 6. The Council's actions further divided the Hopi.

Navajo-Hopi Relations

Mineral leases also reopened hostilities between Navajo and Hopi. With the cessation of Navajo raids in the 1870s and the end of their use as Hopi "police" by the United States government, Navajo-Hopi relations had for the most part been worked out by each household. Conflict did not erupt again until the Progressives realized that the land occupied by the Navajo was vital to the Hopi because of its mineral resources.

In 1961 the Peabody Coal Company expressed interest in leasing an area in the northwestern corner of the 1882 Hopi Reservation near Kayenta. But in 1946 the Department of the Interior had decided that the mineral estate in this area belonged to both the Navajo and the Hopi. The land in question had belonged to the Hopi reservation in 1882 but had been ceded to the Navajo when the reservation boundaries were redrawn in 1942 to correspond to District 6. The Department of Interior's 1946 ruling asserted that excluding District 6, which was under sole Hopi jurisdiction, both the Hopi and the Navajo owned the mineral estate within the 1882 Hopi Reservation, since the Navajo had settled in the area with the knowledge and approval of the Secretary of the Interior. Mining leases would therefore have to be approved by both the Navajo and the Hopi. The two tribes had attempted to negotiate their mutual claims but had failed. In 1961 Dewey Healing, Chairman of the Hopi Tribal Council, filed a suit against Paul Jones, Chairman of the Navajo Tribal Council. In September 1962 a three-judge federal district court decided the case, affirmed the following year by the Supreme Court. The 1962 decision upheld the 1946 decision, further ruling that the Hopi and the Navajo had an undivided and equal interest and that all of the 1882 Hopi Reservation lying outside District 6 was to be known as the Joint-Use Area.

After the 1962 decision naming all of the 1882 Reservation outside District 6 for joint use, the Tribal Council began to press for the partition of the area into exclusive Hopi and Navajo sections. The Council's main intention apparently was to secure full leasing revenue for the estimated twenty-two billion tons of unmined coal in the Hopi Sector of the Joint-Use Area. In 1974 the partition of these lands was authorized along with $31,500,000 to relocate any Hopis or Navajos who found themselves on the wrong side of the boundary. Since the 1974 partition of the Joint-Use Area (J.U.A.), however, the government has spent more than $100 million on the relocation of approximately one thousand Navajo families and one hundred Hopi families.

From 1974 until 1980 the Tribal Council, its attorneys, and its public relations counsel waged a media battle against the Navajo. Mark Panitch noted in the *Washington Post* (July 21, 1974):

Both the Hopis' energetic and effective lawyer, John Boyden, and their public relations counsel, Evans and Associates, are headquartered in Salt Lake City. . . . Through their Mormon allies, the [Progressive] Hopis also have developed allies in the worlds of industry and government. . . . While Boyden was lobbying in Congress and arguing in the courts, Evans and Associates virtually stage-managed a range war on the borders of the Hopi Reservation.[2]

Relocation has created considerable individual hardship especially among the Navajo, and has been another bone of contention between Hopi Progressives and Traditionalists. Opponents of relocation founded the Big Mountain Defense/Offense Committee to represent Navajos, particularly from the Big Mountain area, who have continued to defy the federal relocation order. The richest undisturbed coal deposits nearest to the surface are believed to be at Big Mountain. At present more than 15,000 Navajos await or resist relocation. While Hopi Progressives have railed against the constant delays in Navajo relocation and have impounded Navajo stock, Traditionalists have supported the Big Mountain Navajo (*Voice* July 29, 1986) and continue their opposition to mining. Although it is sometimes overlooked, mining is the larger issue behind relocation.

Once the Tribal Council was empowered to negotiate mineral leases in 1961 it proceeded to do so. The leases negotiated by the Tribal Council were to dramatically change its position and role in Hopi life.

During the 1950s the Traditionalists were at least as powerful as the Progressives and may have formed a majority. Although they had failed to stop Docket 196, the reconstruction of the Tribal Council, or the Navajo-Hopi Act, they had succeeded in two areas. They had abolished stock permits and negotiated conscientious objector status for Hopis initiated into the Kachina Society. They had also continued to fight the existence of the Tribal Council, although their opposition was, for the most part, simply ignored. Then they went to court.

Despite some Traditional religious leaders' opposition to using United States courts, they finally agreed in 1964 that the only way to force the removal of the Tribal Council and to stop the leasing of Hopi land for mineral development was to challenge the legality of the Council. They did this based on its own constitution. A lawsuit filed by representatives of Mishongovi, Shipaulovi, Oraibi, Shongopavi, and Hotevilla named the Hopi Tribal Council and all the lessees as defendants. A few months later the case was dismissed by Judge Walter M. Bastain, who ruled that the Hopi Tribal Council was a sovereign government and, therefore, an indispensable party immune from suit. In 1964 despite the pending lawsuit, the Tribal Council had granted a drilling and exploration permit to Peabody Coal Company and had entered into leases with more than ten oil and gas companies. A coal lease with the Peabody, still in effect, was signed in 1966. But the Traditionalists had not given up. In 1971 they filed another suit that challenged the legality of mineral leases granted by the Council. The plaintiffs in this case were more than sixty Traditionalist Hopis, religious leaders, and kikmongwis of all traditionally organized villages.

Once again the court's argument was that the Tribal Council was a legitimate sovereign Indian government, and thereby immune from court review. In 1975 the United States Court of Appeals approved the dismissal of this case, and in 1976 the Supreme Court declined to hear it. The Indian Law Resource Center (1979: 166) therefore concluded, "the United States courts had thus ruled that there was no judicial forum in which the Hopi traditional leaders could have their day in court to challenge the strip-mining leases."

Clemmer (1979: 536) notes that between 1961 and 1964 leases brought $3,139,104.43 in royalties. The leasing ventures were undertaken in an attempt to create jobs for the Hopi and to provide the council with income. Clearly there was no way that the money from oil and gas leases could be equaled by the Anglo-American environmentalists, lawyers, and anthropologists who had made donations to the Traditionalist cause.

PROGRESSIVE AND TRADITIONALIST: 1979–1987

Since the late 1950s more and more Hopis have felt that they could do nothing to stop the ever-encompassing blanket of Anglo-American culture. The continued legal rebuttals of the Traditionalists' position may have helped to influence the attitudes Traditionalists and Progressives hold today. The last ten years appear to have witnessed a calm resignation by Traditionalists and a growing respect for their position by Progressives. Some Traditionalists have even changed their attitudes as they enjoy such conveniences as electricity, running water, and western medicine.

But others have continued to oppose utilities, even when this position has led to confrontation with the Bureau of Indian Affairs as it did at Hotevilla in 1968. Traditionalists, realizing that in order to pay utility bills a cash income is necessary, successfully blocked the Arizona Public Service Company's attempt to install electricity there (Clemmer 1978: 73).

Underlying the disagreements between Traditionalists and Progressives over the Tribal Council and mineral exploration was the more basic conflict over the extent to which Hopis should become involved in the American cash economy. This has always been a major issue separating the two Hopi factions, and this is what lay behind the Traditionalist opposition to electricity at Hotevilla.

Both Progressives and Traditionalists desire and use some Anglo-American goods. Traditionalists argue, however, that a dependency on goods and services will prohibit their independence from Anglo-American domination. The Progressives, on the other hand, conceive of independence as Tribal control of these goods and services. To illustrate:

Following World War II returning veterans frequently found themselves alienated from both Hopi and Anglo-American society, and alcoholism for the first time became a problem among the Hopi. This problem has continued. In the 1970s the Tribal Council partially funded an alcoholic counseling center staffed by Hopis because they felt that the federal government Indian Health Service was not adequately meeting the tribe's needs. From the Progressive point of view, cash acquired by the Tribal Council made this independent action possible. The Counseling Center not only helped Hopis but provided a cash income to the Hopis employed.

Traditionalists, on the other hand, blamed cash for the very existence of the problem. Cash made possible the purchase of alcohol. If the alcoholic needs help, the Traditionalists reason, he should turn away from the cash economy and to a medicine man and traditional religion. "Counseling" is always available within the kiva, and an alcoholic's kiva association would not only support him but, if necessary, remove him from the destructive Anglo world of which alcohol is a part. For the Traditionalist, cash not only causes the initial problem of alcoholism but also maintains such social problems because it continues to separate the Hopi from their traditional religion and values.

Traditionalists further argue that the pursuit of cash and the goods that it can purchase has caused other social problems, particularly the dividing of families and the dividing of villages. For instance, women and men increasingly live near their place of employment rather than in the village of their, or their wives', lineage. On First Mesa this has led to the growth of Polacca because of its proximity to jobs at Keams Canyon, and has brought about the physical separation of families. The mesa-top villages are now mainly inhabited by the generation of grandparents who farm the valley below, while the younger wage earners have moved into the more modern houses along Route 264.

Nowhere on Third Mesa has the impact of the Anglo-American cash economy been more acutely felt than at Moencopi. Moencopi agriculture compared to that of the mesas is almost entirely dependent on irrigation, demanding village-wide participation in maintenance and rotation.

But by the late 1920s the growing number of Hopis engaged in wage labor began to be a threat to farming (Nagata 1970: 49). As more and more people failed to use and, therefore, failed to help maintain the village irrigation system, factionalism developed. The farmers still recognized the authority of Oraibi to settle disputes while the younger wage earners, who usually lived in the newer upper section of the village, did not. Frustrated by this growing factionalism, the village established a council in an attempt to unify the divided Moencopi. It was soon dominated by the younger people of the upper village, however, thus further separating the new area from the traditional lower village. In 1936, as a result of the Indian Reorganization Act, Upper Moencopi became a separate political unit governed by its own Village Council, while the lower village still answered to the religious and, therefore, political leadership of Tewaquaptiwa of Oraibi.

Wage labor has had another kind of impact on the Hopi household. Cash has made it easier to acquire a separate house, and this has sometimes led to the abandonment of matrilocal residence in favor of residence near the place of the husband's employment. The husband is therefore no longer in his traditional ambiguous position and, since cash is increasingly necessary, his role within the nuclear family becomes increasingly important.[3] His wife and children, however, are now not surrounded by members of their lineage. With lineage ties no longer reinforced by close working relationships, clan affiliation has become even more important as it provides "relatives" in the new community. Thus, while the clan remains the primary social unit for Hopis, emphasis has shifted from the lineage or village clan segment to the clan as a whole.

Before 1875 and the establishment of the trading post at Keams Canyon, Hopi trade both with Anglos and other Indians was based on barter. But during the next twenty years barter for transacting business with Anglos gradually declined because of the increase in wage labor.

From an early date Keam had employed Hopis at his trading post and had paid cash as well as given barter for crafts. The construction of the Atcheson, Topeka and Santa Fe Railroad, which reached Albuquerque in 1880, brought tourists to the Southwest, greatly increasing the Native American craft market and opening up further opportunities for Hopi wage labor. Hopis now commonly worked as teamsters hauling Mormon produce and Navajo wool from Tuba City, and Navajo and Hopi crafts and wool from Keams Canyon to the railroad towns of Flagstaff, Winslow and Holbrook. The Mormon community of Tuba City employed Hopis as farm workers and coal miners and the school at Keams Canyon provided other jobs.

Although the Hopi economy of today remains based on subsistence farming, it has, since Anglo-American contact in the 1850s, been increasingly supplemented and partly replaced by a cash economy. The three primary sources of cash income for Hopis are wage labor, livestock and crafts. Although some Hopis own stores, restaurants, or auto repair shops, full-time wage labor is the most common form of income. Most Hopis who have jobs work for the tribe or the federal government and so employment is concentrated around Keams Canyon, New Oraibi and Tuba City.

Keams Canyon is the Hopi Agency town and contains the offices of the Bureau of Indian Affairs (B.I.A.), the boarding school, and the hospital, all of which employ a number of Hopis. On Second Mesa the Hopi Cultural Center, containing a motel, restaurant, museum, shops, and the silversmiths' "guild," also provides employment. The offices of the Hopi Tribal Council are located in New Oraibi on Third Mesa. The Council administers federal programs, such as CETA (Comprehensive Employment Training Act) through the Departments of Aging, Health and Human Services, and the Department of Education. In Tuba City there is also a B.I.A. office, a boarding school, a large high school, a public health service hospital, and several shops and garages.

Employment is high around these centers. In New Oraibi and Bacavi on Third Mesa, forty percent of the population aged sixteen and over are employed. The Hopi average employment of those sixteen and over is fifty percent. These two Progressive villages contrast significantly with the Traditional Third Mesa village of Hotevilla where only nineteen percent are employed.

Another important source of cash income for Hopis is the sale of livestock. Herding replaced hunting as a male occupation after the introduction of sheep by the Spaniards in the sixteenth century, and now livestock is the exclusive domain of the men, who own all horses, sheep, goats, and cattle. In 1891 Donaldson (1893: 46) estimated from trading records that 26,000 pounds of wool were sold at from eight to nine cents a pound and that 20,000 sheep, 5,000 goats and 800 cattle belonged to the Hopi of First, Second, and Third Mesas. The size of these herds increased dramatically after the federal government initiated construction of windmills around 1915. Until the 1950s, one of the principal sources of income was from the sale of sheep and wool.

In the last twenty years, however, there has been a marked decline in the number of sheep within the Hopi area and a growing preference for cattle (Nagata 1970: 165–66), which do not demand the daily care and attention that sheep require. Many cattle ranchers now may also maintain full-time employment.

The ever-increasing Hopi participation in the national cash economy has caused concern among the more traditional Hopis who foresee a continuing decline in the interrelationship of subsistence farming, social organization, and the religion that for so long has served to integrate Hopi culture. For this reason strict adherents to the traditional religion oppose the Tribal Council that sees increased employment, as opposed to subsistence farming, as one of its primary goals.

As citizens of the United States, both politically and economically, the Progressives have maintained their efforts to increase wage labor. As mineral leases and strip-mining brought more and more income, the Tribal Council engaged in another business venture. Through a grant-loan from the Economic Development Administration and some of its own money, the Council built the motel-restaurant-museum-craft shop complex on Second Mesa known as the Hopi Cultural Center. The Tribal Council is now apparently the single largest employer on the Hopi Reservation, and so it is not surprising that as more and more young people desire Anglo-American goods they seek wage labor, and soon find themselves dealing with the Tribal Council. Still, a young person from a Traditional family will

A.	Mesa/Area	Village/villages	Total Population	Male	Female	House-holds	Over 15	Over 15 Employed
	First Mesa	Hano, Sichomovi, Walpi	521	251	270	121	407	102
		Polacca	627	311	316	103	424	97 + ?
	Second Mesa	Mishongovi, Toreva Shipaulovi Shongopavi	471	215	256	91	309	109
		Second Mesa "downstairs" ?itá·ki·tpik	154	79	75	30	93	31
	Third Mesa	Oraibi	133	68	65	31	90	27
		Lower Oraibi	477	200	277	144	287	116
		Hotevilla	443	243	200	109	326	62
		Bacavi	217	112	105	61	147	59
	Moencopi Area	Upper Moencopi Lower Moencopi	670	327	343	158	424	141
	Keams Canyon	Sample only ED 70 15	211	105	106	71	104	36 + ?
	TOTAL		3,924	1,911	2,013	919	2,611	780 + ?

B.	Mesa/Area	Village/villages	Total Population	Male	Female	House-holds	Over 15	Over 15 Employed
	First Mesa	Hano, Sichomovi, Walpi	496	248	248	89	264	3
	Second Mesa	Mishongovi Shipaulovi Shongopavi	596	306	289	105	294	0
	Third Mesa	Oraibi	905	445	460	170	560	3
	TOTAL		1,996	999	997	364	1,118	6

Figure 4. Population, households, and employment, 1980 and 1891. A. 1980 (U.S. Department of Commerce, Bureau of the Census). B. 1891 (Donaldson 1893: 45).

usually refuse to work for the Council although he will work for the Bureau of Indian Affairs or the Public Health Service.

Some Traditionalists fear that theirs is a losing battle. The rapid increase in wage labor and the concurrent use of cash in the last ninety years is dramatically illustrated by comparing the data from the 1891 census with those of the 1980 census in Figure 4.

Before World War II wage labor was sporadic and frequently seasonal (Nagata 1970: 186). Since World War II, however, routine wage labor has come to dominate the lives of many Hopis. Cash, to a greater or lesser degree, is now a necessity.

What struggles the Traditionalists do win seem to be Pyrrhic victories. At present, neither electricity nor running water has been installed either in Hotevilla or Oraibi on Third Mesa, nor at Mishongovi on Second Mesa. As a result, these villages are beginning to develop "suburbs" of houses with utilities. Walpi, on First Mesa, is also without electricity and running water and is frequently cited by Progressives as an example of what will happen to Traditionalist villages. Walpi is now occupied by only eight people; the rest of the residents have moved to the new community of Polacca in the valley below.

In recent years Progressive-Traditionalist tensions have been greatest between 1974 and 1979, during which time Docket 196 (the Hopi land claim petition) was settled (1976) and the partitioning of the Joint-Use Area was approved by Congress (1978). Docket 196 is still bitterly debated by Traditionalists and Progressives, and Traditionalists have continued to maintain their opposition to both partition and relocation. By giving their support to the Navajos of Big Mountain who are refusing relocation, Traditionalists have supported "the enemy" in the eyes of most Progressives. Although Progressives and Traditionalists can be regarded as two political factions advocating two different economic approaches, the Traditionalists have always seen their differences as

religious ones. They accept being called Traditionalists in English because, as they say, they follow the traditional Hopi religion. They argue that their myths validate their status as true followers of the Hopi way.

Many Progressives, however, believe that the inevitable increase in wage labor will soon bring about some modification of the Traditionalist position. For their part, the Traditionalists believe that the Progressives, having discovered that self-interest is the primary concern of both their Mormon lawyers and the mining companies, will move closer to the Traditionalist point of view.

Shared beliefs and concerns as well as family and lineage ties do sometimes succeed in cutting across political and religious differences between the Traditionalists and Progressives. One such occasion occurred when both the Traditionalists and the Progressives joined other Indian groups in legal action to prevent further development of the San Francisco Peaks as a ski resort. But their differences may remain unbridgeable, and have led many a Traditionalist to lament that indeed the Hopi "are two different peoples now."

NOTES

1. It should be pointed out that although the bahana myth was probably a nineteenth-century introduction, the concept of "Judgment Day" is very recent. It is interesting to note that in the letter from the Traditionalist chiefs and religious leaders to President Truman in 1949 the origin myth is basically the same as that recorded by Cushing (1923) in 1883, Voth (1905) in 1902, and Titiev (1944) in 1935, but the role of the bahana has

changed. He will now bring about "Judgment Day" when "all people" who have mistreated the Hopi will be judged. Thus, the "white brother" must identify Hopis and Anglos who have lived properly—in other words, Hopis and Anglos supporting the Traditionalist point of view. The Judgment Day concept may have been specifically inspired by the Mormons who, like the Traditionalists, also emphasize the importance of prophecy. It is now argued on Third Mesa that prior to Judgment Day all the true followers of the traditional Hopi way will return to Oraibi.

2. Mormon interest in, and influence among, the Hopi recurred in the 1950s, almost a hundred years after Hamblin's first missionary efforts. In 1951, the same year that Boyden became the Hopi claims attorney, the "first full-time Mormon missionaries came to [New] Oraibi" (Udall 1969: 240). These missionaries also attempted to work at Hotevilla where the doors were evidently slammed in their faces (ibid. 241). The Mormon missionaries, Virgil and Ruth Bushman, who came in contact with the Sekaquaptewa family at this time, were evidently as concerned with spreading the "Mormon way" of education and political organization as they were the Gospel. By 1953 Emory and Helen Sekaquaptewa were baptized as were their sons Wayne, Emory Jr., Abbott, and Edward, and their two daughters, Allison and Marlene. This remarkable family was to play an important role in the Tribal Council and Hopi acculturation.

In 1953 Emory Sr. became a key figure within the Tribal Council, acting as one of the first chairmen and as tribal judge. His two eldest sons, Wayne and Eugene, had both served in the military during World War II. Wayne returned to Hopi in 1963 to found, with his brother Emory Jr., the overlay jewelry manufacturing shop known as Hopicrafts. Emory and his brother Abbott were both active in the Tribal Council in the 1960s. Abbott was one of the first representatives to the Tribal Council from New Oraibi in the 1950s and has been actively involved ever since. He has alternately acted as Executive Secretary or Chairman. His last Council term expired in 1982.

In 1973 Wayne Sekaquaptewa started the Hopi newspaper *Qua'Töqti*. "In 1976 he started a tour company, Hopiland Tours, and an Indian construction company, Pueblo Builders. . . . His first concern in all this economic activity was to provide jobs for his people" (*Qua'Töqti,* Sept. 13, 1979). At the time of Wayne Sekaquaptewa's death in 1979 it was noted that, "As time went on he more and more saw his obligation to his people in spiritual rather than economic terms. He died without fulfilling his main objective, getting land for a new Mormon LDS [Latter Day Saints] chapel between Old Oraibi and Hotevilla" (ibid.).

3. Although the Hopi husband has taken on a new and important role as a wage earner, this change has not led to male dominance. Schlegel (1977) has noted that in households where both the husband and wife work reciprocal interdependence has likewise been maintained.

Plate 1. Butterfly dancer and partner, Lower Moencopi.

Plate 2. Prehistoric Hopi Ceramics. *Upper left:* Tusayan Black-on-White jar. *Lower left:* Sikyatki Polychrome bowl. *Right:* Sikyatki Polychrome jar.

Plate 3. Historic Hopi Ceramics. *Left:* San Bernardo
Polychrome jar. *Center:* San Bernardo Polychrome jar.
Right: Payupki Polychrome jar.

Plate 4. Polacca Polychrome and Mishongovi Variety.
Left and right: Polacca Polychrome jars. *Center:* Mishongovi Brown-on-Buff jar.

ERRATA

Plates 2, 3, and 4 courtesy of Peabody Museum, Harvard University.
Photographs by Hillel Burger.

Plate 5. Domestic wares. Jar made by Terry and duck
bowl made by Vera.

Plate 6. Style B stew or serving bowl. Vessel 32 (ht. 18.0 cm), made by Loren.

Plate 7. Jar. Vessel 200 (ht. 32.0 cm), made by Terry and (left) decorated by Cindy and later altered (right) by Terry.

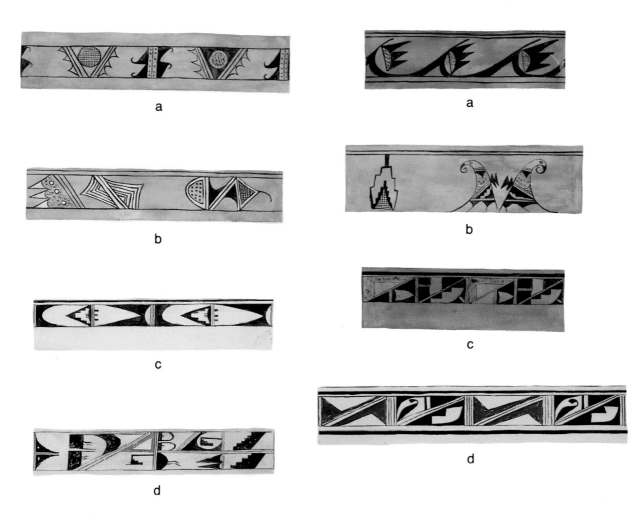

Plate 8. Roll-out drawing of Style A and Style B framed-bands used on small bowls. a. Vessel 12 (ht. 7.0 cm), made by Diana and decorated by Betty. b. Vessel 34 (ht. 6.5 cm), made by Diana and decorated by Betty. c. Vessel 31 (ht. 6.0 cm), made and decorated by Lucy. d. Vessel 28 (ht. 4.9 cm), made and decorated by Cindy.

Plate 9. Roll-out drawings of Style A and B small bowls. a. Vessel 97 (ht. 6.3 cm), made by Terry. b. Vessel P.M. 248952 (ht. 6.9 cm), made by Terry c. Vessel P.M. 249053 (ht. 6.5 cm), made by Lucy. d. Vessel 143 (ht. 6.6 cm), made by Loren. *Note:* a., c., and d. are frame-band designs; b. is a discrete unit design.

Plate 10. Raised Decoration Style. Vessel 58 (ht. 7.0 cm), made by Faith.

CHAPTER FIVE

HOPI CERAMICS

INTRODUCTION

While wage labor and cattle ranching have replaced subsistence farming for many Hopi, crafts remain a significant tie that binds the Hopi to the American cash economy. Starting with the revival of Hopi pottery in the style of Sikyatki Polychrome of the fourteenth century by Thomas Keam at the turn of this century, crafts have been the main way for Americans to become acquainted with this Native American group. And until quite recently, pottery has been the most popular of the Hopi crafts for the American consumer. When tourism to the Southwest was first beginning on a large scale, what spurred interest in the handicrafts of a people who had been recently dismissed as primitives was the British Arts and Crafts Movement.

Started by William Morris as a protest against mass production and industrialization, the arts and crafts movement of the 1870s and 1880s aimed to restore English handmade crafts to their former quality. Morris felt crafts had been compromised by mass production, so he and his group printed their own books by hand, made wallpaper and wove fabric. One of the most important by-products of this movement was the belief that crafts could be art.

The definition of Hopi pottery as art could only have come after white people became involved with the marketing of the craft. Hopi pottery as "art" is strictly a concept of the white marketplace, and it was particularly the British Arts and Crafts movement that created a market for Indian crafts. By the 1880s Hopi women were manufacturing pottery for sale at Keam's trading post. By the turn of the century Hopi men were weaving rugs—usually in the Navajo style—for distribution through the Fred Harvey Company (Wade 1976: 70). By 1920 Hopi men were manufacturing Kachina dolls for sale.

Most of the ceramic production was "tourist ware," to be sure, but not all of it. In 1893 for instance, Indian pottery was exhibited as art in the Palace of Fine Arts at the Columbian Exposition in Chicago, an extremely important commercial distinction, establishing the level and wide range of pottery prices today.

While crafts have become an important part of the Hopi economy, it is significant that ever since the end of the nineteenth century they have been almost entirely under Anglo control. In the 1920s when Mary Colton, a founder of the Museum of Northern Arizona, lamented that the introduction of commercial materials and market pressure had led to the deterioration of Hopi ceramics (Breunig 1978: 9), the Museum of Northern Arizona organized the first annual Hopi Craftsmen Exhibition of 1930, which significantly increased the market value of First Mesa ceramics and other Hopi arts (McKenna 1983).

The annual Hopi show has remained an essential outlet for Hopi crafts and painting. Since the 1920s when such well-known Hopi artists as Fred Kabotie attended the Santa Fe Indian School, Hopi painting and Hopi ceramics have been the primary means for most Anglo-Americans to learn about the Hopi.

In 1946, also under the guidance of the Museum, seventeen Hopi World War II veterans learned silversmithing. Although a number of Hopi silversmiths work in their houses, a "guild" was established in 1949 on Second Mesa (M. N. Wright 1972). By 1965 this group included seven full-time silversmiths and another twelve who worked mainly during the winter (Kennard 1979). Well-known jewelers and potters may now earn in excess of $50,000 a year (Wade 1976: 263; Dept. of Commerce, Bureau of the Census, 1980). In the last twenty years gold and silversmithing have rivaled pottery as a cash commodity.

The most important person in the history of Hopi crafts, however, and the man who forged the link between craft and cash, was Thomas Keam. Keam was but one of a number of trader-collectors working in the West at the end of the nineteenth century. Keam was pivotal in bringing both tourist curios and art pottery to the tourists and collectors visiting the now accessible West at the end of the nineteenth century. His collection of historic and prehistoric pottery acquired by the Peabody Museum at Harvard is one of the finest collections of Hopi pottery of the nineteenth century. We have already seen how important he was in starting the first Hopi trading post and arranging for the first boarding school. Keam also shaped the course of the modern

history of Hopi pottery.

Keam virtually invented the ceramic tile mold which, like the miniature, was an item small enough to be easily toted home in tourists' suitcases. More importantly, he showed First Mesa potters examples of Sikyatki Polychrome ware from the fourteenth century and suggested that they copy it. Keam undoubtedly worked with the First Mesa potter Nampeyo, one of the finest and most widely recognized of all Hopi potters, whose works are priceless today.

Keam's association with First Mesa potters who sold their wares through his trading post put First Mesa in a position to control the manufacture of Hopi pottery. The First Mesa cartel dominates Hopi pottery today. Keam's interest in pottery was commercial and the pottery produced then and now on First Mesa is primarily for tourist consumption, whether it be cheaply made curios or highly skilled works of art.

Third Mesa, the object of this study, remained outside the sphere of Keam's influence and the pottery revival he spurred. Many Third Mesa Hopis were hostile to Americans like Keam and the cash economy he represented. From a more practical point of view they were also simply too far away to trade at his post in Keams Canyon. Consequently, the pottery they manufactured differed in style from the Sikyatki Revival ware Keam first encouraged First Mesa potters to make.

Since Keam's intervention the stylistic evolutions of Hopi pottery on First Mesa and Third Mesa have pursued different courses. The stylistic differences that originated at the turn of the century still persist in the two different styles associated with Traditionalist and Progressive potters. The differences in their pottery reflect deeper differences in the way they view the world.

PREHISTORIC POTTERY

Although pottery has been made in the Southwest since the seventh century none can be directly linked to the Hopi until the latter part of the twelfth century. The decorated ceramics produced then were usually slipped with a white clay on which there were black designs. Some of these black-on-white types, for example, Tusayan Black-on-White (Kayenta Variety) and Walnut Black-on-White are associated with archaeological sites to the north and south of the Hopi Mesas, supporting the Hopi argument that they occupied these sites during their migrations.

The designs on these ceramics, particularly the Tusayan pieces, were frequently created by surrounding an area of the white surface with black paint. Thus, negative white designs appear in large black zones (Pl. 2: upper left). These white designs were commonly of scrolls, frets and what potters today identify as a rain cloud (Chapter 6 Fig. 18). Black hatching and dots within a negative white square are also common. These designs are also found on the orange, black and white polychrome vessels (Kayenta and Kiet Siel Polychrome). Twelfth-century pottery was fired with wood. Later it was to be fired with coal, profoundly affecting its appearance.

Rather abruptly, around 1250, a new type of pottery was made. These ceramics, termed Jeddito Black-on-Orange, differed in form, temper and the method of firing from the earlier black-on-white pottery (Smith 1971: 353). These ceramics were probably fired with coal instead of wood.

The longer firing made possible by the use of coal aided in oxidation, a chemical change necessary for ceramics of the highest quality. The designs on these ceramics were similar to those of the black-and-white pottery which gradually declined as the black-on-orange pieces became more popular.

The period between 1350 and 1540, when the Spanish arrived, has been called the "Golden Age" of Hopi Ceramics, so named because of the extraordinary technical excellence and beauty of Jeddito Black-on-Yellow and Sikyatki Polychrome then produced. These wares undoubtedly were greatly admired when they were made, for they were not only used by the Hopi but were traded.

Around 1350 the Hopi stopped making the orange ware and simultaneously began producing a yellow ware made from a lighter colored paste. This paste was exceptionally fine and was either lacking temper (non-plastic material, such as sand, added to the clay to counteract excessive shrinkage during drying and firing) or was tempered with ground untempered sherds (Wade and McChesney 1981: 20). The paste was then fired at extraordinarily high temperatures—around 1000°C (Nobles 1978)—and was completely oxidized. These two technical achievements resulted in a high quality ceramic with a smooth surface for painted decoration. The paste itself fired to a beautiful light creamy-yellow to brownish-pink which acted as the background for the painted designs.

Although at first the black designs were not unlike those of the earlier Jeddito Black-on-Orange, the layout or composition of these designs was different. This was particularly true of the decoration on the interior of bowls. The interior of earlier bowls, which were higher than the bowls produced after 1350, had commonly been decorated either with a band of decoration around the rim or with designs that rotated around the center. Now, the design area on these low bowls was sometimes divided either into two or three sections (Pl. 2: lower left). This type of interior bowl layout was to become a distinct feature of Sikyatki Polychrome which appeared around 1375.

Most connoisseurs of Native American art consider Sikyatki Polychrome the most beautiful of all prehistoric pottery (Pl. 2). It is technically excellent, the forms are beautiful as are the finely painted designs in black and red against the light creamy-yellow background. The designs themselves were now either geometric or life forms. Many of the geometric designs as illustrated in Figure 21 (Chapter 6) are still in use today.

The decoration on this pottery is in marked contrast to that produced a hundred years earlier in terms of layout, designs used and decorative techniques. Rigid geometric, zonal compositions were replaced by curvilinear designs. Bowl interiors were frequently divided into two sections as seen in Plate 2. Sometimes the design layout included three sections. Sometimes the design was just a single design unit or life form, ranging from naturalistic and abstract bird, animal, and plant motifs to isolated human anatomical parts including hands, legs and heads (Wade and McChesney 1981: 20). Although many Sikyatki designs are still in use today, the striking combination of the geometric and curvilinear is the innovation and contribution of Sikyatki Polychrome.

There were also new decorative techniques such as splattering, stippling and the use of the dry brush. The dry brush containing remnants of paint was used, as was splattering, to add both depth and texture to the decorated surface, specifically on bowl interiors (Pl. 2: lower left). Although the exterior of these low bowls was frequently decorated with simple bands and/or two to four designs, elaborate exterior decoration was confined to jars.

Sikyatki Polychrome jars, in contrast to those produced earlier, were not globular but were squat with flaring shoulders. The difference between these two jar shapes is seen in Plate 2. The decorated area on these jars was either at the shoulder, as seen in the San Bernardo Polychrome jar in Plate 3 or on the area from the rim, or just below the rim, to the shoulder (Pl. 2). Although decoration at the shoulder was usually geometric and confined to a band, when the upper half of the jar was decorated curvilinear designs were also used.

Much of the pottery produced during this period (1350–1540) was not decorated. Like the utility pottery produced today it was made from coarse or tempered clays that fired either a light yellow or brownish-red. The surface is not rubbed and smooth but simply scraped down. The bowls and jars are deeper and the jars have taller necks.

This common utility pottery, as well as the painted pottery, continued to be produced after the Spanish arrived and the mission was established at Awatovi (Smith 1971: 608) but by the time the Spanish arrived the "Golden Age" of Hopi ceramics was already coming to a close.

HISTORIC CERAMICS

In 1629 the mission of San Bernardo de

Aguatubi was established at Awatovi. This mission and the subsequent missions at Shongopavi and Oraibi brought about a number of changes in Hopi ceramics.

With the introduction of sheep the fuel for firing became dung instead of coal, which resulted in a softer ceramic. This new type of pottery, San Bernardo Polychrome, was probably used by the friars at the missions as well as by the Hopi themselves. Hopi potters now started making candlesticks, cups and saucers, and Spanish shaped soup bowls and pitchers. Although most jars and bowls continued to be shaped the same way they had been before the Spanish arrived, the shoulders on some jars became more pronounced.

Spanish influence is also seen in ceramic design. As laborers at the mission, Hopis made ceramic drain pipes and painted interior-wall decoration. This included wide bands of continuous and running floral designs and the simulation of glazed Spanish tiles (Smith 1949). These "tiles" were sometimes plain, painted with a diagonal band, a cross, or a central flower or dot. Sometimes the design was such that four of these simulated tiles produced a design similar to a Maltese cross with the central arms of the cross formed by the painted division between the individual "tiles." This type of discrete design, along with Spanish style rosettes and flowers, curvilinear floral patterns and the eight-pointed Vallero star, now began to appear on ceramics. Sometimes these designs are combined with earlier ones as seen on the bowl interior in Plate 3 where the flower petals around a central dot design are "feathers" of the type seen on Sikyatki Polychrome. The rim on this bowl is painted red in contrast to Sikyatki Polychrome which generally had undecorated rims. Rims continued to be painted red from the founding of the mission until 1850. Until around 1780 these rims also usually had black ticking (Wade 1980: 58).

Following the Pueblo Revolt in 1680 Hopi ceramics again changed in response to foreigners. Although the band of geometric decoration on jar shoulders continued, a secondary design band suspended from the jar's lip was added (Pl. 3: left). This addition and the more pronounced jar shoulder are features similar to those found in Upper Rio Grande ceramics and may be the result of the arrival of the Tewa from New Mexico who founded the village of Hano on First Mesa.

Tewa influence is also seen in the plain utility ware. Jars or *ollas* are now shaped so that there is an abrupt change between the narrower neck and bulbous body. This shape is similar to that of Sankawi Black-on-Cream (1550–1650) made by the Tewa of the upper Rio Grande (Harlow 1970: 42). Wade (1980: 58) notes that on some Hopi vessels an attempt was made to approximate the gray-cream tone of these Tewa vessels. Others were fired in a reducing atmosphere, in which little air was allowed to enter so that smoke surrounded each piece, turning it a dark gray to black in imitation of the Tewa Kapo Gray and Kapo Black (1650–1750) ceramics. The impact of the arrival of the Tewa on ceramic decoration was short lived, lasting about sixty years. The Tewa potters in Hano may have started making other decorated wares or they may have restricted their production to unpainted storage jars and ollas. This was the case by the close of the nineteenth century.

Following the Pueblo Revolt, Keresan influence is also seen in Hopi ceramics.

This is most pronounced in Payupki Polychrome (Pl. 3: right) which by 1740 had replaced San Bernardo Polychrome.

Keresan influence is seen in both the shape and decoration of Payupki Polychrome vessels. Although simple globular bowls and stew-soup bowls with out-flaring rims continued to be made, a distinctive new shape of jar like that of Puname Polychrome from Zia appeared at this time. This jar is lozenge-shaped as the triangle of the lower body and that of the upper body are approximately the same size and shape (Pl. 3: right). The neck is small and out-flaring and the base concave.

Unlike San Bernardo and Sikyatki Polychrome, Payupki Polychrome vessels are slipped. The color of the slip is usually orange but may range from yellow to cream. On this background feathers and other designs similar to Puname Polychrome are abundant. The most common of these designs is found on the jar body in Plate 3 (right). These include, from left to right, "S frets," "split feathers," and the "fringed apron." "Checkerboards" as seen in the neck band are also common but the neck band itself is not. Designs are painted in dark red and black or, as with the "checkerboard," are orange negative designs. Although negative designs are commonly found on prehistoric and earlier historic ceramics there is a shift away from this type of design, as seen on the body of this jar.

The gradual abandonment of negative designs is an important stylistic change that began with Payupki Polychrome. Until the end of the nineteenth century the background of the vessel was increasingly seen as such rather than as a color area from which negative designs could be constructed. This change was to culminate in a Polacca Polychrome decorative style where the potter appears to have conceived of the vessel rather like a painter's canvas on which discrete designs and kachinas are painted. These two different ways of utilizing the background of a vessel represent a fundamental difference between the Progressive and Traditionalist styles of today.

HISTORICAL DEVELOPMENT OF STYLES A AND B

During the mid-1870s when Thomas Keam established his trading post in what was to become known as Keams Canyon, the Hopi produced the pottery that is now termed Polacca Polychrome.

Polacca Polychrome first appeared around 1780 when Hopi potters abandoned the cream colored slip used on Payupki Polychrome and started slipping their vessels with a white kaolin that scabbed on firing, creating numerous fine lines called "crazing." This distinctive slip is characteristic of Hopi ceramics until the 1900s.

At first Polacca Polychrome vessels were similar to Payupki Polychrome in both shape and decoration but this was soon to change. Around 1820 Hopis began to experiment with new shapes and designs and as Keresan influence weakened, Zuni influence increased. The lozenge-shaped jar was abandoned and in its stead globular jars, sometimes with an acutely tapering lower body and a small neck, were made. These vessels retained the concave bases and red rim of Payupki Polychrome until around 1850. Thereafter the bases were rounded and the rims were painted black.

This new shape of jar demanded the delineation of different design areas (Pl. 4:

left and right). Instead of painting just the upper half of the jar, its bulbous body was painted with black and red designs and the smaller underbody section merely slipped red. The neck, rarely decorated on earlier historic ceramic jars, was now also decorated. The design area on the vessel body was commonly divided into four panels. These panels were not of equal size as they had been but were now two pairs of panels, one large and one small. Sometimes this panel arrangement was doubled so that there were eight in all. Occasionally a series of panels encircling the midbody was also added (Pl. 4: right). This type of layout is like that used on Zuni Kiapkwa and Zuni Polychrome as is a white slip and many of the designs themselves. Prominent among these is the "Rain bird" and variations thereof (Pl. 4: left and right), dotted and solid crescents and birds, as well as rosettes and petal flowers (Pl. 4: left).

Based on Keam's collection of more than 1,400 vessels now at Harvard University, Wade and McChesney (1981: 119) concluded that "with the exception of native clays and pigments, some Hopi pots are identical copies of contemporary Zuni vessels." They attribute the similarity between Zuni wares and Polacca Polychrome to interpueblo marriage, trade, and to the Hopi migration to Zuni during the 1863 drought and smallpox epidemic.

Hopi potters, however, did not just slavishly copy Zuni ceramics. Zuni layouts and designs are simplified with the painted design appearing in marked contrast to the white or, in the later quarter of the nineteenth century, occasionally gray to buff background. Some Hopi designs were only part of a more complex Zuni design; others were Hopi innovations like paintings of Kachinas, clowns or other mythic beings. The Zuni shape of jar was also modified to become more squat (Pl. 4: left).

Although most of Keam's collection was acquired from First Mesa, the closest settlement to his trading post, Polacca Polychrome, or what could be considered varieties of this pottery type, were also being produced on Second and Third Mesas. In fact, in the Keam collection there are some pieces which, according to Keam's friend, Alexander M. Stephen, were made in the Second Mesa village of Mishongovi. Some of these vessels have the white kaolin slip of Polacca Polychrome; on others the slip ranges from gray to buff (Pl. 4: center). These jars usually have short vertical necks and red-painted rims. As can be seen in Plate 4 some of these jars have a design painted only in the area between the shoulder and the neck of the jar, with the lower body painted red. Wade and McChesney (1981: 512) have observed that vessels from this village are technically inferior to those from First Mesa and that although Polacca designs are used, specifically the Polacca-type bird, "no attempt is made to integrate such motifs into the larger linear composition. . . . At best, an empty space has been provided within which the alien birds reside."

Since the people of Oraibi did not trade as much with Keam as did the residents of other villages and, for the most part, remained hostile to American policies, there are few ceramic collections from this village. In 1909, however, Reverend Voth, the Mennonite missionary at Oraibi, collected a number of Polacca Polychrome pieces made in Oraibi for the Fred Harvey Company (Wright 1979: 5). The collection was sold in 1918 to George C. Heye and is at present at the Museum of the American Indian in New York.

The Polacca Polychrome pieces in this collection are in many ways similar to those acquired by Keam and Stephen at Mishongovi. Compared to earlier works from First Mesa, the painted decoration is crude, the lines irregular and wide, and the design units are not arranged in the First Mesa manner but are more isolated. One vessel (M.A.I. 9/627), for example, is decorated with three Zuni deer with the heart and arrow motif, and three rain cloud motifs (Chapter 6, Fig. 18). The deer are isolated rather than portrayed within a central curvilinear design or "house," and they look more like pigs. In 1912 Voth made yet another collection of Oraibi ceramics for Harvey. Within this collection (Wright 1979: 72–73) there are also a number of Polacca Polychrome pieces, some of which bear such Polacca designs as the "split feather" and the "horned Kachina" (Wade and McChesney 1981: 584, 97).

The difference in technical excellence between the ceramics from First Mesa and Second and Third Mesas by the turn of the century is probably the result of Anglo trade. When Hopis first started making Polacca Polychrome it was clearly for their own use. With the advent of Keam's trading post near First Mesa two things happened: durable metal pots and buckets became available and the opportunity to sell or barter decorated ceramics for trade goods was created. That metal containers were replacing ceramic vessels is indicated by a decline in the production of large decorated vessels, although undecorated "red ware" storage jars remained common (ibid. 143). The number of unused Polacca Polychrome pieces within the Keam Collection at Harvard has led Wade and McChesney (1980: 80) to argue that by the 1880s First

Mesa ceramics had become a commercial product. Their argument is further supported by the similarity between vessels suggesting "the origins of mass-produced tourist trade objects" (ibid.).

Thomas Keam not only encouraged the commercialization of Polacca Polychrome by paying cash or, more likely, giving trade goods for them, but can be credited with instigating the Sikyatki Revival on First Mesa. It is the twentieth-century variant of this commercial ceramic type that is commonly known as "Hopi pottery" by Anglo-Americans.

In 1880 Keam commissioned seven reproductions of Sikyatki and San Bernardo Polychrome vessels that he had excavated from local ruins (ibid. 455). He may have had the copies made as an experiment to see if potters could in fact reproduce these wares, and he may have foreseen the interest in and demand for "Indian antiquities" that was to take place ten years later.

In 1879 Col. James Stevenson (1883) had collected Hopi ceramics for the Smithsonian. In 1892 the Second Hemenway Expedition under the direction of the anthropologist Jesse Walter Fewkes purchased Keam's own collection, now at Harvard. By this time, however, not only museums but tourists were demanding Hopi pottery.

When rail service reached Flagstaff in 1882 it brought tourists to the Southwest. Keam now encouraged the production of small, easily transportable "curios," predominantly miniature vessels and tiles, usually with a Kachina painted on them. To make the tiles even-sided Keam introduced the tile mold. According to Wade and McChesney, the original catalogue of the

Keam collection written by Stephen "indicates that premium prices were paid [by Keam] for superior tiles, so it is likely that good commissions were given for reproductions [of antique ceramics] as well" (1981: 455). The effect this had on the number of potters can readily be determined from the accompanying tabulation by comparing their numbers in relation to the population of First Mesa and Second Mesa villages and Oraibi in 1891.

Pueblos	Population	Females	Pottery makers
FIRST MESA			
Walpi	232	115	67
Sichomovi	103	52	30
Tewa Hano	161	81	37
SECOND MESA			
Mishongovi	244	118	66
Shipaulovi	126	64	33
Shongopavi	225	107	60
THIRD MESA			
Oraibi	905	460	73

Population and Pottery Makers for the
Hopi Mesa Villages in 1891
(from Donaldson 1893: 45)

Except for Oraibi, where few people traded with Keam, half the women in the Hopi villages were engaged in pottery making.

Besides increasing the number of potters and pushing the Hopi into the American cash economy, Keam helped establish First Mesa as the center of ceramic production for the Anglo tourist and the art market. First Mesa's prominence was further reinforced by the Sikyatki Revival begun by Keam. The Sikyatki Revival was greatly stimulated by the Tewa of First Mesa, specifically the famous Tewa potter Nampeyo whose ceramics, decorated in the Sikyatki Revival style, soon came to be known as "Hopi pottery," and

overshadowed the Polacca Polychrome style that had been produced until then on all three mesas.

Nampeyo's contribution to the Sikyatki Revival was in part stimulated by Hopis of First Mesa who were jealous of her economic success. Hopis particularly resented the fact that Nampeyo's success was dependent on the sale of Polacca Polychrome which the Hopi considered to belong to them, as opposed to the undecorated vessels which had been made by the Tewa since their arrival on the Hopi Mesas. The Hopi Nequaptewa recounts the events that took place as follows:

At that time Nampeyo was the only potter in Hano who made Hopi-type pottery [Polacca Polychrome] and this made the [Hopi] women very jealous, for they saw she was making good money on her work. Then all the women in Hano started making the Hopi-type pottery and stopped making their own [undecorated] Hano wares which were still in demand by the other villages where they traded, for to get money for their work was much more tempting than to trade their cook pots and water carriers among the other villages (1943: 41).

Evidently, even though Nampeyo had learned how to make Polacca Polychrome at Walpi from her Hopi paternal grandmother, other Hopis considered it "stealing" for her to make Polacca Polychrome especially as she was "making good money." The criticism would prompt her to seek "different kinds of designs" (ibid.) that First Mesa Hopis would not consider theirs. Predictably, because Keam had already established the cash value of prehistoric wares, prehistoric Sikyatki Polychrome ware was then highly admired, and Nampeyo turned to them as models.

Stephen's catalogue of the Keam Collection describes his "Polychrome" class, which consisted primarily of Sikyatki and San Bernardo Polychrome and a few Jeddito and Polacca pieces:

> The best productions of the ancient potter are presented, superior in texture, finish, and symmetry. The designs are in many specimens very complicated, but are preserved from any appearance of crowding by the nicety with which the details are laid in (Wade and McChesney 1980: 25).

Fewkes, who excavated the ruins of the village of Sikyatki, also admired Sikyatki Polychrome. In his note of warning to tourists who might purchase pottery from "Harvey and dealers in Indian objects along the Santa Fe Railroad" (1919: 279), he states that the prehistoric pieces are superior to the "modern" because of the care and attention to detail with which they were made, as well as the fact that they are unslipped. Fewkes also made it clear to Nampeyo, whose husband worked for him at Sikyatki, and to other First Mesa potters, that Anglo-Americans appreciated a smooth polished surface and carefully executed designs.

Anglo-American admiration and its accompanying cash reward was further expressed by the Reverend Voth. It was he who, through his association with the Field Museum in Chicago, arranged for Nampeyo to demonstrate pottery making at the Santa Fe Railroad Fair held in 1895. By 1910 Nampeyo had demonstrated pottery making for over a year at the Harvey House hotel El Tovar at the Grand Canyon, and had returned to Chicago for yet another demonstration (Nequatewa 1943: 42), and by then Sikyatki Revival style pottery had come to be known as "Hopi pottery."

Although the first to make "Hopi pottery" were Tewas, First Mesa Hopis soon began to produce the commercial Sikyatki Revival Ware. The potters of Second and Third Mesa continued to make some pottery for their own use, but domestic demand was further reduced as trade goods increased.

As early as 1939, M-R. Colton notes (pp. 6–15) that "the production of decorated types of pottery is limited almost entirely to First Mesa." Thus, just thirty years after Voth had assembled his large collection of Third Mesa ceramics, most of which are painted (Wright 1979: 5), painted decoration had apparently declined on Third Mesa. What was produced was either not valued or not made available to the Museum of Northern Arizona, which played a major role in the development of First Mesa ceramics (Walker and Wyckoff 1983). The consequence of First Mesa control of painted ceramics produced for the Anglo market was that Third Mesa Progressives had to create their own unpainted style of decoration or align themselves in some way with First Mesa.

Today the First Mesa cartel of Sikyatki Revival ceramics is rigorously maintained and has been given mythological status. The myth asserts that before the arrival of the Tewa from the Rio Grande around 1700 Hopis did not know how to make pots and that the Tewas agreed to teach the residents of First Mesa, who gave them a site for their village. On Second Mesa, the women only knew how to make coiled yucca containers; on Third Mesa, containers were made of woven rabbitbrush. Although its origin is difficult to determine this myth is believed by the residents of First and Second Mesa and is often repeated by the younger Progressives of Third Mesa.

First Mesa Control of the Ceramic Market

The primary means used by First Mesa potters to maintain control of the ceramic market is witchcraft. In one case a Progressive potter completely stopped ceramic production when told that if she continued to sell her wares her grandchildren would suffer from incurable impetigo. Another potter I knew also feared that witchcraft was the cause of the pain that developed in her leg after a number of my visits.

But First Mesa potters have other means to exercise their control. In 1971 the Hotevilla-Bacavi school decided to include ceramics in their fine-arts program, and pottery wheels and kilns were acquired and installed. A number of people, including some at the Keams Canyon Police Department, say this was done over the objections of First Mesa potters who, when they were not heeded, went to the Hotevilla school and destroyed the kilns. As a result, hearings lasting two days were held by the Tribal Council. The two-page official report (Hopi Tribal Council minutes, July 1–2, 1971) summarized the position of both Hotevilla and First Mesa residents. M. Vernon Masayesva, Administrator of the Hotevilla-Bacavi Day School, testified:

> Pottery is one of the fine arts programs, a ceramic program which is put out by the Bureau [of Indian Affairs], and what the Hotevilla school is trying to accomplish is to give a child an emotional satisfaction. . . . Pottery-making is strictly based on educational experience for the children, with no economic interest. They are not attempting to duplicate what the First Mesa people are doing.

Masayesva also explained that he believed the potters of First Mesa were upset by the program because "they were disturbed about losing the [ceramic] market, which is not the intention of the program." On behalf of the potters of First Mesa, Mrs. Carlotta pointed out that

> according to the old tradition . . . each village was delegated to make different craft. . . . To some people at First Mesa this is the only income they get from making potteries and they depend on it. This is the reason why they came to the school.

Everyone finally agreed that the First Mesa potters had acted to protect their cartel of ceramics for the Anglo market. It was also made clear that no pottery should be produced on Third Mesa. But disputing the First Mesa argument that Hopis did not know how to make pottery before the arrival of the Tewas, some older women said that they and "their grandmothers before them" had made pottery.

Pottery production is considered by the residents of First Mesa to be the property of these residents and must be shared only on their terms: Third Mesa women who want to make ceramics for sale may do so only if they are married to men from First Mesa and have been taught by a First Mesa potter.

Initially Third Mesa potters were probably not interested in making Sikyatki Revival wares for ideological reasons. As we shall see later, Third Mesa potters get around the First Mesa embargo today in different ways. Some potters who wish to sell pottery to Anglo-Americans create entirely different designs as Nampeyo was forced to do a hundred years earlier. Others are aligned with First Mesa through marriage. Traditionalist potters usually don't sell their pottery but prefer to barter it with other Native Americans. These potters decorate their ceramics in a style reminiscent of Polacca Polychrome. They still don't desire to make First Mesa Sikyatki Revival style pottery because of ideological differences. Thus, stylistic differences associated with First and Third Mesa at the turn of the century are still maintained.

There can be little question, especially in light of Voth's support of Nampeyo, that Third Mesa potters were aware in the early part of this century of the Anglo-American value placed on Sikyatki Revival-style pottery.

But from the very beginning of the Sikyatki Revival, Third Mesa potters did not use Revival designs. Their initial rejection is not surprising since many of the designs were created by Nampeyo. To the Hopi of Third Mesa, Nampeyo's success would surely have exemplified all that was *qahópi* (not Hopi—not good).

Since their arrival in 1700 the Tewas had probably been considered inferior by the Hopis. As Dozier (1966: 30) notes: "The Hopi no doubt had little respect for this religiously poverty-stricken society." Furthermore, the Tewas were more aggressive and self-assertive than Hopis. These traits, considered progressive and proper by Anglo-Americans, were disdained by the more passive and conformist Hopis. Although Anglo-American approval of Tewa values "altered the value system in favor of the Tewa [on First Mesa]" (ibid.), it further alienated many of the residents of Third Mesa.

There was another reason for Third Mesa dislike of Nampeyo. At the same time that Nampeyo was enjoying the support of Anglo-American traders, missionaries, and anthropologists like Dr. G. A. Dorsey of

the Field Museum, her brother Thomas Polacca was acting as interpreter for United States government agents. Thomas Polacca accompanied Keam and the school superintendent on their trip to Oraibi in 1890, and it was he who seized "the great medicine man of all the Moquis" (Donaldson 1893: 58) and turned him over to the government as a "hostile" leader.

Third Mesa Traditionalists would therefore have been particularly opposed not only to Tewa values but also to their support of government programs. While First Mesa Hopis may have emulated their Tewa neighbors, Third Mesa Traditionalists stood mainly in staunch opposition. It is highly unlikely that Third Mesa Traditionalist potters would ever have asked permission to use Sikyatki Revival designs. First Mesa men, after all, had aided Agent Daniel in dipping Hotevilla women in Black Leaf-40 in the 1920s. And the passage of the Hopi Constitution that Third Mesa Traditionalists opposed was made possible by the First Mesa vote. Third Mesa also disdained Sikyatki Revival designs because they were produced for the Anglo-American cash economy and therefore according to Anglo taste.

During the past seventy years, the Sikyatki Revival Style has undergone changes which may reflect a change in Anglo taste rather than that of the Hopi-Tewa of First Mesa (Wyckoff 1983). This is also true of Third Mesa ceramics produced by potters aligned with First Mesa. Today ceramics made by these potters are indistinguishable from much of the pottery produced on First Mesa.

This style of painted decoration, used by Progressive potters aligned with First Mesa, I have called Style B (Fig. 5). It is very different from the pottery made by

Figure 5. Style B roll-out drawing of a framed-band design on a small bowl. Vessel 17 (ht. 5.8 cm), made by Lucy.

Traditionalists on Third Mesa whose style I have called Style A (Fig. 6). This style of decoration was not considered as "artistic" by Anglo-Americans and it has been ignored until now.

Third Mesa Traditionalist pottery was not manufactured for the tourist market nor recognized as art pottery by the Museum. It has probably always been used as an inner- or interpueblo barter item, is consequently seldom sold, and so no collections of Third Mesa painted pottery were made. But based on the few isolated examples available and on a comparison between current production and ceramics manufactured in 1909, Traditional Style A decoration appears to be a gradual development of the Third Mesa Polacca Polychrome Style.

There are some differences, of course. At the time Voth made his collection in 1909, Oraibi potters had ceased to use the white Polacca slip and had begun to paint directly on the polished reddish-brown clay surface. Although it is possible that on Third Mesa the extreme stress of the period—the forced schooling, the removal of Tewaquaptiwa the village chief, and the division of Oraibi—had discouraged the potters from

making the effort to slip their vessels, I think it more likely that they felt that a slip was just not necessary for the technical excellence of a painted vessel. Unslipped pottery had long been a Third Mesa tradition; unslipped culinary wares, for instance, had been and still were being produced. Although potters abandoned the slip they did not abandon Polacca Polychrome designs. Many of the Polacca designs, or closely related designs, are still in use today.

For example, except for motifs 6 and 7 (sun and feather) all of the motifs illustrated in Figure 18 (Chapter 6) are also found on Polacca Polychrome, as are the tadpole and corn plant illustrated in Figure 19. Kachina masks, like the Sun Kachina (Chapter 6, Fig. 19) are identifying features of Polacca Polychrome produced between 1860 and 1890 (Wade and McChesney 1981: 143). Conspicuously absent is the Polacca Polychrome bird which seems to have been replaced by the feather motif, although birds are occasionally painted. It is interesting that although these birds' heads are in the Sikyatki Revival form (Fig. 5), the round head with central eye of the

Figure 6. Roll-out drawing of a framed-band design on a Style A stew bowl. (Vessel P.M. 248946, ht. 9.9 cm, made and decorated by Betty.)

Polacca bird is now used for the Humpbacked Flute Player motifs (Fig. 10) apparently first used on pottery in the late 1940s.

The similarity between Polacca Polychrome, specifically the Second and Third Mesa variety, and contemporary Style A ceramics is not, however, confined to shared motifs. Other common traits include the use of dots and crosshatching within the rain cloud motif (Fig 6 and Fig. 8, Pl. 8a; Fig. 18, Chapter 6), the use of scrolls attached to rain clouds (Plate 7), and serial repetition or translation of design units and motifs. These shared traits produce a stylistic continuity that can be most clearly seen by comparing the vessels from Mishongovi in the Keam Collection (Wade and McChesney 1981: 512–45) with

contemporary vessels. One particularly striking example is illustrated in Plate 4 (center). The design on this vessel closely resembles the contemporary design illustrated in Figure 6 which is a roll-out drawing of the upper vessel in Figure 8.

It is not surprising that Traditionalist potters have chosen to maintain Polacca Polychrome designs, which were produced before intensive Anglo-American contact and the division of Oraibi, for this is seen as the time when things were "the way they ought to be." In all likelihood, Sikyatki Revival designs have always been consciously rejected and Polacca Polychrome designs deliberately maintained, thus the reference back to Zuni and Polacca designs by some contemporary Traditionalist potters.

CHAPTER SIX

TRADITIONAL AND PROGRESSIVE STYLES OF CERAMIC DECORATION

INTRODUCTION

When I began my research on Third Mesa in 1979 I had no idea that Traditionalists and Progressives decorated their pottery differently. I knew that the well-known potter Elizabeth White was from New Oraibi and during an earlier visit I had met a potter from the Traditionalist village of Oraibi. Also, Michael Stanislawski, an archaeologist who has conducted research on First Mesa (1969a, b, 1973, 1978), told me that some pottery was manufactured on Third Mesa. This pottery, he said, was commonly for local use and he had heard from the potters of First Mesa that it was decorated quite differently than their own.

During the first few months of my stay I met a number of potters and observed that indeed some potters decorated their wares in a style different from the potters of First Mesa. The difference between these two styles, which I have called Style A and Style B, was not only observable by me but was recognized by other Hopis and the potters themselves. Their statements regarding these two styles as well as the relationships between potters is presented in Chapter 7. Over the course of the following year and in my many conversations with Third Mesa potters I learned that their religious-political affiliation as either Traditionalists or Progressives is reflected in their two different styles of pottery decoration.

Although the potters acknowledged the two different painting styles, at first they refused to comment to me on each other's work, true to the Hopi ideals of equality and unity. As I came to know them better, however, they frequently expressed their disapproval of the style different from their own in moral terms. Thus it became clear that these different styles expressed two different ways of looking at the world.

All potters made a variety of ceramics.[1] These I divided into two categories: trade wares, which are only produced for the Anglo market, and domestic wares, which are either for Hopi use or for sale. I was able to observe not only the different function of the pieces within these categories but found that linguistic data supported this classificatory division.

Trade wares were always decorated and included such items as ash trays, vases and boxes, while domestic wares were bowls, jars and bottles. Some of these vessels are decorated, others are not. Within the general group I call domestic wares were clearly different classes of vessels. In order to determine if certain vessels required painted decoration and, if so, a particular style of decoration, I solicited their classification in Hopi. In order to establish a folk classification all of these vessels were classified by no fewer than sixteen potters and non-potters.

One class of vessel usually painted was

85

decorated only in the Traditionalist style. This vessel was a ceremonial bowl, and its style of decoration further indicates the significance of Styles A and B as expressions of cultural values.

An analysis of the two Third Mesa styles reveals that these two styles differ in both their symbolic content and in their use of space. It is at this fundamental structural level that two different world views are clearly expressed in ceramic design.

THE POTTERS

In 1980 there were ten Third Mesa potters, including five Traditionalists and five Progressives. The most well known Progressive potter is Elizabeth White whose pieces frequently sell for over a thousand dollars. Elizabeth White was born in Oraibi in 1892 and has a house, a summer home, in the Progressive village of New Oraibi. Her principal residence is in Flagstaff where she is a highly respected member of the artistic community.

While Elizabeth White lives in New Oraibi only part of the year, the other potters are full-time Third Mesa residents. Because these potters either do not consider themselves individual artists or want to remain anonymous, fearing the First Mesa cartel, they are identified here by pseudonym.

The five Traditionalist potters are Anne, Terry, Betty, Vera, and Amy. (Betty was teaching her granddaughter Diana to pot in 1980, and since at that time Diana's vessels were finished, fired and decorated by her grandmother she has not been included.) These five potters use Style A painted decoration on their ceramics. This style of decoration continues the Polacca Polychrome tradition in the separation of the figures from the background.

Anne, Terry, and Betty live in the Traditionalist village of Oraibi. Vera and Amy live in Hotevilla, which continues to be the religious and political center of the Traditionalists of Third Mesa. All of these potters married men from Third Mesa who are also Traditionalists.

Some Progressive potters, like Lucy, Loren and Cindy, paint decoration on their vessels, while others decorate their ceramics by manipulating the clay itself. These potters paint in Style B, a contemporary variant of the Sikyatki Revival style begun on First Mesa at the turn of the century.

Lucy and Loren are both married to men who are Progressives from First Mesa. Their marriages establish important connections that encourage relationships with First Mesa potters. Cindy, Lucy's daughter, is married to a man from Second Mesa who is, likewise, a Progressive. They both live with Cindy's mother in New Oraibi. Loren lives in Upper Moencopi, the Progressive community which split from the Traditionalist lower village in the early 1930s.

The two Progressive potters who do not use Style B are Elizabeth White and Amy. These women did not marry men from First Mesa and do not have kin there. Elizabeth White was married to a man who was part white and part Cherokee (Carlson 1964: 146) and Amy's husband is a Progressive Hopi from New Oraibi, the village where they now live.

Before analyzing Styles A and B, it is important to first establish on what class of vessels painted decoration occurs.

THE CERAMICS

To judge by the ceramics produced by

Third Mesa potters during my stay, I believe two categories can be distinguished. The first consists of ceramics made solely for trade. Within this category are tiles introduced in the late 1800s by Thomas Keam; "wedding vases," a Hopi-Tewa vessel form introduced about fifty years ago; and ashtrays, plates, vases and rectangular lidless boxes. The second category consists of pottery made either for Hopi use or for sale or barter, and includes bowls, jars, and bottles. These two categories are not mutually exclusive; in fact, apart from crenelated ceremonial bowls, all ceramics may be sold or bartered.

These two categories, which I call trade wares and domestic wares, are defined by the observed difference in their use—trade wares being made exclusively for sale. There is linguistic evidence that the Hopis themselves perceive these two categories—trade wares are named in English, the language of the marketplace, while domestic wares are readily named in Hopi.

The terms Hopis use to classify different kinds of ceramics reveal how they perceive of them, and this, in turn, affects the ceramics' use and such attributes as decoration. In order to establish that none of these terms was idiosyncratic the ceramics studied were identified by at least six potters and ten non-potters, usually by all of the nine resident potters and many more non-potters. In soliciting the terms used for these ceramics I was able to construct a tentative folk classification of domestic wares (Appendix II). This folk classification is based on 115 vessels which represent virtually the entire year-long production of most Third Mesa potters. Analysis revealed the physical attributes necessary for class inclusion. Thus, this folk classification provides the art historian and

the archaeologist with a model against which analytic classes can be compared.

The distinction between trade wares and domestic wares is a very important one. Trade ceramics—tiles, wedding vases, vases, ashtrays, and lidless boxes—are not treated to hold water or resist charring and are produced only for sale. These ceramics are made only by Progressive potters. Except for the boxes, which are known to have been in use prior to Anglo contact (Smith 1971: 243), these ceramic forms have all developed since ceramics became a cash commodity.

Domestic wares, unlike trade wares, were made by both Progressive and Traditionalist potters. All of these various types of bowls and jars were seen in use in Hopi households. Bottles, also called canteens in English, were seen in Hopi houses and, I was told, they are also taken to the kiva. Although the specific shapes are somewhat different, these three types of vessels were all made before Anglo contact. Thus, trade wares and domestic wares differ in their historical development, in the language used in their terminology, and in their potential use; and they are made by potters of different political-religious factions.

Boxes and miniatures are transitional from one group to another. Although I have classified boxes as a trade item they were occasionally referred to in Hopi and I saw one in use in the house of the potter who made it. Likewise, miniatures, which I have classified as a domestic item, were commonly made for sale and were frequently referred to in English. They were, however, also found in use in Hopi houses and referred to in Hopi; thus, their classification as a domestic item. They are also known prehistorically.

TRADITIONAL AND PROGRESSIVE STYLES OF CERAMIC DECORATION

Trade Wares

Decorated rectangular tiles. These were introduced between 1875 and 1890. Loren was the only potter who made these tiles, designed to be sold to tourists for use under hot plates. They came in two shapes—rectangular (9.5 cm × 13.8 cm) and square (9.6 cm)—and of a uniform thickness (0.4 cm to 0.5 cm). Loren achieved this uniformity by flattening the clay with a rolling pin and cutting the tiles (like cookies) with a wooden frame. She was also the only potter who poured clay into commercially purchased molds to form standard eight-inch plates.

"Wedding vases." Lucy and Loren both made double-spouted jars surmounted by a loop handle. Both potters made "big ones" (about 28 cm in height at their maximum point and 46 cm in circumference), as well as smaller wedding vases (between 7 and 15 cm high and from 16 to 24 cm around). When I asked Lucy about these vessels, which I never observed in a Hopi household, she said, "We don't use anything like this here but maybe they do over by the Rio Grande. Some people say that over there the bride drinks out of one side and the groom out of the other—but we just make these for tourists."

Vases. Lucy also made vases. These neckless jars (from 5.8 to 7.2 cm high) taper toward the base; they were made either for direct sale to tourists or for the Heard Museum Hopi Show. Lucy chose this shape because "museum people like it, but we would never use it," which was why there was no Hopi term for it.

Ashtrays. Lucy and her daughter frequently made ashtrays, as did Terry.

These can be rapidly fashioned by pressing the clay on the palm of the hand, and occasionally adding one coil. They range in size from 8.0 to 13.7 cm in diameter, with an average height of 2.2 cm. Hopi ashtrays are never used in local households since the Hopi themselves prefer the more durable heavy glass variety. Moreover, as Lucy said, the decoration would be ruined if you used the piece.

Rectangular lidless boxes. Prehistoric boxes have been discovered but now they are made only for trade. Lucy and Cindy also made these. Three sides of the boxes were of equal height, between 3.0 and 5.2 cm; the fourth side was about double this height. On the interior of the higher side there was usually a painted decoration. Lucy sometimes provided suspension holes in the taller wall. Apart from the one attached to the wall of Lucy's sitting room, I saw no others in a Hopi home.

Domestic Wares

Domestic wares were defined in Hopi according to their shape—bowls, jars and bottles—and more specifically according to size (large or small) or function. One class of vessel, the "duck bowl" was qualified according to its shape. A quantified folk classification of domestic wares is in Appendix II.

Within the general bowl (*caqápta*) category I was able to quantify eight classes. During my stay, ceremonial bowls may also have been made but if so I had no access to these. Although domestic wares were made by all Progressive and Traditionalist potters, different classes were preferred by one group or another and by particular potters. (Appendix V is a list of domestic wares and their makers.)

Traditionalists produced more undecorated mixing bowls, sometimes called piki bowls, and stew bowls (large bowls for serving stew) than Progressive potters did. Decorated serving bowls were more commonly made by Progressives. This is not surprising considering that traditionally the only vessel used to eat from was the communal stew bowl. Progressives also made many more decorated small bowls than Traditionalists did. These were usually manufactured for sale.

Piki bowls (paqwíscaqapta). These are large (average height 12.6 cm, rim diameter 26.9 cm) open bowls with polished interiors and an incurving rim. These were not made for sale but commonly given as gifts to be used by the recipient.

Stew bowls (nöqkʷíscaqapta). Most of these bowls are similar to piki bowls but smaller (average height 9.7 cm × rim diameter 22.1 cm). These bowls hold between six and twelve cups whereas piki bowls usually hold between eighteen and twenty-five cups. These stew bowls were the bowls that were placed on the table during ceremonies, or when family and friends gathered to eat. At such times one was expected to eat at every house that was visited. Occasionally an older person would eat just a little stew by dipping some piki directly into the dish. This once standard form of eating has now almost disappeared and people are served individually from these bowls.

All Traditionalist potters made piki bowls and stew bowls. The only Progressive potter who made piki bowls was Lucy who, along with Loren, a Progressive from Moencopi, also made stew bowls. Five of the sixteen stew bowls were decorated. The two made by Loren were painted in Style B.

The other three were made by Betty and Terry who used the Traditionalist Style A.

Serving bowls (Oyâ:pi). Although the smaller stew bowls were sometimes called serving bowls, compared with stew bowls these bowls were lower in relation to their rim diameter (average height 6.2 cm × 21.3 cm), and were all decorated. Considering that a serving bowl used to transfer food from a cooking vessel to the table and from which food is again transferred to individual plates is a modern innovation, it is not surprisng that this class of vessel is primarily made by Progressive potters. In Progressive households these bowls were the locally produced "china" of the Hopi table. Only one Traditionalist potter, Terry, made a serving bowl.

Duck bowls (pá·wikʷocaqapta). These figurine bowls (Pl. 5, center) ranging from 7.5 cm to c. 24.0 cm in length were made by Progressives and Traditionalists. Their use appeared to be entirely decorative, and they were usually made as gifts for children. Potters delighted in making these pots, laughing over the expressions of the ducks they created. At First Mesa over Easter weekend, duck- and rabbit-shaped vessels were filled with Easter eggs and given out by Kachinas. Rabbit-shaped vessels were made by Lucy for the occasion.

Small bowls (caqáphoya). All Third Mesa potters made these bowls. Although there is considerable variation in the class, most of the bowls, like other vessels in the *caqápta* category, have a proportionately large rim diameter in relation to their height. The average height of these bowls is 6.0 cm and the average rim diameter 9.8 cm. Most

Figure 7. Style A and B small bowls. *Upper:* Vessel 23 (ht. 10.0 cm), made by Lucy. *Lower:* Vessel 11 (ht. 7.0 cm), made by Betty.

were decorated, manufactured for sale, and made by Progressive potters.

One vessel made for sale by Lucy was lozenge-shaped and is commonly called a "volcano pot" (Fig. 7). This shape declined in popularity around 1820 (Wade 1980) and was made again as part of the Sikyatki Revival of the 1900s. No vessels of this shape were seen in a Hopi household. This vessel and two others, also made for sale by Lucy, were the only small bowls whose height exceeded their rim diameter.

Progressive Style B potters were extremely productive, Lucy frequently making twenty small bowls a day. These were primarily for sale to tourists. During my stay only seven of this type of bowl were produced for Hopi use.

Except for plain coffee mugs (*homícaqaphoya*) made by Traditionalists, as the size of the vessel decreases the likelihood that it will be decorated and sold to tourists increases. Accordingly, the more likely they are to be made by Progressives.

Decorated miniature vessels. These, like all domestic wares, are known prehistorically. They average 3.4 cm in height and are primarily made for sale, although I saw eight miniatures in use either as children's toys or as decorative items; one was used as a salt container. An undecorated miniature was also made as an offering to Spider Mother (see Appendix I). Miniatures were sometimes used as weights for the string of feathers attached to the back of the Long-Haired Kachina masks.

Miniatures, which were either bowls or jars, were made by all Progressive potters and Terry.

Jars (sí·vi). Like bowls, these were also sometimes qualified as being either large or small. Small jars (average height 6.4 cm) were used as children's toys or sold to tourists. These were made by Faith, Anne, Cindy and Terry. Large storage type jars (average height 24.9 cm) were made by Anne and Betty—both Traditionalists.

Seed jars (*poshímsivi*).   These containers were used to hold the seeds, predominantly corn kernels, given out by the Kachina dancers at the night dances preceding Powamu. The seeds were kept in these jars until planting time when a few were placed in each field as an offering to the Kachinas. The spot where the seeds were left is considered sacred and, along with prayer sticks, or prayer feathers attached to a bush, it constitutes the field shrine. The jars containing seeds (and frequently prayer feathers) were hung from the house beams or on walls "to protect the corn," presumably from rodents or children.

These vessels, ranging between ten and fifteen centimeters in height, were made by Anne, Betty and Terry, and were usually decorated.

Bottles (*wikóro*).   These bottle-shaped vessels are rounded, with one flat side, and a loop handle on each side of the vessel. When a leather strap is attached to these loops and the opening is plugged with a corn cob, like a cork, these vessels may function as canteens. There can be little doubt that these pots are ceramic versions of the gourd water containers that were once carried to the fields or on journeys.

While still warm from firing, these vessels are usually coated with piñon sap to make them water resistant. They are not decorated. Small bottles (*wikórohoya*) were evidently taken to the kiva. One may have been a child's toy. Larger (height 29.0 cm) bottles are made for barter with Santo Domingo traders. These vessels are made only by Traditionalists.

I think it is most significant, especially if archaeologists (Binford 1962; Deetz 1965; Hill 1966; Longacre 1964, 1970; and Whallon 1968) are going to attempt to reconstruct kinship from ceramic remains, that neither Progressive nor Traditionalist potters are concerned with producing ceramics for their own use, but rather, rely on the reciprocal exchange of gifts to fill their needs. All potters used their own wares only if they were faulty or, occasionally, if they particularly liked them. Betty, for example, used six Third Mesa Hopi vessels, of which only one was of her own design; the others had been gifts.

Religious and social obligations, then, as well as economics, play a critical role in the distribution of ceramics. Economics can be said to have been of critical importance in the development of the Sikyatki Revival Style in the 1900s and in its maintenance. The desire to become part of the Anglo-American cash economy also stimulated the development of the Raised Decoration Style by those Third Mesa Progressive potters who lacked in-law relations on First Mesa. Economics cannot, however, explain the Traditionalist style of decoration. Just as the distribution of ceramics conforms to and is part of Traditionalist attitudes vis-a-vis Anglo society, so their decorative style conforms to and is part of their concepts of beauty, spatial relationships, and the world around them.

THE STYLES

Design analysis, according to "formal aspects" (Shepard 1956: 259–60), concentrates on design layout or type, the designs within this layout, and the symmetrical arrangement or composition of design parts. In accord with these analytical techniques, I have examined Third Mesa ceramics. I looked at fifty-nine of the 115 domestic ware vessels within this study sample that were painted. They support the frequently proven contention that different types of design are found on vessels that differ in function and/or shape (MacNeish et al. 1970); Shepard 1956; Washburn 1977) and that iconographic motifs are commonly associated with specific design types (ibid.), as well as the fact that some potters prefer one compositional arrangement of design parts to another. But none of these analytical approaches reveals the underlying design structure.

The structure of a design is its most fundamental organization. Anthropologists, archaeologists and art historians have considered various organizational principles as design structure (Adams 1973; Arnold 1983; Fernandez 1966; Graves 1982; Hanson 1983; Hole 1984; Kent 1983; Washburn 1977, 1983). I found the relationship between the design or figure and the surrounding space or background to be the design structure. It is only at the level of structure that design becomes a reiteration of a group's concept of natural and social order.

Two distinctly different design structures are found on Third Mesa pottery. These different design structures are the fundamental difference between Style A and Style B.

In order to determine if the figure-ground relationship was in fact the design structure and not merely a question of different designing principles used on different kinds of vessels, the relationship between design and vessel class was examined (Appendix III). I found that the design structure of ceremonial bowls is consistent with Style A, the style used by Traditionalists.

In contrast to ceremonial bowls are the bowls made for secular use. These bowls commonly use a different type of design,

the framed band instead of the discrete unit, and may or may not be decorated with symbolic motifs, which are always used on decorated ceremonial bowls. Within the framed-band design, however, the two different design structures are maintained. Thus, although vessel function or shape may influence the type of design used it does not determine the design structure.

Considering the small size of the sample another concern was that the observable difference in the figure-ground relationship was because of individual preference (Appendix IV). It is my contention that this is not the case, but rather, that the difference can be equated with two different groups of potters—Traditionalists and Progressives. The different ways in which these two groups of potters present objects in space parallel their differing views of the world.

According to Geertz (1958), world view is not just the way a group believes "things in sheer actuality are" but also "the way things ought to be." As we have seen during the last one hundred years, Hopis have become so divided that they no longer completely share the same view of the world. It is these differences that are expressed in design structure.

Associated with the two different design structures are design types and the use of symbolic motifs. These differences as well as differences in framed-band symmetry, negative design and width of line are all attributes of two different painting styles. Style A is the style of Traditionalists and Style B of Progressives.

Elements of Style A and Style B

Design Structure.   In examining the

differences between Style A and Style B Third Mesa Hopi pottery, it becomes clear that two different design structures are used. Style A prefers a separation between the design and the space surrounding it, so that the design—a rain cloud, bird, feathers or whatever—stands out clearly from the background and is easily recognizable (Pl. 5: left).

In Style B pottery, on the other hand, the design structure is quite different as can be seen in Plate 5: right and Plate 6. In Style B there is an integration between the design and the space that surrounds it, so that it is difficult to distinguish design from space.

This is the most profound difference between the decoration of Style A and Style B pots. It lies deep in the potter's subconscious and is a material expression of how these different potters as Traditionalists and Progressives conceive of the world. When we look at the pots more closely, we become aware of other differences between these two styles but none is as fundamental as design structure.

Style A Prefers Discrete or Hanging Discrete Unit Designs more than Style B. A discrete unit design is created when a motif, or a number of elements and/or designs, forms a discrete area of decoration surrounded by space. The decorated area, when it is facing the viewer, can be seen in its entirety. In addition, the other discrete areas or units of decoration are usually not visible (Pl. 5: left). The overall effect, therefore, likens the body of a vessel to a sheet of paper containing a central figure.

On some vessels discrete units are attached to an encircling band, thus becoming hanging discrete units; the relationship between the decorated area or

figure and the surrounding space or ground remains the same (Fig. 8: lower). Thus it is impossible to have more than four units on the exterior body of a bowl because, as these bowls do not have a neck, there is only one exterior design area.

Bands are used in both Style A and Style B. Bands are simply "a belt of decoration encircling a vessel" (Raynolds 1939; Muriott 1942) and as such do not define a design field other than that of the vessel surface itself.

The bands are either lines of various width that encompass the vessel or lines to which are attached design elements placed along the line without change in their directional orientation. A single band can constitute the entire decoration on miniatures and small bowls, but they are more commonly used along with what I have called framed bands.

Framed bands (Fig. 9) create a design field within the total design area of the vessel surface.[2] As I employ the term here, it accords with Amsden's (1936: 9) definition:

> Taken as a form of pattern layout, a [framed] band must have certain characteristics. It must have definitely greater length than width . . . it must have an upper and lower boundary line of generally parallel trend, to preserve its strip-like form. It must encircle or cross the whole field of design, lest it become a mere sectional area, as a pendant rectangle. [Framed] banding then must be defined as a division of available decorative area by the drawing of parallel lines to create a zone of decoration.

Both Style A and Style B use framed bands but when Style A uses them it organizes the designs within them in a

Figure 8. Style A stew or serving bowls. *Upper:* Vessel P.M. 248946 (ht 9.9 cm). *Lower:* Vessel 29 (ht. 11.4 cm) made by Betty.

Figure 9. Style B serving bowl. Vessel 91 (ht. 6.6 cm), made by Lucy.

manner quite different from that of Style B.

Style A prefers a single figure; Style B prefers an overall pattern. Although Style A and Style B potters both use framed bands, they handle the disposition of figures within the bands quite differently.

In Style A framed bands, the space between figures is such that usually only one figure can be seen in its entirety. But in Style B framed bands, the figures are closer together and the emphasis is on the overall pattern as opposed to a specific figure.

This stylistic difference can be seen in the two small bowls illustrated in Figure 7. The lower bowl is decorated with a Style A framed band and was made by Betty, a Traditionalist. The upper bowl is unusual both in shape and in that the design is not within framing lines. However, although this is not a framed band the effect of an overall pattern in comparison to the lower vessel can be clearly seen. This bowl is in Style B and was made by the Progressive potter, Lucy.

That Traditionalists prefer designs in which figures can be seen in their entirety is evident within the framed band and in their preference for the discrete unit design types. The discrete unit type of design occurs more frequently (28 percent) in work by Style A potters than by Style B potters (12 percent). Style A potters also prefer independent figures. This can be seen by

comparing two *sí·vi* (Fig. 10: upper and lower). The Style B discrete unit design is on a miniature. In spite of its diminutive size (height 4.7 cm), two rectangles and an interlocking key were added to prevent too large an open space between the birds. This is in marked contrast to the larger (height 20.0 cm) lower vessel painted in Style A where there is an isolated figure constructed on a diagonal "spacing line."

Style A potters think in terms of independent figures rather than overall pattern. Discrete or hanging discrete units decorate the only two bowls, other than miniatures, and these were painted by Style A potters. Style A's preference for isolated figures is also evident on the interior of a serving bowl (Fig. 11). The upper vessel is in Style A: five distinct figures are painted individually and not abutting an adjacent figure. The lower vessel is in Style B: twenty-one figures are in close association.

The preference for independent figures by Style A potters is not based on technical limitations. Their preference for commercial brushes, which produce a wider line, does not make it more difficult to create the overall pattern favored by Style B potters. Independent figures are preferred by Style A potters for their own sake. This is apparent in their frequent criticism that on Style B ceramics "You can't see what it [the decoration] is." Terry went so far as to repaint the painting done on one of her jars

Figure 10. Style A and B miniature and jar. *Upper:* Vessel 90 (ht. 4.7 cm), made by Cindy. *Lower:* Vessel 86 (ht. 20.0 cm), made by Terry.

CHAPTER 6

Figure 11. Style A and B serving bowls. *Upper:* Vessel P.M. 248945 (rim diameter 19.3 cm), made by Terry. *Lower:* Vessel 27 (rim diameter 27.6 cm), made by Lucy.

TRADITIONAL AND PROGRESSIVE STYLES OF CERAMIC DECORATION

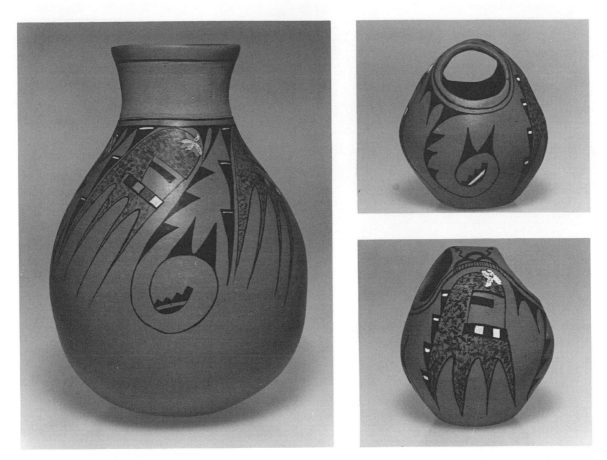

Figure 12. Jars. *Left:* Vessel 200 (ht. 32.0 cm), made by Terry and decorated by Cindy and Terry. *Right:* Vessel P.M. 248951 (ht. 14.5 cm), made by Terry.

by a Style B potter (Pl. 7: left). In order to isolate the Long-Haired Kachina more clearly, Terry added white and commercial paint to this figure (Pl. 7: right).[3] When she re-used this figure in another of her pots she chose to reorganize the pattern so that part of the design became one independent figure, and the Long-Haired Kachina mask, with a string of prayer feathers, became another (Fig. 12). These two independent figures became, in fact, discrete units.

Style A prefers a wide line; Style B prefers a narrow line. Another distinction is the quality of line. Style A is bolder. It uses wide brush strokes and large, frequently isolated figures clearly placed on the ground of the vessel. Moreover, frequently the composition of the parts within these figures isolates them from the surrounding ground. The width of the Style A line is not accidental; it is a deliberate choice. Both Style A and Style B potters use commercial and yucca brushes. Style A potters prefer the wider commercial brush, although the wide brush stroke occurs whether a commercial or a yucca brush is used (the yucca brush is 0.4 cm wide). The difference

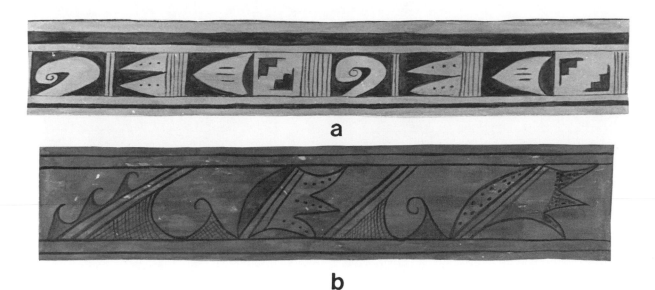

a

b

Figure 13. Roll-out drawings of Style A and Style B framed-bands used on small bowls. *Upper:* Vessel 142 (ht. 5.7 cm), made by Loren. *Lower:* Vessel 85 (ht. 8.3 cm), made by Betty.

in line between Style A and B can be seen by comparing the two framed bands in Figure 13.

Style B potters, on the other hand, use the narrow (0.05 cm), single-strand yucca brush for lines because they prefer thin, fine lines. They use commercial brushes only to fill in a figure. As opposed to the Style A single figures, Style B has many lines, used to create a mass of motifs, elements, and Sikyatki designs which frequently abut or interlock. Style B, therefore, proportionately uses a greater number of figures than Style A does.

Third Mesa potters are aware of these two painting styles and make comments, usually negative, about the other group's painting. These criticisms usually refer to the number of figures used and their arrangement in space. Style A potters, for example, criticize Style B as "too fancy." "There is painting everywhere," they complain.

In Style A framed bands there is more unpainted area than in Style B framed bands. The Style A potters are actually quite correct in their criticism of Style B pots. There *is* a real difference in the amount of painting, one that can be measured. More paint is used in Style B framed bands than in Style A. I measured the painted area on sixteen bowls with a polar planimeter from roll-out drawings (Pls. 6, 8, 9; Figs. 5, 6, 7, 9, 13, 14) of framed bands. Since these are all bowls with the maximum circumference at the rim, this measurement was used as the length on all these drawings. The exterior area of the vessel itself has therefore been standardized and does not represent the actual surface area.

I found that the size of the framed band in relation to total pot area was in part dependent on the presence or absence of rim bands and vessel shape, and had no relation to Style A and B. But when I looked at the painted area *within* the band, the bowls fell

Figure 14. Roll-out drawings of framed bands. *Upper:* Stew bowl, vessel 80 (ht. 12.0 cm), made and decorated by Terry. *Lower:* Small bowl, vessel 30 (ht. 4.1 cm), made by Diana and decorated by Betty.

into two distinct groups (Fig. 15). In Style A, the average painted area was 33.5 percent and in Style B it was 53.9 percent, indicating that Style B bands have more figures, they are in closer proximity, and nearly half of them are filled. The difference the filling makes can be seen in vessel 34 (Pl. 8b). On this Style A pot a framed band was painted in black, and then the potter atypically decided to use some white paint and filled in other areas. This increased the painted area and, as a result, 51.3 percent of this band is painted instead of the former 42.0 percent.

Because of the differences in the numbers of figures used, in the thickness of the lines that depict them and in the sheer amount of paint as applied to the pot's surface within a framed band, there are stylistic differences between Style A and Style B framed bands that are apparent to any viewer. Furthermore, there are two other differences that arise out of the ones we have already discussed. One of these has to do with the phenomenon known as "figure-

ground reversal." The other has to do with the type of symmetry achieved in the painted framed-band design.

Style A designs are easy to read; Style B designs show figure-ground reversal. Because Style B vessels typically show a greater use of figures, many of which are filled in, Style B vessels frequently show a figure-ground reversal or "negative design" (Shepard 1956: 288–93). This means that when you look at the pot, the figure and the background against which it is placed keep changing places, the figure becoming the background and the background becoming the figure.

To create this reversal, the figures must be filled, and the size of the filled area must be greater than, or approximately the same as, the ground area. This can be seen on Vessel 143 (Pl. 9d). The two panels in which two negative white triangles and diagonal lines appear on a red ground are divided almost equally between the red painted area and the white ground. Measurements with the polar planimeter

Vessel	Vessel Area (cm²)	Band Area (cm²)	% Band Area	Area of Band or Panels (cm²)	Painted Area (cm²)	% Painted area within band or panel area
Style A						
1	758.6	614.8	81.0	536.3	256.0	47.7
11	375.6	261.6	69.6	252.3	64.4	25.5
12	249.2	143.9	57.7	143.9	38.1	26.5
30	135.0	97.3	72.0	97.3	38.7	39.7
34	223.1	143.2	64.2	143.2	73.5	51.3
80	1,380.0	855.0	61.9	720.8	177.4	24.6
85	396.0	247.5	62.5	227.0	61.2	27.0
97	205.1	139.4	68.0	139.4	47.0	33.7
Style B						
17	744.8	593.2	79.6	566.6	335.4	59.2
28	187.2	152.9	81.7	149.0	43.4	29.1
31	211.5	87.1	41.2	82.1	43.7	53.2
35	796.2	421.1	52.8	460.6	244.7	53.1
91	688.8	203.4	29.5	190.5	93.0	48.8
142	243.0	156.8	64.5	134.4	76.5	56.9
143	308.6	162.4	52.6	130.0	79.7	61.3
PM249053	212.0	87.4	41.2	83.4	52.3	62.7

Figure 15. Style A and B framed-bands with vessel area/band ratio and band/painted area ratio.

show that red covers 17.2 sq. cm and the exposed ground (white) area is 16.8 sq. cm in the panel on the far left. In the same type of panel on the right, 20.2 sq. cm are red with 15.4 sq. cm white.

Figure-ground reversal can also be created by surrounding the negative figure with a large filled area, as is seen in the lower triangle of the other two panels on Vessel 143. The painted area in the lower triangle in the left panel is 8.4 sq. cm and in the right panel 8.0 sq. cm. Both techniques—that of surrounding a negative figure with paint, and that of equally dividing the area between painted figures and unpainted negative figures—are commonly found in Style B ceramic painting (Figs. 5, 13a; Pls. 8c, 9c and d). But figure-ground reversal is *not* found in Style A, where figures are clearly placed on a background.

The fact that Style B uses figure-ground reversal with such frequency while Style A completely avoids it means that in appearance Style A and Style B are radically different. But the differences are deeper than merely the look of the pots. Shepard (1956: 291) says that these differences seem "basically psychological. . . . To draw independent motifs [figures] is quite different from laying off a framework and tinkering with it to obtain interesting effects [negative figures]."

While Shepard is correct that these differences have a psychological basis in that they reflect the potter's view of the world, Style B's "interesting effects" are not the result of mere tinkering but are part of the thinking process itself. Style B potters do not "tinker" to create negative figures but have a preconceived plan based on subdividing the framework of bands and

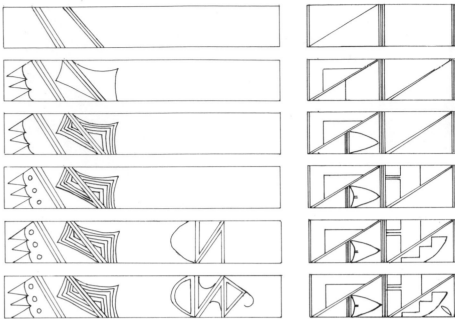

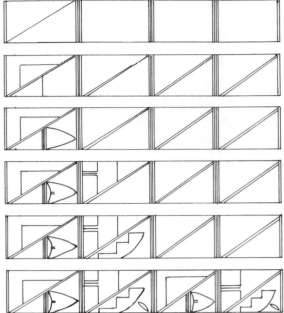

Figure 16. Style A designing (Vessel 34).

Figure 17. Style B designing (Vessel P.M. 249053).

panels. Style A potters, likewise, have a preconceived plan before they begin to paint the independent figures which decorate their pots. The order in which lines are applied in framed bands perhaps clarifies the basic difference between these two approaches (Figs. 16, 17).

Style A potters use lines within banding lines and occasionally panel lines to establish the placement of figures (Fig. 16). Style B potters, by contrast, continue to narrow the field of design by subdividing the panels (Fig. 17). They frequently do this with diagonal lines which divide the panel into two sections. Additional lines further subdivide the panel or create a specific figure within it. Style B potters then fill in figures themselves or the area around the figures, which changes the positive figure to a negative one. The final

product (Pls. 8b, 9c) is the creation of framed bands in two distinctly different styles: Style A vessel 34 (Pl. 8b) contains independent figures while the Style B vessel P.M. 249053 displays an overall pattern.

Style A prefers translation, Style B rotation, as symmetry. The final stylistic distinction between Style A and Style B pottery has to do with framed-band symmetry.

Style A potters use an organizational technique known as translation, which consists of repeated figures translated along a band without change in directional orientation. This class of symmetry (Shepard's symmetry Class 1, 1948: 219–20) has the same organization as a band as defined here, with the difference that the figures are confined within two framing lines. This symmetry can be seen on the

CHAPTER 6

102

upper band in Fig. 14.

Style B potters, on the other hand, commonly use the organizational technique of rotation. This means that figures rotate around a series of point axes. This class of symmetry (Shepard's Class 4) can be seen in framed bands c and d, Plate 9. A comparison of these two Style B bands in this illustration with the upper (a) Style A framed band, in which translation is the symmetry, clearly shows the difference between these two types of organization.

Although Style B potters use a variety of other classes of symmetrical organization as defined by Shepard (ibid.), frequently changing the symmetry from one panel to another within the same framed band (see Appendix III), Style A potters do not. Only three Style A framed bands do not use Class 1 symmetry but they are all constructed on the principle of translation. One of these (Fig. 6, Chapter 5) has two abutting bands along which figures are translated. As these figures are the same in both panels they are horizontally reflected across the central axis between the two bands. Thus, according to symmetry analysis as developed by Shepard (1948, 1956) and Washburn (1977), the symmetry is not one of translation. I would argue, however, that in this case the primary organizational technique remains that of translation.

The other two vessels that have not been classified as using translation are the only examples of rotation used by Style A potters and this has to do with the way the pot was held when painted, rather than a matter of design decision. On these vessels an exterior design of water, motif 5, is painted along the rim and base bands. These two designs move in opposite directions. This occurs, however, only because the vessel is held upright when the lower band is painted,

and upside down when the upper band is painted. Since painting is done from left to right, a rotational structure has resulted.

Motifs, Design Units, and Sikyatki Revival Designs

Until now we have been looking only at observable stylistic differences. These are quantifiable differences, easily seen by anyone looking at the pots, and are in fact often discussed by the potters themselves. In the most general terms, Style A descends from Polacca Polychrome and Style B from the Sikyatki Revival.

So far we have discussed only what might be called the "form" of the decoration. These stylistic differences don't have a "meaning" in the iconographic sense. Now, however, we will see that Style A and Style B wares also differ in what might be called the "content" of their designs.

Style A pots use more of what I have labeled motifs, meaning depictions of natural objects that have symbolic meaning. Style B pots, on the other hand, use more designs derived from Sikyatki Polychrome and frequently use them without specific symbolic reference or spiritual meaning.

This critical distinction between Style A and Style B rests on the determination that motifs are symbols. Ruth Bunzel, who conducted research among pueblo potters in the 1920s, did not then recognize the symbolic content of motifs. In her discussion of Zuni ceramic design, Bunzel noted that the Zuni potter conceived of patterns which were "psychological elements" and that these might be called a "design vocabulary." The design vocabulary represented material objects and nothing more. Bunzel then concluded that most

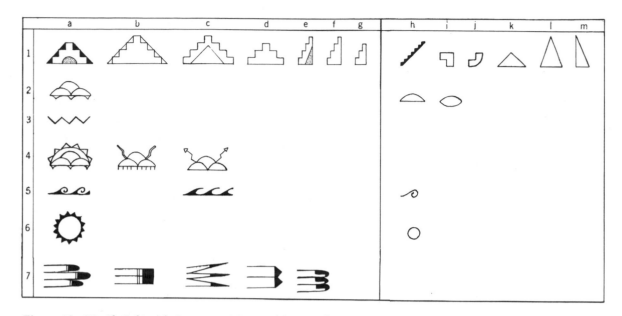

Figure 18. Motifs (left) and elements (right) used by Third Mesa potters. Motif (1) rain cloud: ʔó:mauɨ, (2) rain cloud: ʔó:maɨy yó·ya leki ʔat, (3) lightning: talwí·pi, (4) rain cloud with lightning: ʔó:maɨy yó·yaleki ʔat, (5) water: pá:hɨ, (6) sun: tá·wa, (7) feather/prayer feathers: nakʷa/nakʷákʷisi.

pottery decoration was not symbolic because "the same name is applied to elements having nothing in common from a stylistic point of view, and conversely, the same elements may be differently designated in different contexts" (1929: 69). The seemingly arbitrary association between term and design that Bunzel encountered among the Zuni potters was very similar to the situation found among the Third Mesa potters working today.

My research, however, shows that Bunzel's conclusions that these "psychological elements" were not symbolic is not true for Third Mesa potters today. Both Style B and Style A potters *do* use symbolic designs on their pots. I have labeled these symbolic designs "motifs."

All motifs are symbols in that the referent *is* commonly agreed upon. And, each referent carries with it several

associations that can be a given myth, a ceremony, or some facet of Hopi religious thought. An analogy in our own culture might be a picture of a Christmas tree which summons up associations of religious thought, family, and gifts. In fact, all but five of the motifs used in Third Mesa pottery decoration function like the picture of the Christmas tree and refer specifically to the Kachina cult.

Motifs may have a single referent but in some ways they are like texts.[4] A tadpole motif, for example, will always be called that, although one informant may emphasize that tadpoles appear in rock pools only if the Kachinas have brought the spring rains, while another informant will emphasize that without rain (brought by the Kachinas) there cannot be life. Hopi motifs do, therefore, represent "material objects" as Bunzel (ibid. 70) hypothesized,

Figure 19. Motifs used by Third Mesa potters. Motif (8) Four Corners/Hopi (land): *hoysícvi,* (9) tadpole: *pavátya,* (10) corn plant: *hímiꞌiyi,* (11) bird: *círo,* (12) Sun Kachina: *Ta·wáqacina,* (13) Long-haired Kachina: *Angáqacina,* (14) Humpbacked Flute Player, (15) One-Horned Humpbacked Flute Player, (16) Bear's Paw. Motifs 14–16 were seldom identified in Hopi.

but associated with these material objects are Hopi religious beliefs and the associated ceremonial cycle.

Sixteen motifs are used by Style A potters in the decoration of their pots. I began my research into the meaning of these motifs by showing pictures of them to a number of Hopi people, including both Traditionalists and Progressives.

Immediate and unanimous identification was made of all motifs (Figs. 18, 19) by thirty-seven Hopi, who were asked to name them.

The motifs are:
1. Rain clouds
2. Rain clouds depicted differently
3. Lightning
4. Rain clouds or rain clouds with lightning
5. Water
6. Sun
7. Feather, prayer feather
8. Four Corners, Hopi land
9. Tadpole
10. Corn plant
11. Bird
12. Sun Kachina
13. Long-Haired Kachina
14. Humpbacked Flute Player
15. One-Horned Humpbacked Flute Player
16. Bear's paw

How the motifs were presented made no difference to their identification. The motifs were painted on pottery, on file cards, or on Kachina costumes. Regardless of the context, all terms were agreed upon.[5] The rain cloud motifs (2, 4), the sun, the Sun Kachina, and the corn plant motifs (6, 10, 12) are all found on Kachina costumes (see B. Wright 1973: 90, 93, 124). Tadpoles (motif 9) are frequently painted on rattles and rasp gourds (195) as well as on ceremonial bowls. The "Four Corners" motif is found on the shield carried by the Kachina Ewiro (63). The Sun Kachina is also frequently drawn by school children, as are others of their favorite Kachinas, including the Long-Haired Kachina (motif 13).

The observed use of motif 4, rain clouds, motif 5, water, as well as motif 9, tadpole, and 10, corn plant, on ceremonial bowls confirms the religious significance of these motifs. Furthermore, the rim of these bowls was always in the shape of motif 1c or d on four sides (Fig. 18). The sacred use of these motifs—which are also doodled by school children in the margins of their copybooks—and the ready identification of these and all motifs, show how important these symbols are to the Hopi.

Different motifs may have similar labels (motifs 1 and 2, Fig. 18), as both a stepped pyramid and a configuration of three semicircles can mean rain clouds.

Motifs can be considered as words, and the elements that make them up as the letters. The elimination of decorative elements and reduction to the structural part or "core" (Munn 1966: 943) necessary for meaning to be maintained can be seen in motif 1 (Fig. 18), rain clouds. The basic design of rain clouds is either a two- or three-step terraced pyramid (Fig. 18: 1a, b). Decorative elements can be added to the exterior and interior of this form (1a), to the exterior only (1b), or only to the interior (1c) without changing its meaning. The form may be reduced by dividing it longitudinally in half (1e–g). This half may or may not be decorated on the interior, but still the identification of the shape as a rain cloud remains possible. However, if this motif is further reduced it is no longer labeled as a rain cloud, but becomes simply an element (1h–m). Potters recognize most elements as derived from motifs and that these, conversely, can be built up to make motifs, but they do not think in terms of elements any more than we think of words in terms of letters. Motifs, not elements, are, to use Bunzel's term, the potter's design vocabulary.

Motifs are usually recognizable by their outline. Rain clouds or corn, for instance, are easily identified this way. Shape alone identifies the Humpbacked Flute Player (14) and the One-Horned Humpbacked Flute Player (15), as well.

While some motifs like rain clouds can

be reduced and still remain motifs (Fig. 18), others are identifiable only by the inclusion of what in other contexts would be elements. This is the case with motif 7, which in order to be recognizable as "feathers" or "prayer feathers," must have two or three triangles, rectangles, or finger shapes solidly filled at the tip. This solid area was essential for identification. None of these shapes could be recognized as a feather or prayer feather *without* this solid tip, whereas a single triangle, rectangle, or finger was occasionally recognized as a feather or prayer feather as long as it *had* the solid tip.

Other interior elements essential to the identification of a motif were the four circles and crossing parallel lines within the "Four Corners" motif (Fig. 19.8), the dot for the eye of the bird (11) and the two lines, eyes and nose of the Sun Kachina (12).

In other cases elements can be added that do *not* change the motif, as with the interior and exterior decoration of rain clouds and the addition of triangles to the lightning of motif 4c (Fig. 18), rain clouds with lightning.

One motif may be added to another (Fig. 18) to form a third, as lightning (3) has been added to rain clouds (2) to form the motif of "rain clouds with lightning" (4). The feather/prayer feather motif (7) when found in association with the bird's head motif (Figs. 18, 19) is distinguished as "feathers" as opposed to "prayer feathers." This shows that context as well as motif association affects identification of the feather/prayer feather motif. This was clearly demonstrated in the discussion of vessel 27 (Fig. 11: lower). In every case, Hopis who determined that the upper portion was a bird's head classed motif 7 as "feathers." Hopis who considered this portion "a design" or "maybe water," classed motif 7 as "prayer feathers."

An apparent change in motif identification does occur when motif 7 (feathers) or 10 (corn) is attached to motifs 1, 2, or 4 (Figs. 18, 19), either design of rain clouds or rain clouds with lightning. When indicated separately these motifs remain prayer feathers, corn plant, rain cloud, or rain clouds with or without lightning. But together, whether on Butterfly Dancers' robes (Pl. 1), on Kachina costumes (B. Wright 1973: 174), or on ceramics (Fig. 8: lower), they are identified as "wet earth." Action in this instance has taken place to produce a different condition. Prayer feathers have produced rain which creates wet earth; rain produces corn which is the product of wet earth.

Beyond the identification of motifs, is their spiritual or symbolic significance. Motifs 1–7 and 9–12, specifically rain clouds, lightning, water, sun, prayer feathers, tadpole, corn, bird and Sun Kachina, are all associated with the ethereal spirit world and its gifts, referring specifically to the Kachina cult. The sun is the face or manifestation of Tawa, the Father and Creator. Lightning foretells rain, and the rain clouds are brought by the Kachinas. Rain occurs only if ceremonies, prayers, and prayer feathers have been correctly prepared, performed, and offered. Birds are also important to the Hopi religion. Hawks, red-shafted flickers, meadowlarks, flycatchers, and other small birds are shot for their feathers, used as prayer feathers or on Kachina costumes. Eagles, which are ceremonially caught, kept and fed, are also killed and stripped of their feathers for use as prayer feathers or on costumes. Macaw feathers are also

purchased for Kachina costumes.

There are four other motifs commonly used by Style A potters that do not refer to the Kachina cult. These are the Humpbacked Flute Player, the One-Horned Humpbacked Flute Player, the Bear Paw and the Four Corners.

The first three may be taken as a group. While all the people I asked agreed that motif 14 was a Humpbacked Flute Player, as a design it could be "the sign of the migrations" or "the sign of the Flute Clan." Humpbacked Flute Players are associated with the migrations because they led the Hopi before they were divided into four separate groups and clans. The flute players carried seeds in their humps, which they planted for the people as they traveled. This motif as well as the One-Horned Flute Player and the Bear's Paw (motifs 15, 16) were not termed as "being" something but rather as representing an event (the migration) or a group of people. The One-Horned Flute Player is the sign of the Gray Flute Society[6] and the Bear's Paw print the sign of the Bear Clan.

These motifs can be said to stand for groups of people joined in a clan, a society, or in the activity of migration. They are the only motifs used by Christian potters (see Jacka and Gill 1976: 45), who would naturally avoid reference to the Kachina cult since they are no longer supposed to believe in it. This very avoidance shows the emotional strength of the Kachina cult motifs.

The only motif that is neither related to the Kachina cult nor a sign for a group or activity, is motif 8, termed *hoysícvi* (*hóy* = move, *sícvi'o* = crosswise, roundabout) by Hopi speakers. Hopi- and non-Hopi-speaking Hopis frequently referred to it as "the Four Corners." All Hopis agreed, however, that it means, "It is here," or "it is our land—our place." Or, "It is the sacred circle, it is the land given to us, when we first arrived, by Masaw. We came from the four corners to this land. We all met here [where the lines intercept].[7] Our land is sacred and these [the four circles in the motif] are the four sacred mountains." (The four mountains at the four cardinal directions are Loloma Point, east; Bill Williams Mountain, west; Navajo Mountain, north; Woodruff Butte, south.) This land, like rain and corn, is a divine gift; it lies within the four corners of the Hopi world, for which the Hopi looked so long.

It seems possible to conclude that some of the peculiarities of motifs—the fact that they may change their referent when associated with other motifs, or that some elements are added purely as decorative devices—led Bunzel to remark that "there is no consistency in nomenclature [of Hopi motifs], not even within the same pattern" (1929: 70). Bunzel did recognize the pictorial nature of some motifs. She says that designs, if they have any significance at all, are pictures of objects (ibid.). But because of what she saw as a lack of consistency, Bunzel concluded that Hopi designs were not symbols, since "the association between the design and the object or idea" was not "fixed and recognized" (69).

The discrepancy between Bunzel's interpretation and mine may perhaps be because Hopis consider motifs either as representations of a natural object or as "signs." If I asked a Hopi "the meaning" of rain cloud motifs 1, 2, and 3 in Figure 18, for instance, I would be told that there was none. If I pointed to motif 1 and asked, "What is this?" I would be told it was a

cloud or a design. If I asked what it was a design of, I would be told it was a rain cloud. In other words, the motifs were not considered as abstract designs but as representations of the object.

Today on Third Mesa motifs are also clearly symbols, not only because the referent is commonly agreed upon but because motifs serve as vehicles for concepts (Langer 1957: 60–61) relevant to Hopi spiritual life.

Both Style A and Style B use motifs, but there is a vast and important difference in the *way* they use motifs. Style A has a greater repertoire, regularly employing sixteen motifs, while Style B, on the other hand, uses only four. Further, Style A will frequently use two or more motifs on a single vessel, while Style B will usually use only one motif on a vessel. (For a listing of vessels and the number of motifs used and their makers see Figures 29 and 30 in Appendix III, *Design type and compositional symmetry in relation to vessel class.*) Style A's use of motifs seems to indicate the potter's interest in the meaning generated by these motifs. Style B motifs are quite different in that, with one exception, all Style B motifs were initially borrowed from Sikyatki Polychrome ware of the fourteenth century. The use of these motifs may have been a source of confusion for Bunzel.

Another reason Bunzel may have concluded that Hopi motifs were not symbols was because she conducted her research on First Mesa at the time of the Sikyatki Revival of the 1920s.[8] Consequently, while her conclusions may well describe the situation among First Mesa potters working in the Sikyatki Revival style, they are not applicable to Third Mesa, especially not to Traditionalist potters. These potters shun the Sikyatki

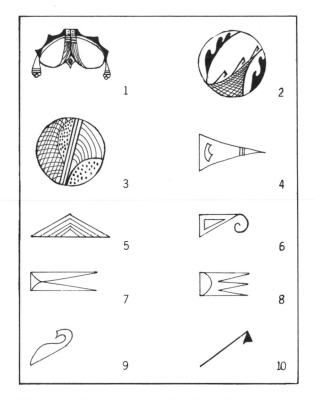

Figure 20. Design units used by Third Mesa potters.

and so are fraught with spiritual meaning.

But there are other things on pots besides motifs. Large portions of some ceramic designs consist of elements or a number of elements arranged to form a *design unit*. I have used this term in accord with Mera who stated that "basic elements through elaboration often become what may be termed design units" (1937: 1). Mera, however, used this term to refer to the Rain Bird design which, as he pointed out, was formalized. In contrast, Third Mesa design units (Fig. 20) are not standardized although they could certainly become so.

A design unit (Fig. 20) is simply a shape, not a representation of a natural object and certainly nothing that would call up spiritual associations in the mind of the beholder. Potters either make up design units as they paint the pot (design units 1–4), or adapt designs from Polacca Polychrome. Design units are not commonly used and are frequently created as part of the designing process and to "fill in the space," which was a commonly given reason for including single elements in a design.

Design units 5 and 9 are adaptations of Polacca Polychrome designs (see Wade and McChesney 1981: IV, 19; V, 19). The "Maltese Cross" found on one vessel (Fig. 6) is also a survival from the nineteenth century but this design was recognized as an early one, and since it is considered by the potter to be a formalized Polacca design, it has not been considered as a design unit.

Design units 6–8 are all reminiscent of Sikyatki Revival designs. Unit 8 is similar to the Sikyatki Revival design illustrated in Figure 21c. This design makes use of the triple elongated triangle and single

Revival style since they associate it with white influence. Today, revival designs are still extensively used on First Mesa which initiated the revival, while on Third Mesa, by contrast, a greater variety of motifs is used.

Another factor which may have skewed Bunzel's research is that Bunzel did not distinguish between motifs, design units, and Sikyatki Revival designs and so the importance of motifs could easily have been overlooked. Motifs are, to re-emphasize, a representation of a natural object, usually abstracted, that is recognizable by anyone. Motifs are more than just pictures of natural objects, however; they also make specific reference to the Hopi Kachina cult, to the Hopi migrations or to the Hopi land itself,

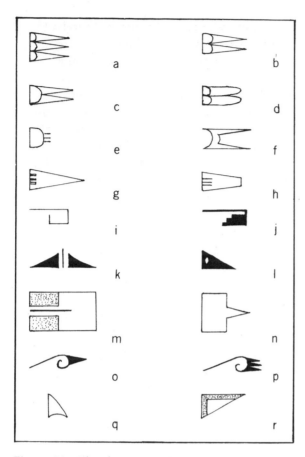

Figure 21. Sikyatki Revival designs used by Third Mesa potters.

semicircle characteristic of Sikyatki Revival design (Fig. 21a) but, although it is occasionally found on Sikyatki Revival wares it is not used in the same manner. The triple elongated triangles of the Sikyatki Revival design commonly intermesh with two elongated triangles of a like design with only two triangles (Fig. 21b). The contrast between them can be seen by comparing Plate 9a with Figure 9. Unit 6 is clearly similar to the Sikyatki designs o and p, the triangle and scroll being reversed.

Except for the Progressive potter Loren, design units were only used by

Traditionalist Style A potters. Again, there is a difference in the approach to design between potters working in Style A and potters working in Style B. Style A potters when not using motifs are more inclined to make up their own design units as they go along. Style B potters use designs taken ultimately from Sikyatki Polychrome ware, and handed down through Sikyatki Revival wares.

Progressive potters working in today's descendant of the Sikyatki Revival style recognize and label the Sikyatki Revival designs they use as coming from the prehistoric ware. Early copies of this ware made on First Mesa at the turn of the century lack its fine line, high polish, and overall elegance (Wade and McChesney 1981; Fewkes 1898). But by the time of Bunzel's visit in 1924, the Sikyatki Revival was well established, with not only the thin line and high polish characteristic of prehistoric Sikyatki Polychrome but also many of the same designs.

What is interesting about these Sikyatki Revival designs is that some of them are actually symbolic motifs. Feathers (motifs 7a, b, c) and rain clouds (motifs 1e, f, g), for example, dominate the Revival designs; other designs that may have been motifs used by the First Mesa potters and the Progressive potters of Third Mesa over the years have lost their meaning. Many of what might have been considered motifs are instead considered by the Progressive Hopi potters "just designs." Although a clear stylistic relationship between motif 2 rain clouds and Sikyatki design a–e exists, these designs are not labeled as rain clouds. Likewise, design j is often not labeled, but if a potter is questioned about the half-stepped pyramid within the crook, it will be identified as a rain cloud.

We do have examples of how, over time, formerly important motifs lose their meaning and become reduced to "just designs." Design i, according to Stephen (Wade and McChesney 1980: 31), represented either a hunting weapon or the god Muingwa in the 1890s. This was an important symbol, evidenced by the fact that it was extensively painted on kiva walls at the same time it was used on Sikyatki Polychrome (Smith 1952). Today, it carries none of its earlier meaning.

Although one potter did copy designs directly from Sikyatki Polychrome ware— she showed me sherds decorated with designs d and e and motif f—Revival designs for the most part are no longer taken from Sikyatki Polychrome ware. Rather, they have become part of the standard First Mesa design vocabulary. That they have enjoyed long use is apparent when Sikyatki Revival wares of the last sixty years are compared. I examined seventy-nine pieces from the Melville Collection at Wesleyan University, acquired during the late 1920s and early 1930s (Walker and Wyckoff 1983). Forty-seven percent of them bore Sikyatki designs used by Third Mesa potters, as illustrated in Figure 21. By 1959 these designs had become even more popular. At that time 130 vessels made by First Mesa women were brought to the Museum of Northern Arizona Hopi Show; 51.5 percent were painted with Sikyatki designs as judged from illustrations of the vessels (Sikorski 1968). Motifs 1e, f, g; motifs 5a, 7a, and 11 were also used on these Sikyatki Revival wares.

In other words, during the earlier period of the Sikyatki Revival a little less than half the pottery collected on First Mesa used these Revival designs. More than a quarter

of a century later slightly more than half the pottery collected on First Mesa bore such designs. These designs have truly become part of the First Mesa design vocabulary, and by extension that of Progressive potters working on Third Mesa in Style B. It is this style that is used on the ceramics commonly produced for sale to tourists. Style A pots, on the other hand, are bartered among Hopis.

CONCLUSION

Two distinctly different styles classifiable by the attributes of line width and of figure/ground ratio, and by the use of motifs as opposed to Sikyatki Revival designs, exist among Third Mesa potters and are recognized by them. The traits that make up these two styles can be identified and quantified.

Style A prefers discrete unit designs which may be seen clearly and completely, while Style B favors an overall pattern. Discrete unit designs are found on twenty-eight percent of Style A vessels as opposed to twelve percent of Style B vessels.

Since discrete unit designs are almost always used in association with two or more motifs, Style A vessels are also more inclined to have one or more motifs than Style B vessels have (seventy-nine and fifty-six percent). Style A also displays a greater variety of motifs.

By contrast, Style B is confined to only four motifs and on more than half of these vessels only motif 1, rain clouds, appeared. This motif is commonly found on Sikyatki Revival wares and is used by Style B potters with Sikyatki Revival designs, which are characteristic of Style B. They are found on seventy-two percent of these vessels, and on only eighteen percent of Style A pots.

Compared to the variety in the Style A sample, Style B decoration was far more standardized (the degree of standardization is not evident in my sample because I chose to include as many different designs as possible). This is probably because so many were rapidly produced for the tourist trade. Lucy commonly produced vessels almost identical with vessel P.M. 249053 (Pl. 9c), whereas Loren consistently produced vessels similar to 143 (Pl. 9d) and 32 (Pl. 6).

Style A uses translation as symmetry and avoids rotation, while Style B uses it frequently. Style A vessels commonly use motifs, whereas Sikyatki Revival designs dominate Style B. Most important, however, is that these two styles demonstrate two different structures: Style A is one of isolated figures surrounded by space, thus the preference for hanging or discrete unit design types. Style B structure is one of overall pattern which acts to create negative figures. Within the framed band this distinction is closely related to another, the figure-ground ratio.

The basic structural difference between these two styles, therefore, is not simply the symmetry of design parts (Washburn 1977), or the spatial division of the design field itself (Graves 1982), but rather, the spatial relationship between the design or figure and the design field or background. This relationship is a material expression of a given group's concept of space, which is an integral part of world view.

Now we are ready to look at who these potters are, what relationships exist among them, and how they are aligned with respect to Traditionalist and Progressive thinking. When we have done that we will see why these potters have different world views. We will then also look at other ways in which these different world views are physically expressed.

NOTES

1. See Appendix I for a detailed description of ceramic manufacture including access rights to clay sources, a map of which is included.

2. Although both Washburn (1977: 18) and Shepard (1956: 268) recognize the importance of framing to create the design field, they both emphasize that a framed band has a central axis midway between the two framing lines. This is not always the case with designs I have designated "framed bands."

3. In order to illustrate the relationship between these two designs, this vessel has been depicted in Plate 7 with 50 percent roll-out at maximum vessel width and should be compared to Figure 12, left.

4. That "pictographs" served this function has been noted by Stephen for the Hopi (Mallory 1894: 604) and by Mallory (ibid. 468–73) for the Micmac.

5. The Long-Haired Kachina I showed informants was uncharacteristically painted on a pot. I have included it as a motif despite the fact that it apparently had never been used on ceramics previously.

6. Waters (1963: 38) argues that the Humpbacked Flute Player is associated with the migration of the Hopis, and the Blue Flute Clan and the Blue Flute Society were named after him. Thus he is the symbol of the migrations, the clan, and the society. According to my data, the Two-Horned Flute Player is the symbol for the Blue Flute Society, not the Gray Flute Society, as claimed by Waters. In accord with Waters, however, the Humpbacked Flute Player Kachina is distinguished by two antennae instead of horns.

7. Some Hopis consider the center to be the three

mesas they now occupy, while some Traditionalists consider the center to be Oraibi itself. The design of two crossing parallel lines signifying the migration and meeting of the Hopis is commonly drawn on the legs and arms of Kachinas (see Wright 1973, also Pl. 1).

8. The type of interpretive problem Bunzel faced in Sikyatki Revival designs exists today. The vessel produced by a Third Mesa potter illustrated in Figure 11, lower, was given a number of different interpretations as a complete design. The most common was that it is a bird. Some saw a bird's head in the upper left-hand corner, others did not. However, when shown the design in isolation, all the Hopis claimed it was "just a design," which was also said about the "bird's crest" in the upper right-hand corner. The feathers were called either feathers or prayer feathers, depending upon whether the viewers discerned a bird's head. As previously discussed, feathers were commonly defined as prayer feathers in isolation. Everyone identified the rain clouds both in and out of context. These motifs were

certainly in use at the time of Bunzel's visit, and almost assuredly were given the same labels. Stephen, although he identifies motifs 1a, c, f, g (Fig. 18) as "cloud symbols" (Wade and McChesney 1980: 31), refers to them in Hopi as "nak-tci," the term used today for a headdress, specifically the one shaped like motif 1d as commonly used by the Butterfly Dancer (Pl. 1). In Hopi this motif, be it painted or in the shape of a headdress, or attached to a Kachina's armband (see B. Wright 1973: 201), is referred to as ʔó:mawi̵ (cloud). In contrast to motif 1, motif 2 is more commonly called ʔ'ó:mai̵y yó·yalekiʔat (a cloud from which rain is falling), although in English they are both referred to as either "rain cloud" or "rain clouds." Stephen does not note feather motifs per se, but he does state that "the Mythic Um-toc-ina, the thunder . . . [whose] body is a rain cloud with lightning darting through it, which discloses the origin of the angular cloud symbol so universally depicted upon all classes of pottery," has a "tail of an eagle" (Stephen in Wade and McChesney 1980: 26).

CHAPTER SEVEN

THE POTTERS OF THIRD MESA

INTRODUCTION

In the last chapter we were introduced to the potters and examined the differences between Style A and Style B. The potters who use one of these styles will, when asked, criticize the style different from their own. The language of their criticisms shows not only how they look at pottery but how they look at what it means to be Hopi. Before we examine these aesthetic judgments, however, we should look at the relationships between the potters and how they learned to work in the styles they espouse. We will see how the potters' political and religious differences are not only reflected in the styles of Style A Traditionalist potters and Style B Progressive potters, but also how these differences help to determine the intended uses of the pots, the number of pots a potter will make each year, and from whom the potters will learn their craft.

The political strength of the First Mesa pottery cartel has played a part in the third style of Third Mesa, the Raised Decoration Style. This style must be discussed singly, since its genesis was so completely different from that of Style A and Style B. Its existence says much about the politics of pottery on First Mesa today.

Different potters decorate their vessels in diverse styles. This comes from the difference in values shared by groups of potters who frequently are kin and learn from one another. The fact that a Style A potter, for example, learns from another Style A potter does not dictate the style in which the potter works, for there is a constant exchange of ideas among many of the potters.

The motivation to make pottery and distribute it represents a critical difference between Style A and Style B potters. Style B, used by Progressives, is primarily made for sale to tourists. Although occasionally sold, Style A vessels are made for Hopi use or for barter with other Native Americans. Both Style A and Style B potters learn from their kin; however, Progressive Style B potters have kin on First Mesa who allow them access to the First Mesa ceramic markets. Raised Decoration Style pottery is similar to Style B in that it is made for sale, but its evolution is unique since these potters do not have access to the First Mesa market.

KINSHIP, LEARNING AND PRODUCTION

The five Style A potters are Traditionalists and live in Oraibi and Hotevilla; the oldest are Anne who lives in Oraibi and her sister Vera who lives in Hotevilla. Anne and Vera still make pottery in their respective villages although, because of failing eyesight, they seldom decorate their work. They are daughters of Qöyawaisi and are members of the Corn Clan, and were separated in 1906 when the split occurred at Oraibi and the Corn or *Pikyas* Clan was divided. Qöyawaisi, who is now deceased, and her daughter Anne remained at Oraibi (Anne is the same person referred to as Anita by Titiev, 1972). Vera and another of their sisters moved to Hotevilla. Two of Anne's daughters, Terry and Betty, are potters. Like Anne they live at Oraibi. Both were sent to boarding school, worked off the Reservation during World War II, and returned to their village to marry and raise families.

After the war Betty married the son of a Traditionalist leader from Hotevilla and returned to Oraibi. Terry also married a Traditionalist from Lower Moencopi, and after living for some time in Tuba City where her husband worked for the Bureau of Indian Affairs, likewise returned to Oraibi. At about the time of their return, Terry's husband, who like so many Hopis suffers from diabetes, had to undergo dialysis. The village chief therefore agreed that to avoid the long trips to the hospital at Keams Canyon or Tuba City, Terry and her husband could install electricity for a dialysis machine in their home. The machine was provided by the Veterans Administration. Terry's family does not have electric lighting; they use electricity only for the dialysis machine, their television, and Terry's electric kiln.

None of Terry's or Betty's daughters is a potter but Betty is currently teaching her daughter's daughter Diana.

Apart from Anne's sister Vera, the only other active potter in Hotevilla is Amy. She is related to both of these older women because her maternal grandmother was Vera's older sister, the woman from whom Vera learned pottery-making. Amy married Elmer from New Oraibi and lived there for some time, but she and her husband became disillusioned later with the increasingly "progressive" changes that took place there. With the establishment of the Tribal Council and the growing division between Progressives and Traditionalists, they decided to return to Hotevilla where Amy began to learn the craft.

The kin relations and the teachers of these Corn Clan potters are shown in the accompanying diagram. Except for Vera, who learned from her sister because of her move to Hotevilla in 1906, all the potters learned from preceding generations.

No diagram, however, can indicate the constant exchange and learning that also take place among contemporary potters. Sisters Terry and Betty, for example, constantly help each other as well as their mother Anne. At one time or another all the Style A potters used Terry's electric kiln. Vera and her grand-niece Amy frequently work together and on occasion pass pieces back and forth for "help." These potters identify as teachers those older women from whom they learned, but in fact they may learn as much from contemporaries.

The work of Style A (Traditionalist) potters is in marked contrast to that of Progressive or Style B potters. Style A potters learned from members of their lineage and they frequently helped one another. Their pottery is rarely sold, not because it is valued less or is primarily produced for home consumption but because Traditionalists are less concerned than Progressives with the cash economy. The greatest part of the production of the Traditional potters between 1979 and 1981

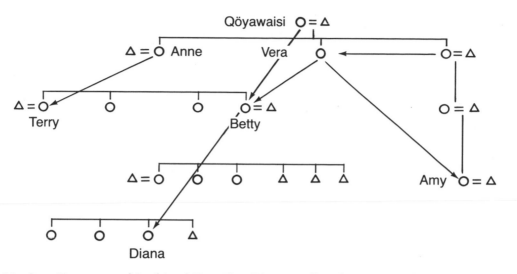

Figure 22. Corn Clan potters of Oraibi and Hotevilla. (Direction of learning ———➤ .)

was for gift-giving or barter.

Gift-giving was commonly a formalized gift exchange. For instance, pottery was exchanged by the girls who performed in the Butterfly Dance. Pottery was also given on many occasions in gratitude for, or in anticipation of, another gift, or was used in interpueblo barter in exchange for the services of, for example, a medicine man or a dressmaker.

The contrast between the role of pottery as a cash commodity for Progressives and as one of many items used for barter by Traditionalists can be demonstrated by comparing the ceramic production from July 1, 1979 to July 1, 1980 by the Progressive potter Lucy and the Traditionalist potter Betty.

During this period Lucy made only seven vessels not for sale. Three of these were mixing bowls (vessels 13, 14, 15) made to repay lineage members of her daughter's Butterfly Dance partners; two were commissioned by New Oraibi residents (27 and P.M. 248954); the other two were

Christmas gifts to staff members of the Hopi Day School where Lucy works as a cook. The hundreds of pots produced by Lucy, usually small bowls, were sold to tourists and traders for more than $7,000. Lucy's total income, including her salary and cash received for her other ceramics during the year, exceeded $20,000.

During the same period Betty made thirty vessels. Her total ceramic production and its intended and actual use are listed in Figure 23. Although Betty received $210 from the sale of her pottery, all of the purchases were made by me, usually on behalf of the Peabody Museum, Yale University. Had they not been purchased, Betty would probably have used them for intra- or interpueblo barter with other Hopis or with one of the Santo Domingo traders who come from time to time.

All the Style A Traditionalist potters (except for Betty's granddaughter who is still learning the craft) barter with these traders. Betty, as is common, has established a particularly close relationship

9 *paqwíscaqapta*

Four vessels (3, 4, 5 and P.M. 248957) were made to "pay back" her daughter's Butterfly Dance partner's lineage. Three of these served this purpose and one was purchased for the Peabody Museum for $20.

Two others were made in exchange for the services of a medicine man. As these slightly cracked upon firing, one (146) was given to a friend, also a member of the Corn Clan, and the other (147) was kept for Betty's own use.

One *paqwíscaqapta* (138) was made to pay back the men who wove the wedding robes of Betty's sister's daughter's daughter.

8 *nöqkʷíscaqapta*

All were made to pay back her daughter's Butterfly Dance partner's lineage; these include sample vessels 6, 7, 8, 9, and 10. Seven of these were used for this purpose but one was used as payment to a dressmaker from Lower Moencopi, who made a dress for Betty.

3 *nöqkʷíscaqapta* or *oyâ:pi*

One of these (P.M. 248946) was intended as payment for the dressmaker. The intended use of 2 and 29 is not known. All three were purchased for $50 each.

6 *caqáphoya*

These were all made as sale or barter items. Two were used to exchange with Hotevilla women for plaques. Two (11 and 85) were purchased for $40. Two were exchanged with a trader from Santo Domingo for four pairs of earrings and a ring.

1 *caqápta*

Made and given as a gift to me.

1 *sí·vi̇*

Made and used as payment to the medicine man.

1 *oyâ:pi*

Potter was unwilling to state for whom the vessel was made.

1 *wíkóro*

Made for and bartered with a Santo Domingo trader.

Figure 23. Intended and actual use of ceramics produced by Betty between July 1, 1979 and July 1, 1980.

with one of them. In an earlier visit this trader had requested that Betty make a large *wikóro* (bottle), and told her it would be taken to Santo Domingo where it would be painted and used in a ceremony. I was unable to discover what Betty received in exchange for this piece, which she made some time later, but one can assume that it was equal to its local retail value of $150. Betty also traded two of the six *caqáphoya* she made that year with the Santo Domingan woman. She received three pairs of earrings and a ring and, since Betty "had traded with her before," the trader gave her another pair of earrings. These were of the type assembled with materials acquired from a jobber and commonly found on roadside stands. These earrings were made from turquoise, silver, plastic, and shell beads that hung from silver earhooks and usually sell for $5 or $6. Betty's ring was also of a common type, usually defined as Navajo. It was made from silver and inset with a piece of coral and a piece of turquoise; it would have sold for about $20. Thus the retail value of these items was about $40, the same as the market value of Betty's bowls and the same price for which, in fact, she sold two similar small bowls.

In other trades, Betty paid with a stew bowl the equivalent of $20 to $30 to have a dress made, and with a jar a like sum to the medicine man. This is a very small sum indeed to pay a medicine man and must have been only a partial payment. Betty perhaps shared payment with her husband since they had both visited the medicine man after the death of their grandchild. The medicine man may also have received a serving bowl.

In conclusion, Betty and other Traditionalist potters, like Progressive potters, produce ceramics for ceremonial exchange or to acquire goods and services. Progressive potters, however, also sell their wares to Anglos for cash to acquire goods and to pay for such services as electricity and telephones. Since Traditionalists don't care for costly utilities, they need less cash income.

There is a question, however, about the impact of the First Mesa cartel on Third Mesa potters. Do Third Mesa Traditionalist potters refrain from producing ceramics for cash sale because of their fear of First Mesa potters? Or do they stay out of the cash economy because of different attitudes? I suggest that it is because Progressive and Traditionalist potters have different values. Pottery, to the Traditionalists, is not considered an element in a cash economy. Independence from the dominant white society can be maintained only if cash income does not become a necessity. For the Traditionalist, life should be regulated by the ceremonial and agricultural cycle.

Thus, these potters distribute their pottery in accord with the Traditionalist position, while Progressive potters, with their desire for Anglo-American goods and services, sell their pottery for money. Evidence that Third Mesa potters are not simply inhibited from production by the First Mesa cartel is the fact that there are outlets for Traditionalist pottery. Not only are there outlets, there is also an unmet demand for these wares. Third Mesa ceramics are sought by the Museum of Northern Arizona and by the Second Mesa Cooperative, both of which are eager to sell Third Mesa bottles and mixing bowls. As traditionally made and "glazed" with piñon sap, the *wikóro* is now made only on Third Mesa. These simple domestic pieces which only thirty years ago were not considered of value or sought by the Museum have now, because of declining production, become rare. But now neither the Museum nor the Cooperative can often acquire them. The only decorated wares acquired by the Museum were commissioned in 1973. Traditionalist potters seldom submit pottery to the annual Museum of Northern Arizona Hopi Show. The Museum "only wants fancy things," the potters say, and the financial benefits of barter are greater. This in fact is true, since the barter exchange is at retail rates, whereas both the Museum and the Second Mesa store add a minimum of 25 percent to the listed price.

Third Mesa potters also spurn the Second Mesa Cooperative which could be an important outlet for their work. Since the Second Mesa Cooperative is under the control of the Tribal Council, Traditionalist craftsmen see it as yet another way that the Council enriches itself at their expense.

The Third Mesa potters are not entirely opposed to selling their work, however.

Betty's son, a well-known carver of Kachina dolls, established a craft shop on Arizona Road 264 across from the entrance to Oraibi in 1981. The shop may prove to be a future outlet for Third Mesa Traditionalist ceramics. Another new retail outlet is in Oraibi itself. Tourists were first permitted there in 1980, and had asked if there were anything for sale. "They wanted something from the oldest town in America," I was told. Betty now has a box of small pieces for sale to tourists, made by her mother Anne or her granddaughter Diana. Selling to tourists, however, has not really compromised the Traditionalists anti-cash attitude. All of Betty's sale items are clearly inferior ones. Diana is just learning the craft and Anne's eyesight is failing. Terry also gave one piece to Betty to sell—because the black paint had fired poorly. None of these pieces was good enough to be bartered but Betty and Terry thought they "might as well get something for them."

Although Traditionalist potters who work in Style A seem to be outside the sphere of the First Mesa cartel, the influence of this cartel is a factor in Progressive pottery, both in Style B ceramics and in the Raised Decoration Style.

The primary motivation for the production of both Sikyatki (Style B) and Raised Decoration Style ceramics is for cash income. But because of the economic importance of the Sikyatki Revival Style to the residents of First Mesa, who claim it as their own, it was taught only to potters whose spouses were from First Mesa. This in turn forced the creation of the Raised Decoration Style by Progressive potters who were married to men from Third Mesa but who wished to produce pottery for the Anglo market.

First Mesa potters vigorously maintain control of the ceramic market. Threats of witchcraft are the primary control mechanism. However, when this failed, as it did at Hotevilla in 1971, violence was used and Hotevilla kilns destroyed. So, although potters on Third Mesa are divided into Traditionalists and Progressives by attitude toward cash income, Progressives are further divided by whether or not they have a relationship to First Mesa. The three Third Mesa Style B potters are Lucy, Loren and Cindy and they all have ties to First Mesa either through their husbands or their father. Lucy and Cindy are mother and daughter and members of the Fire Clan. They live in New Oraibi. Lucy learned pottery making from her mother's sister and then from her mother-in-law from First Mesa. Lucy said that she knew how to make pottery but "didn't tell them on First Mesa; they just thought I learnt quick." They did, however, teach her Sikyatki Revival designs and layouts which in turn she taught to her daughter, Cindy, who is married to Nelson from Second Mesa.

Both Lucy and Cindy know the Traditionalist potters on Third Mesa. Lucy and Cindy occasionally pay Terry to fire their pottery in her electric kiln and, at least on one occasion, Cindy has painted one of Terry's vessels for her.

The third Style B potter is Loren from Upper Moencopi. Like Lucy, Loren's husband Samuel is from First Mesa. Loren says she did not know how to make pottery until she was taught by her husband's First Mesa kin. Her teacher was her husband's mother's sister. Apart from her First Mesa colleagues, Loren has no contact with other Hopi potters and was apparently unaware of any at Oraibi, although she said she "had heard" that some pottery was made in Hotevilla. Unlike Lucy and Cindy who participate in the Hopi ceremonial cycle on First Mesa, Loren is a Mennonite and her husband Samuel is a member of the Church of Jesus Christ of Latter-day Saints. Samuel is also involved in the traditional religious activities of First Mesa.

Style B, as practiced on Third Mesa, is therefore a Sikyatki Revival style originating at First Mesa which, through marriage ties, has been learned by women from Third Mesa. These potters have been taught with the understanding that it is a First Mesa craft and their wares must therefore be sold as First Mesa pottery. Thus Lucy and her daughter return to Lucy's husband's family house at Walpi to sell their pottery directly to tourists. Loren travels seventy miles to sell her wares at her husband's village of Polacca. Most Anglo tourists believe that First Mesa is the only place "Hopi pottery" is made and one must go there to buy it. Even when Lucy and Cindy sell their pots to a dealer in Winslow, or Loren takes hers to sell in Utah, their pottery is sold as a First Mesa product.

The two other potters active at Third Mesa are Faith and Elizabeth White. Since neither Faith nor Elizabeth White had ties with First Mesa, they created their own style of unpainted ceramics for sale. Apart from the fact that decoration of Raised Decoration Style pottery is achieved through the manipulation of the clay itself, ceramics made by Faith and Elizabeth White do not look alike. Faith's low serving bowls are daubed so the clay rises in peaks on the exterior (Pl. 10). Although Elizabeth White decorated her vessels in a similar manner in the 1960s, today her bowls and vases are elegantly decorated with corn cobs or flute players in relief.

Both Faith and Elizabeth White are Progressives and devout Christians who reside in New Oraibi, although Elizabeth White spends the winter in Flagstaff. Of all the potters on Third Mesa these two potters have the most Americanized idea of what their pottery means. They both regard their pottery as works of art, the product of their own inspiration. They both developed their own unique style although this may be force of circumstance. The emphasis on individual expression in potting and decoration may be due not only to the progressive "white man's" attitude adopted by Faith and Elizabeth White, but also because they had to produce ceramics that appealed to Anglo-Americans.

Both Faith and Elizabeth White emphasize that it is the individual's creative ability, rather than instruction, that makes a good potter. Faith learned from her maternal grandmother's sister, but what was important to her was that she enjoyed working with clay. "You have to love clay," she said. "The person has to feel the shape in her hands." The only person that Faith acknowledges as having helped her was "the man from the Museum, maybe Mr. Wright," who admired the exterior daubing on some of her vessels, which she claimed had occurred by accident. By remaining in New Oraibi she is under the eye of First Mesa potters. In spite of the fact that Faith does not paint her pottery or use Sikyatki Revival designs she feels that First Mesa potters are resentful that she "may make some money." Elizabeth White similarly believes that no one can teach someone else how to make pots, and that many potters are not talented because "it does not come from within." Elizabeth White is clearly an individualist and works alone.

Elizabeth White never made pottery as a

child, perhaps because she spent years in boarding school followed by studies to become a Mennonite missionary. It was not until she retired from "more than a quarter of a century" (Carlson 1964: 168) of teaching that she decided to become a potter. She inquired about clay sources from the potters of First Mesa but was told to find her own since it was everywhere. Elizabeth White thus did seek assistance from First Mesa potters but was clearly rejected. Her contemporaries believe that she would probably have also been rejected if she had sought assistance from Traditional potters. As she herself notes, Chief Tewaquaptiwa referred to her as the "one who wanted to be a white man" (ibid. 3). Elizabeth White had little choice, then, but to be helped by her Anglo friends, as Faith had been. Her association with these friends, and the close contact maintained by her residence in Flagstaff, have provided her with sale outlets, first through art galleries or the Museum of Northern Arizona. In recent years, however, because of poor health, Elizabeth White's production has declined so that most of her sales have been directly to collectors. In 1979 her small vase (c. 8 cm high), decorated with a single raised ear of corn, was offered for sale through the Museum's shop for $300.

Although Faith is married to Elizabeth White's sister's son, they have little contact, perhaps because of their individual attitudes, but more likely because Elizabeth White is a member of the Coyote Clan (sometimes called the Fox Clan) and Faith is a Reed Clan member. Faith was once on friendly terms with Lucy but this is apparently no longer the case. Faith and Elizabeth White have virtually no contact with the other potters of Third Mesa.

CONCEPTS OF BEAUTY

Both Faith and Elizabeth White claimed that their individual styles were artistic achievements. Style A and Style B potters did not make such a claim, and so I decided to ask these potters about each other's pottery and showed them pictures from a book to discover their aesthetic. I learned that both Traditionalist and Progressive potters preferred their own style and that aesthetic judgments for the Traditionalists have an element of moral approval and disapproval to them. A word of caution, however. As all the potters, except Loren and Elizabeth White, recognized the work of others, I was unable to persuade any of the Hopi women to rank another woman's vessel. Reluctance to rank vessels reflects the value the Hopi place on the ideal of equality, rather than their lack of discrimination.

When I asked both potters and non-potters, "How would you say in the Hopi language that this bowl is beautiful?" all replied "qahíncaqapta."[1] For a bowl to be considered a qahíncaqapta it has to be technically excellent: the rim must be even, the walls symmetrical, and the surface evenly smoothed. The morpheme qahin is a significant one. Voegelin and Voegelin (1957: 43) note its use as a prefix to designate a generous person (qahín-ʔinaẙa). The use of qahin to indicate a technically excellent vessel is similar. It assumes that a vessel of this quality required more of the potter's time and effort than commoner vessels do. The potter, therefore, has been generous with her labor. Since qahíncaqapta does not refer to what one could call "stylistic" qualities, there was little disagreement among potters and non-potters about what constituted an undecorated "beautiful vessel." Thus, although one person may prefer a certain shape to another—usually because of the way it feels, or "fits in my lap"—a well-executed vessel will always be designated as *qahíncaqapta*. Variations of vessel shape within a vessel folk class seem to be a question of personal preference and do not affect the classification of a vessel as *qahin*.

The unanimity of Hopi opinion regarding the excellence of unpainted vessels was not evident when they looked at painted vessels. They did apply the word *qahíncaqapta* to some painted vessels but it referred only to the technical aspects of the painted design. The color of the pigment has to be strong and even and the lines straight to be *qahin*. Sloppy painting would never be seen on a *qahíncaqapta*. Traditionalists were most generous in their judgments on technical merits of pottery other than their own Style A. Traditionalists, both potters and non-potters, frequently termed Style B and, occasionally the Raised Decoration Style of bowl, as *qahíncaqapta*. The Progressive potters, on the other hand, did not consider that Style A vessels were well painted. Only once did a Progressive Style B potter refer to a Style A painted piece as *qahin*. This is because Progressive potters consider a fine line to be a critically important indicator of technical excellence, and Traditionalist Style A potters prefer thick lines. Raised Decoration Style potters agreed with the Style B Progressives in condemnation of Style A's wide lines. Neither of the Raised Decoration potters considered any of the painted Traditional Style A vessels as *qahin*.

But Style A potters were not content to simply talk about the technical merits of the two styles of Progressive pottery. They introduced a note of moral disapproval even while they were remarking that technically these pots were accomplished. While Progressive Style B and Raised Decoration potters simply emphasized the lack of technical ability demonstrated in Traditionalist pottery decoration, Style A potters referred to their works as *qahópi*.

The word *qahópi* is in contrast to the word *hópi*, which can be used to refer to a person or to the Hopi people as a whole, and means that something is "good in every respect" (Voegelin and Voegelin 1957: 43); *qahópi* is its opposite. If someone is *qahópi* (not Hopi) he is demonstrating non-Hopi qualities, he is "bad, mischievous . . . bold . . . lazy."

Traditionalists frequently use this derogatory term for something they consider not done "in the proper way" (for example, a ceremonial dance) with the implication that it is morally wrong. By using this term to describe decorated Progressive pottery, they are stating that it is not the proper way to decorate pottery even though the piece may be a *qahíncaqapta*. They can see that most Style B designs are derived from Sikyatki Polychrome, which they recognize as an earlier Hopi ceramic type, but the style has been influenced by the Tewa, and it is this foreign element that makes it literally *qahópi*. This is not, however, the primary reason for the use of this term. Traditionalist potters rejected the Raised Decoration Style as being a decorative technique contrary to the way pottery should be decorated. Painting is the only appropriate technique for decorating pottery, so the Raised Decoration Style in its very essence is *qahópi*. But Style B, even though it is painted, does not escape condemnation either. Traditionalists level against it such criticisms as "It's too much"; "It's overdone"; "It's just like the dances up there on First Mesa, all they want is to get things. They used to just give a few things away, now it's overdone." "There's so much of it [painted decoration] you can't see what it is [of]; it looks dirty."

The moral quality of these criticisms can be seen clearly in the equation of style with ceremonial dances. Moreover, the parallel drawn between the two is that they are not just overdone but that both are indicative of the *qahópi* or Progressive quest for material gain. Criticism of style thus becomes a criticism of the sale of ceramics for financial gain and of the desire to become part of the Anglo-American cash economy, as well as criticism of the style itself. Because Traditionalist potters disapproved of Style B as a whole, and were loath to rank specific vessels, I could not determine at what point the painted decoration became "too much." So, I tried a different approach. I asked them to examine *Pottery Treasures* (Jacka and Gill 1976), a book of photographs of Pueblo pottery, and indicate the vessels they preferred.

Pottery Treasures contains large color plates of some prehistoric wares (Santa Cruz Red-on-Buff, Sacaton Red-on-White, Tularosa Black-on-White, Kayenta Black-on-White, Kinishba Polychrome, Jeddito Black-on-Yellow, Tonto Polychrome, Gila Polychrome, and Sikyatki Polychrome) as well as historic wares (Cochiti Polychrome, Tinyo Polychrome, Acoma Polychrome, Zuni Polychrome, Santa Ana Polychrome, Zia Polychrome, Polacca Polychrome, and early Sikyatki Revival wares) and contemporary pieces made by such well-known artists as Lucy Lewis from Acoma,

Fannie Nampeyo, Garnet Pavatea, and Joy Navasie from First Mesa; and Elizabeth White from Third Mesa. Although I made some attempt to limit the number of photographs examined, and specifically requested that these photographs be ranked, I met with limited success. Neither of the Raised Decoration potters was willing to do this at all; Elizabeth White said she was too busy in Flagstaff, and Faith feared that further contact with me would subject her to the witchcraft of First Mesa potters. Although Style A and Style B potters kindly consented to examine the book, I was unable to obtain the ranking I wanted, primarily because the potters would not comment on some specified vessels. They wanted to look at all the pictures until finally they became bored or had pressing matters to attend to. As a result, some potters never looked at some of the illustrations discussed by other potters.

I was able, however, to spend many hours in fruitful discussion with these women. Style B potters, without exception, expressed the greatest admiration for the Sikyatki Revival Wares. They especially admired the White Ware by "Frog Woman" Joy Navasie, for the excellence and clarity of the white slip, and the Sikyatki Revival Polychrome by Fannie Nampeyo for the design. Style B potters recognized these as First Mesa designs derived from Sikyatki Polychrome of the fourteenth century. Lucy made this evident when she produced some "designs" made by her husband's sister from First Mesa. According to Lucy, her sister-in-law had had "a big thick notebook of designs that she had taken from things she had seen at Awatovi." The Style B potters were also unanimous in their rejection of Elizabeth White's work, calling her technique of raised decoration "silly." Lucy and Loren both declared that the figures were "funny."

Style A potters were likewise unanimous in their rejection of Elizabeth White's jar and its *qahópi* figures. Individual potters also made specific comments on other pictures in the book. Vera and Terry greatly admired the luster of the San Juan Red Ware. Terry also admired a *wikóro* and bowl made by the First Mesa potter Edith Nash and decorated with Kachina masks, as well as two bowls decorated in the center of the interior with birds. Although these pieces are Sikyatki Revival Polychrome, they all had definable figures, centralized compositions, and the two birds were isolated design units. Terry, Amy, and Betty all admired the designs on the Polacca Polychrome and Zuni Polychrome vessels, further evidence for the idea that clearly defined isolated design units are the preferred type of design. The Polacca Polychrome jar was decorated with a Polik Mana and the Zuni jar with four frogs flanked by butterflies and tadpoles, and with two snakes around the neck.

"These Zunis really know how to make pottery" was a general comment, and Betty and Terry both showed me illustrations of Zuni vessels which they had cut out of magazines. Like the "designs" copied by Lucy's sister-in-law, they considered these exemplary. When I asked if these were *qahópi,* I received surprised looks. They said, "You could call them that, [but] they're not *really qahópi.*"

The fact that Zuni pottery was not called *qahópi* further supports that the use of this term by Style A potters for Style B pottery was not just because it was considered Tewa, and therefore not Hopi, but rather because this type of design was wrong as it was associated with values they opposed.

Betty further argued for the "hopiness" of Zuni pottery by stating that Hopis "used to make pottery this way," which in fact they did in the nineteenth century. During this time Hopis were making Polacca Polychrome, some of which was almost indistinguishable from Zuni pottery, particularly following the 1863 smallpox epidemic when many Hopis took refuge at Zuni. Many of the motifs used by Traditionalist Style A potters are derived from Polacca Polychrome. Furthermore, the design structure of Polacca Polychrome favors isolated figures as opposed to an overall pattern. It is this type of ceramic that was made before the establishment of the trading post and intensive Anglo-American contact, when things were "the way they ought to be" according to Traditionalists. This is why Traditionalist Style A potters, evidently lacking illustrations of Polacca Polychrome, chose to use Zuni pottery as a model rather than Hopi Sikyatki Polychrome as used by Style B potters.

That ceramic design and values are intimately linked and that Betty was not just explaining in historical terms why Zuni pottery was not *qahópi* Betty herself then clarified. She produced Cummings' (1935) *First Inhabitants of Arizona and the Southwest* and explained that she was going to show me some more pictures of Hopi pottery. She then deliberately ignored illustrations of fourteenth-century Sikyatki pieces with designs similar to those used on Sikyatki Revival wares and Style B vessels and pointed to illustrations of Sikyatki Brown-on-Yellow bowls decorated with interior centralized isolated designs. She then explained: "It is the people of the First Mesa who want to make things fancy. The Hopi way is to have things simple. This is the only way—the Hopi way."

I don't know if Betty thought the elaborately decorated Sikyatki pieces were made by the residents of First Mesa and the simpler ones with isolated designs by Third Mesa potters or not. She was, however, adjusting the archaeological record in accord with the Traditionalist view of the world and style of ceramic decoration, thus clearly intermeshing aesthetic and Traditionalist values.

Inquiries into the aesthetic values of Traditionalist and Progressive potters provided an important link between style and world view. A potter's concept of what constituted a beautiful vessel was based on style and technical excellence. Progressive potters criticize Traditionalist pottery as being poorly painted and therefore not *qahin,* but they do not judge it to be *qahópi.* Both Progressives and

Traditionalists when asked about a non-Hopi pot will occasionally call it *qahópi,* literally "not Hopi," but they will usually identify it, for example, as a Navajo, Acoma, or "Rio Grande" piece.

In contrast, Traditionalist potters call all Progressive Style B pottery *qahópi,* although they may admire the excellence of its workmanship and therefore designate it *qahin.* Like Progressive potters they avoid the term *qahópi* for non-Hopi pottery, particularly if it accords with what they consider "good design"—for example, Zuni pottery. The Hopi aesthetic, therefore, can be said to be based on two criteria: technical excellence and style. The two types of painted decoration, Styles A and B, are, however, associated with different values and their development. As we shall see, these different values are not just given material expression in ceramic design.

NOTE

1. The only exception among the twenty-seven Hopis asked this specific question was a man from Lower Moencopi. He said he would call a beautiful bowl *"lolomácaqapta"* and *"a woman would call it sonwáyocaqapta."* Voegelin and Voegelin (1957: 43) gloss *lóloma* (man speaking) and *sónwayoʔ* (woman speaking) as "gentle, well demeanored, beautiful, reasonable." My informant's wife, however, quickly corrected her husband, explaining that although you would use these qualifiers for such things as a beautiful sky or a beautiful young girl, they would not be used to describe a bowl. My informant then agreed with his wife, adding, "Someone made the bowl—that's why she's right." Thus, because a bowl is a manufactured product, it could not be "beautiful," *lóloma/sónwayoʔ,* which also implies "good," but rather *qahin.*

CHAPTER EIGHT

CONCEPTS OF SPACE AND WORLD VIEW

INTRODUCTION

Differences between Traditionalist and Progressive potters are seen in their differing concepts of space. As we have seen, their ideas about what constitutes beautiful or good decoration are not simply opinions as we might express them about the latest hair style, but judgments that penetrate other spheres of life. This is also true for their concepts of space.

The structure and compositional symmetry of Third Mesa painted ceramic decoration express spatial concepts. These concepts are of direction associated with place, and of social distance. Although spatial concepts of direction are an integral part of the traditional Hopi religion, for the most part these are shared by both Traditionalists and Progressives. This is not the case for their concepts of social distance.

Others (Arnold 1983; Fernandez 1966) have found that social space or the distance we maintain between one group and another—those we intermingle with and are close to and those we consider further removed—is often expressed in art. Such is the case for painted Third Mesa Hopi ceramics. Traditionalists and Progressives view Hopi/Anglo-American relations differently. For the Traditionalist this relationship is defined in myth and religion. Social space and directional space are thus not only interwoven with other

spheres of life but are a fundamental aspect of their view of the world around them. The same is true for Progressives, albeit unsanctioned by religious belief.

These differing concepts of social space are so fundamental to the differing world views held by Traditionalists and Progressives that they are expressed not only in ceramic decoration but in furniture placement. I would further suggest that these differences, often expressed in children's drawings, may be acquired at an early age.

CERAMIC DESIGN AND HOPI FURNITURE PLACEMENT

The design structure and compositional and design preferences that lead Traditionalist and Progressive potters to decorate pots as they do are part of each potter's concept of space as a whole. These preferences are therefore not confined to pottery decoration but are also evident in the Hopi placement of household furniture. The floor plans of the houses of Traditional Style A potters are illustrated in Figures 24 and 25. In the typical Traditionalist house all the furniture is ranged along the walls, leaving the center of the room empty and emphasizing the boundary of the walls. The arrangement is intentional and not just the preference of a small group, for the

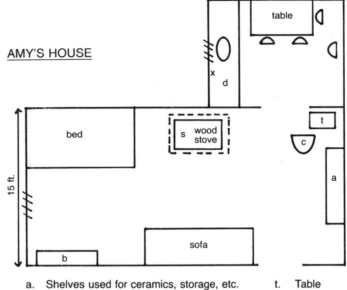

AMY'S HOUSE

a. Shelves used for ceramics, storage, etc.
b. Bookcase filled with plants
c. Chair
d. Kitchen counter with sink
s. "Franklin" type wood stove set on bricks

t. Table
x. Water tap
/// Windows

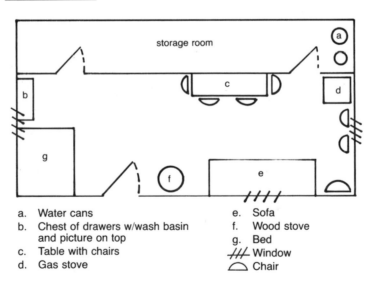

VERA'S HOUSE

a. Water cans
b. Chest of drawers w/wash basin and picture on top
c. Table with chairs
d. Gas stove

e. Sofa
f. Wood stove
g. Bed
/// Window
Chair

Figure 24. Floor plans of Traditionalist (Style A) potters' houses, Hotevilla.

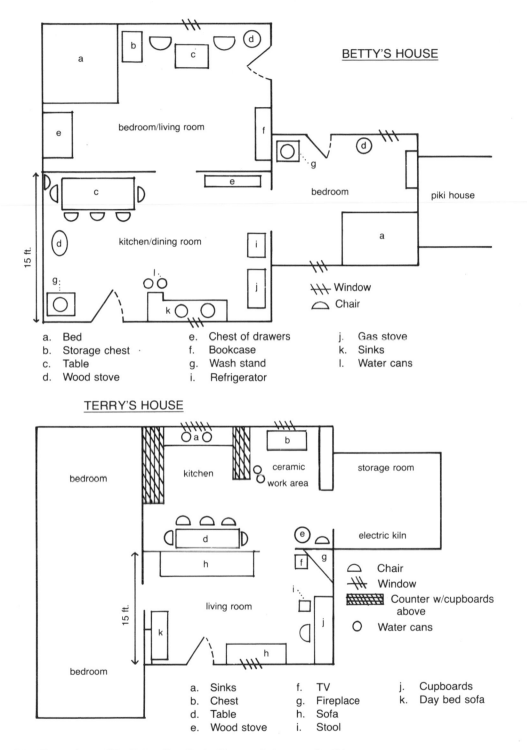

BETTY'S HOUSE

bedroom/living room

kitchen/dining room

15 ft.

bedroom

piki house

Window
Chair

a. Bed
b. Storage chest
c. Table
d. Wood stove

e. Chest of drawers
f. Bookcase
g. Wash stand
i. Refrigerator

j. Gas stove
k. Sinks
l. Water cans

TERRY'S HOUSE

bedroom

kitchen

ceramic work area

storage room

electric kiln

living room

15 ft.

bedroom

Chair
Window
Counter w/cupboards above
Water cans

a. Sinks
b. Chest
d. Table
e. Wood stove

f. TV
g. Fireplace
h. Sofa
i. Stool

j. Cupboards
k. Day bed sofa

Figure 25. Floor plans of Traditionalist (Style A) potter's houses, Oraibi.

CONCEPTS OF SPACE AND WORLD VIEW

furniture in all the Traditionalist households I visited was invariably arranged in this manner.[1] The floor plans of some of the more than twenty households I visited are included in Figures 26 and 27.

Progressive homes are arranged very differently. In fact, the contrast between the placement of furniture by Traditionalists and by Progressives is so marked and so consistent that it was possible to determine the affiliation of the household owner instantly upon entering the home. Progressives, both potters and non-potters (Figs. 28–30) arranged their furniture as Anglo-Americans do, in what can be called "functional units." The eating table, for example, stands away from the wall and is ready to serve its function at all times. Chairs are placed in the room to serve as "conversational units" or, in Lucy's and Faith's houses (Fig. 28), are placed for viewing television sets. The furniture in their houses is placed not only according to function but also to indicate an aesthetic value. This can be seen by comparing Traditionalist and Progressive use of room-corner space. Traditionalists place a piece of furniture in a corner against the wall where it may stand at right angles to another piece, but it does not alter one's perception of a square or rectangular room. The only exception to this was Terry's house, which had a corner fireplace and kitchen cupboards that extended into the kitchen area and divided it from her ceramic work area. This atypical arrangement and the large color television no doubt reflect her years spent in Tuba City.

Unlike the Traditionalists, Progressives place furniture across corners of the room, thereby changing the shape of the usable floor space. The central room area then appears oval, with the furniture rotating around a central axis. This central area, however, is not left as open space, as it would be in a Traditionalist's house, but is punctuated with objects like chairs and tables—most commonly a coffee table. Although Traditionalists might own a television, refrigerator, or stove, they never purchased coffee tables.

The consistency of the Traditionalists' along-the-wall arrangement, in contrast to the more scattered placement of furniture by Progressives, convinced me of its significance. I was unable, however, to elicit clear statements about the reasons for it. So, in an attempt to understand whether an artistic value or practicality was involved, I invited two Traditional friends to help me prepare my house for a Christmas party to which they were invited. They were to arrange the furniture, and both knew who and how many people were coming. They decided that more chairs were needed, and produced four folding chairs. They then set up the room so that everyone had a chair, and placed the food on the table. In Figure 31, top, the original arrangement is diagrammed and below it the rearrangement of the furnishings with the addition of four chairs.

After their rearranging, my furniture lined the walls, and the center of the living room consisted of an empty space ten and a half feet wide! In the course of the furniture moving, I was able to elicit some statements about why this placement was aesthetically pleasing to my friends. First, they said, it looked "nice" because it was neat, and second, it looked "full." They explained: "The Christmas tree is real nice [but] a Kachina is the most beautiful thing, for there are all the colors—nothing is

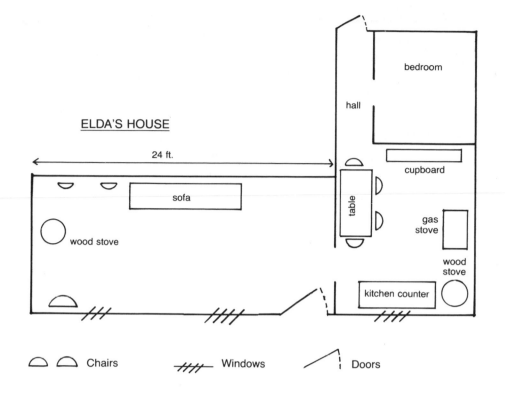

ELDA'S HOUSE

bedroom

hall

cupboard

24 ft.

sofa

table

gas stove

wood stove

wood stove

kitchen counter

◠ ◠ Chairs   ╫ Windows   ╱ Doors

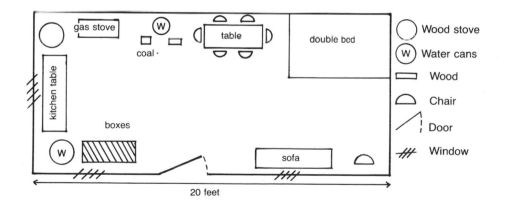

VERA'S OLD HOUSE

gas stove

W

coal ·

table

double bed

kitchen table

boxes

W

sofa

20 feet

○ Wood stove

W Water cans

▭ Wood

◠ Chair

╱ Door

╫ Window

Figure 26. Floor plans of Traditionalists' houses, Oraibi and Hotevilla.

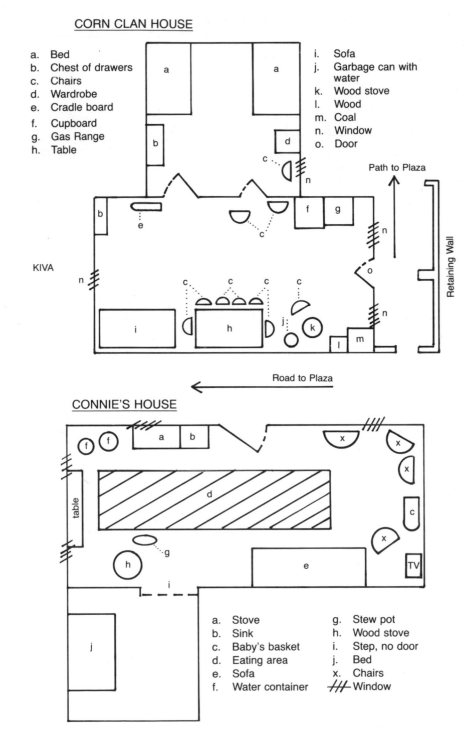

Figure 27. Floor plans of Traditionalists' houses, Lower Moencopi.

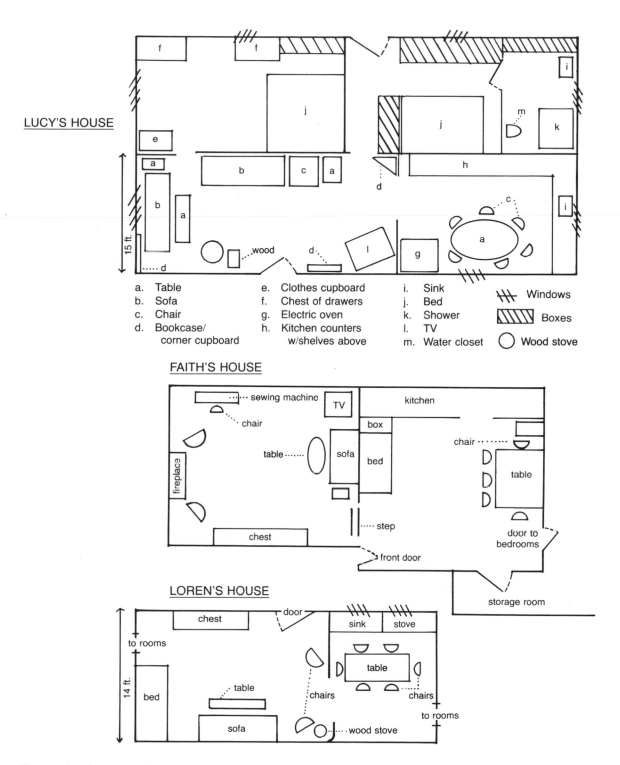

LUCY'S HOUSE

15 ft.

a. Table
b. Sofa
c. Chair
d. Bookcase/
    corner cupboard

e. Clothes cupboard
f. Chest of drawers
g. Electric oven
h. Kitchen counters
    w/shelves above

i. Sink
j. Bed
k. Shower
l. TV
m. Water closet

Windows
Boxes
Wood stove

FAITH'S HOUSE

sewing machine
chair
fireplace
table
chest
TV
box
sofa
bed
step
front door
kitchen
chair
table
door to
bedrooms
storage room

LOREN'S HOUSE

14 ft.

chest
to rooms
bed
table
sofa
door
sink
stove
table
chairs
chairs
to rooms
wood stove

Figure 28. Floor plans of Progressive (Style B) potters' houses, New Oraibi and Upper Moencopi.

CONCEPTS OF SPACE AND WORLD VIEW

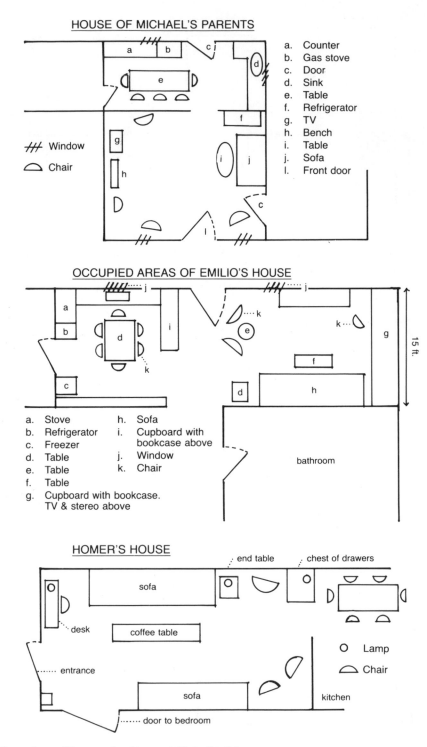

Figure 29. Floor plans of Progressives' houses, New Oraibi.

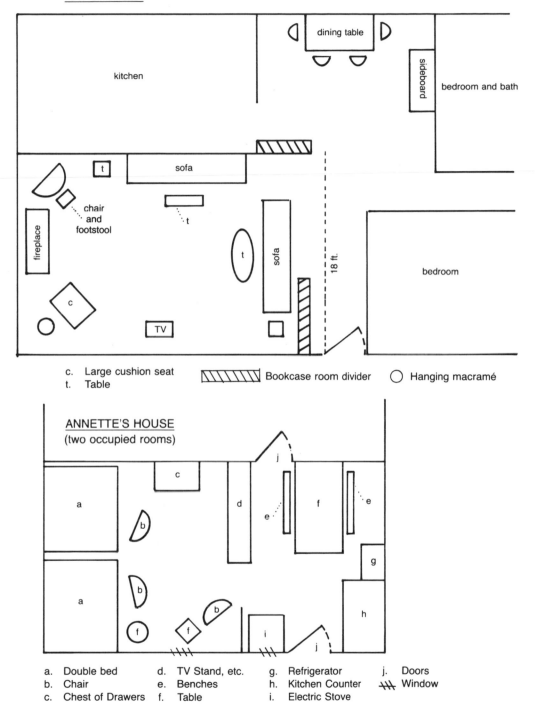

KAY'S HOUSE

dining table

kitchen

sideboard

bedroom and bath

sofa

t

chair
and
footstool

fireplace

t

t

sofa

18 ft.

bedroom

c

TV

c. Large cushion seat   ▨▨▨ Bookcase room divider   ◯ Hanging macramé
t. Table

ANNETTE'S HOUSE
(two occupied rooms)

j

c

a

d

f

e

b

e

a

b

g

b

h

f

f

i

j

a. Double bed   d. TV Stand, etc.   g. Refrigerator   j. Doors
b. Chair   e. Benches   h. Kitchen Counter   ⋙ Window
c. Chest of Drawers f. Table   i. Electric Stove

Figure 30. Floor plans of Progressives' houses, Upper Moencopi.

CONCEPTS OF SPACE AND WORLD VIEW

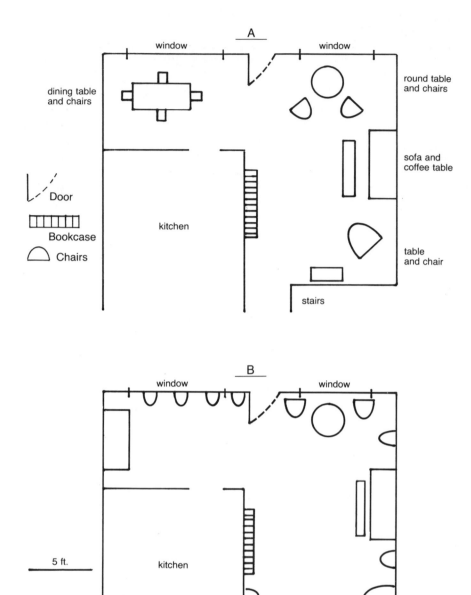

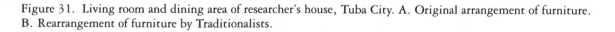

Figure 31. Living room and dining area of researcher's house, Tuba City. A. Original arrangement of furniture. B. Rearrangement of furniture by Traditionalists.

dirty, every color is bright. You can see each thing. Here [in my house] you can [now] see everything." In other words, each object was clearly separate and visible from the center of the room, and the room looked "full" because it was bounded by the furniture along the walls.

It could be argued that this type of furniture placement is aesthetically pleasing because it is what Traditionalists are accustomed to and because it is practical. Although familiarity and practicality may be significant, I do not believe they are chiefly important. Traditionalists, for example, frequently visit Progressives' houses where the arrangement is different. And, the arrangement is not so practical as it once was. The central area is still frequently used for sleeping in cold weather if it allows the family to be close to the fire. It is also where guests may sleep, and may be used for eating when a large group is present. At a Naming Ceremony, for example, the house illustrated in Figure 27 (lower) was used. The furniture did not have to be moved, cloths were laid in the center of the room and the food placed on them. The guests sat around the food on the floor.

Most houses, however, now have an eating table and chairs that are kept pushed against the wall and are laboriously brought out two or three times a day for meals and then carefully returned to the wall. Chairs are also frequently moved into this central space for such activities as rabbitbrush-weaving or pottery-making, and thus create a center of activity from which the room can be viewed.

The difference between Traditionalist and Progressive furniture placement in many ways parallels the contrasting structure of Style A and Style B painted decoration. The differences between Style A, preferred by the Traditionalists, and Style B, preferred by the Progressives, are: Style A uses independent figures as opposed to Style B's overall pattern; Style A has an average painted area, within a framed band, of 33.5 percent while Style B has an average painted area of 53.9 percent; Style A depends on translation for framed-band symmetry while Style B uses rotation; Style A makes extensive use of motifs in pottery decoration, and finally, Style B uses figure-ground reversal.

Furniture arrangements parallel some of these differences in pottery decoration. Traditionalists arrange their furniture to create a marked separation between the furniture ranged along the walls and the empty central space, just as they separate figures from the background in their designs. Progressives, by contrast, do not confine their furniture to the walls but create "functional units," so their furniture is distributed throughout the room in an overall pattern similar to the one found on their pottery.

Progressives also block the corners of a room with furniture, creating an oval or circular visual pattern. The effect is one of rotation, as the furniture appears to rotate around the axis of the room center. This is apparent (Figs. 28–30) in the arrangement of living room furniture. Rotation, therefore, is the symmetry preferred by Progressive potters for their arrangement of furniture as well as for their band designs.

Traditionalists, on the other hand, place their furniture along the walls as if each piece were a motif or element. The symmetry of their furniture arrangement and their framed bands is that of translation in which elements or designs are translated along a framing line as furniture is translated along the wall.

Figure 32. Hopi village houses drawn by Progressive families' children.

CERAMIC DESIGN AND CHILDREN'S DRAWINGS

Children's drawings indicate that these different Hopi concepts of space have been internalized at an early age. The drawings illustrated in Figures 32–34 are by fourth and fifth graders at the Moencopi Day School. Figure 32 shows Hopi village houses drawn by children from Progressive families; Figure 33 shows a house drawn by a Traditionalist child.

If these drawings are analyzed in the same manner as ceramic decoration, the sheet of paper itself becomes the area, or field, for decoration. In the Traditionalist child's drawing, the single house can be equated with the isolated design unit or motif on a pot. As in the composition of motifs, the house does not, except for the smoke, intrude into the surrounding space. Even the ladder is flattened against the wall. The two drawings made by Progressive children, in contrast, occupy the entire design area. In Figure 32, the

Sun Kachina drawing, the house, ladders and smoke cover the entire surface of the paper. In the right drawing (Fig. 32), the Sun Kachina has been replaced by the typical Anglo-American child's "smile-face" sun. Here the design area has been divided into an upper and a lower division, the upper half occupied by the message "To Wyckoff," the lower by the illustration of the village, complete with a Kachina emerging from the kiva. Although these Progressive drawings have incorporated specific Anglo-American concepts—the smile-face sun (right) and an attempt at perspective (left)—what is important is the design structure itself. Unlike the Traditionalist child's drawing, these show overall decoration and, in the right drawing, a dual division of space.

The use of the written message, in contrast to the drawn figure, is also evident in Figure 34, the subjects of which are Kachinas. The lower drawing was made by a child from a Progressive family; like Progressive children's drawings of village

Figure 33. Hopi village house drawn by a child of a Traditionalist family.

Figure 34. Kachinas drawn by a Traditionalist child (*upper*) and by a Progressive child (*lower*).

houses, the subject occupies most of the paper. The lower drawing also creates a rotational composition, or internal symmetry, the preferred Progressive ceramic design class. The very different upper drawing was by a child from a Traditionalist family. Once again the structure of this drawing can be equated with the isolated design unit, or motif, of Traditionalist ceramic design.

These drawings indicate the need for further research to determine whether indeed Hopi children, as part of their development and socialization, internalize one concept of space or another. Although it appears that the drawings reiterate the structures found in ceramic decoration, I was unable to examine such factors as the education and psychological maturity of each child or the furniture arrangement in some of their homes. I did, however, visit the families whose children drew Figures 32 (left), 33, and 34 (upper). The furniture in these households (one Progressive, two Traditionalist) followed the established patterns. I would therefore hypothesize that, at an early age, Hopi children become aware of the differences between Progressive and Traditionalist concepts of space associated with their different views of the world and the aesthetic differences they give rise to.

CERAMICS AND HOPI CONCEPTS OF NATURAL AND SOCIAL ORDER

The reiteration of different styles by Progressive and Traditionalist potters in both their arrangement of furniture and ceramic design indicates that these two styles are part of two different concepts of space. These correlate with their concepts of the social distance between Hopi and Anglo-American societies.

Unlike Traditionalists, Progressives believe that although Hopis are different from Anglo-Americans, they can and should strive to become part of the larger Anglo-American culture and economy. Thus, they believe, given economic opportunity and education, Hopis will be different from but equal to Anglo-Americans as defined by the latter. They believe that American society is a heterogeneous whole based on the shared values of education and the importance of the individual within a democratic capitalist society. This principle was advocated by the Commissioner of Indian Affairs, John Collier, in the 1930s and can be considered the foundation upon which the Tribal Council was constructed. Hence, Progressives view Anglo-American/Hopi relations as a complementary duality, and American society as diverse groups within a unified whole. The Progressives' beliefs about the nature of American society find

an expression in their pottery decoration.

This view of American society as a whole encompassing diverse groups can be equated with the overall pattern of Progressive painted ceramic design. Moreover, their view of Anglo-American/ Hopi relations as a complementary duality can be equated with their preference for figure-ground reversal. It is also significant, as will be seen, that this reversal is commonly structured around a central axis point.

Before we examine how Progressive concepts of space differ from those of Traditionalists it is important to understand how they are similar. Both Progressives and Traditionalists organize the natural world according to the six-fold directional paradigm discussed in Chapter 2. They also share the concept that the four places they associate with the cardinal directions form a circle.

The circle is primarily a concept of time as it is associated with the movement of the sun. However, as the sun moves between places of direction—upper world and lower world, east and west—it is important for the Hopi concept of space. Nonetheless, the most important spatial concept is that of the six-fold paradigm. Central to this schema are the four mountains at the four cardinal directions and the upper world and the lower world at the zenith and nadir. It is this paradigm that provides Hopis with their perception of "natural order" and gives rise to the numerical symbolism found throughout Hopi life.

The space-color-number paradigm governs not only how Hopis see the world but practically every ritual act. It consists of the four cardinal directions plus the zenith and nadir. Each direction is associated with colors and numbers and provides a system of classification for the natural world. Birds, trees, butterflies, and so on, are all associated with the six-directional system. The central position this paradigm occupies in Hopi life is materially expressed in the Hopi Kiva which, when not constrained by the terrain, is constructed along an east-west axis. The four walls of the kiva, therefore, conform to the four cardinal directions. The kiva hatchway is to the "above" of this world and the sipapu leads to the "below." Hieb (1972: 95) has argued as well that before 1890 Hopi houses, like kivas, were consonant with this paradigm. They were entered by a ladder from the roof and all faced east.

Although a ceramic vessel does not follow this paradigm *per se,* the Hopis conceived of it as consisting of six parts (see Appendix II): the top or mouth, the base or bottom, and the stomach, which has four sides. It is conceived of as both square (four-sided) and round which allows the potter to decorate a vessel as a circular continuum or as four separate units, or as both.

Simple bands, and bands along which a motif or design is translated, are infinite designs. They therefore accord with the Hopi concept of a vessel's exterior as a circle, without a beginning or an end. By contrast, discrete design units emphasize the "four sides" of the vessel. When Third Mesa potters use a framed-band design, Progressives will usually divide the band into four panels while Traditionalists will use four separate designs; but in both cases the circular band has been divided according to four sides, paralleling the four cardinal directions.

The circle is also important as a spatial division in Hopi thought. The Hopi concept of a circle encompassing four distinct points is not confined to the design of a vessel. They also consider the path of the sun circular, encompassing the four directions of east, above, west, and below. Horizontal space is also frequently portrayed as a circle along which are the four cardinal directions. The Hopi, for instance, perceive of their land as forming a "sacred circle" along which are the four mountains at the cardinal directions. It is, however, the six-fold paradigm that dominates Hopi concepts of space, generating the importance of certain numbers.

The number four from the four cardinal directions and the four mountains, and the number six, which includes the zenith and the nadir and with which colors, birds and plants are associated, are extremely important to the Hopi. So is the number eight, as the double of four. Framed bands contain either four or eight panels, and the numbers appear consistently as a fundamental part of Hopi culture.

The six-fold paradigm is unconsciously enacted in vessel construction. Traditionalist and Progressive potters always used four, six, or eight coils of clay, placed one on top of another, to build up a vessel. The only time I observed the use of an odd number of coils was when the pinched clay rim of an ashtray needed to be raised. When I asked potters why they had used a particular number of coils I was usually told, "Because it is good this way." Occasionally, I was told it was because of the size of the vessel. I observed, however, that vessel size dictated the size of the coils themselves and not the number of coils used. Very large vessels are made in two halves, apparently with six or eight coils each in the top and bottom halves.

The use of eight, as the double of four, is not confined only to framed-band panels or clay coils, but is a common division within Hopi ritual. It is usual in the ceremonial dance sequence. Ceremonial dances consist of sets of four or eight in a dance sequence in which the dancers move in a counterclockwise pattern. Ceremonies themselves usually last eight days, plus an additional day—not surprising when one recalls that the six-fold paradigm itself consists of three complementary dual divisions.

By looking closely at the manner in which the dances take place in the kiva, we can shed some light on how the Progressives' concept of space departs from that of the Traditionalists. Dances in the kiva are *never* held toward the center or middle, nor do they rotate around a central axis (see Fig. 35).

We have seen how furniture in a Progressive's living room rotates around a central axis and therefore articulates the center. In a Traditionalist living room, by contrast, although something may be moved in the center, the center is not articulated by surrounded objects, as the center is not articulated in a dance in the kiva. The furniture is ranged along the walls of the houses, as the dancers hug the walls of the kiva.

The Progressive emphasis on the center as the point around which all rotates is contrary to the Hopi concept of space as expressed in the six-fold paradigm, where neither the center nor the middle is articulated. Hence, Progressive design is thus not only a material expression of traditional Hopi ordering systems but also of their adaptation to Anglo-American values, as is the manufacture of pottery in order to gain a cash income. The rotational

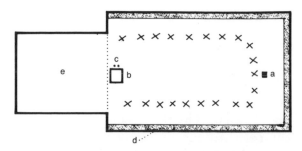

Figure 35. Kiva floor plan showing the position of Kachina dancers during night dances. (a) sipapu, (b) stove, (c) ladder, (d) ledges used as benches, (e) elevated section.

design structure used by Progressives is shunned by Traditionalist potters. Traditionalist potters do not conceive of the center or middle in the same way that Progressives do. The center is not articulated as a specific direction as it is among some pueblo peoples. Independent designs may or may not be placed in the middle, between the rim and the base of a vessel (see Fig. 8). This is similar to the Hopi concept of the middle or center of a traditional village. Each village is considered to have a center, defined by the shrine. This shrine may or may not be in the actual center or middle of the village but this place is regarded as central.

The spatial concept of a center is not fixed in traditional Hopi thought and is expressed in their ideas about the *hoysícvi* motif. This motif (Chapter 6, Fig. 19) depicts a circle representing the sacred land of the Hopi, within which are four smaller circles indicating the four sacred mountains. Diagonally across this circle are two pairs of lines that cross in the center. The center of this design, however, is not conceived of as a fixed place like the four mountains, but was variously identified by informants as Oraibi *or* all the Hopi villages. Each kiva can likewise be said to have a middle or center. This is where the sipapu connects this world with the world below. But this place, which is conceived of as being in the middle vertically, is not in the center of the kiva but adjacent to the western wall.

The actual center of the kiva, like the center of the larger lower kiva floor, is normally empty. Significantly the objects on the lower kiva floor are arranged in the same manner as the furniture in the living room of a Traditionalist's house. Along two or three of the kiva walls in the lower section there are benches. The ladder and fire or stove are adjacent to the step dividing the lower floor from the upper section. The central area is reserved for the construction of altars during ceremonies; it is used at specific times for specific activities, as is the central area of the Traditionalist's living room.

Besides indicating the differences in the way the Progressives and Traditionalists conceive of and use the center or middle, the kiva and the dances held in it also demonstrate the Hopi principles of duality and reciprocity. Reciprocity is an extremely important Hopi value shared by both Traditionalists and Progressives. Progressives and Traditionalists differ, however, in the degree of reciprocity they believe possible between Hopis and Anglo-Americans within the existing system in which Hopi interests are expressed through the Tribal Council. This fundamental difference affects their concept of the actual social distance between Hopis and Anglo-Americans as well as their concept of what it ought to be. It is this difference that is expressed in the two different design structures. Complementary or reciprocal duality is given concrete expression in the very architecture of the kiva. The floor of

the kiva is divided into upper and lower sections. During the night dances the spectators—women, children, and men from other kivas—sit on the banque and stand on the raised floor at one end of the kiva, while the Kachina dancers perform on the lower floor. This division also represents duality between this world and the lower divine world of the Kachinas. The relationship between the Hopis and Kachinas is reciprocal: they feed one another just as most of the women spectators feed the men impersonating Kachinas, and just as these men in turn till the fields of the women.

This internal division within the kiva, as well as the six-fold spatial division of the kiva, makes eight divisions in all. Further research may indicate that doubling of the upper and lower directions and the single use of the four cardinal directions is responsible for the frequent use of two four-fold divisions.

Reciprocal duality is also clearly expressed in figure-ground reversal in ceramic design, a technique used exclusively by the Style B Progressive potters. For figure-ground reversal, either a negative figure must be surrounded with paint or the design area must be equally divided between a painted and a negative figure. Not uncommonly these two figures (Figs. 5, 9; Fig. 10: top) are of the same motif and therefore interchangeable. Traditionalist potters instead clearly separate the painted figure from the background of the vessel surface. This fundamental difference in design structure follows from the difference in values between Progressives and Traditionalists. These values reflect historical events as well as contemporary values.

Progressives believe that under the

current system Anglo-Hopi relations can be, and to some extent are, reciprocal and therefore a complementary duality in which both are equal, as in figure-ground reversal both figure and ground are equal.

Duality is also given concrete expression in Traditionalist design. Within Style A framed bands there are frequently two panels or two design units (Pl. 9b; Figs. 7: lower, 13b, 14: lower). Often, when a vessel is decorated with four design units or motifs, two designs are repeated (Pl. 5: left, Figs. 10: lower, 12: right). As with Progressive Style B design, however, the primary duality is in the design structure or the relationship between figure and ground.

In Traditionalist ceramic design, the separation of figure and ground and the use of isolated design units is a material expression of the potter's concept of the relationship between Hopis and Anglo-Americans. Traditionalists believe in preserving a social distance between the two societies, since Anglo-American values are considered to be in opposition to Hopi values. This is the crux of the Traditionalist position and stands in marked contrast to the Progressive argument of Hopi/Anglo-American reciprocity. In Traditionalist design, therefore, figures are seen as the binary opposite of the surrounding space, as the Hopis are the binary opposite of the American society that surrounds them, a scheme vastly different from Progressive design structure, in which positive and negative figures are interchangeable. In

Style A such duality occurs not within the decorated area, but in the contrast between the decorated figure and the ground of the vessel. Wade and Evans (1973) have noted the significance of undecorated space or "background" in the Kachina sash and kilt. The undecorated white areas depict winter snows whereas the decorated portion depicts summer fertility: the duality between summer and winter, however, is conceived of as reciprocal, for summer fertility depends on winter snows, and when it is summer in this world it is winter below and vice versa.

Although Traditionalist ceramic design is consonant with these precepts, the clear separation between figures and ground in Traditionalist ceramic design and furniture arrangement may be equated with their view, as expressed in Hopi myth, that the ideal relationship between Hopis and Anglo-Americans is one of reciprocal kinship. Traditional Hopis, however, are still awaiting the return of the true bahana, who will be known to their religious leaders. It is the Traditionalist Hopis who will decide, according to their values, when the true bahana has arrived. Thus a reciprocal complementary relationship between Anglo-Americans and Hopis can exist only when Anglo-Americans accept Hopi values. Until this happens, Hopi society must be clearly separated from Anglo-American society and not dependent on its economy.

NOTE

1. The only Traditionalist potter's house I was unable to diagram belongs to Anne, who occupies the Corn Clan house in Oraibi. A brief visit confirmed that this home also followed the typical Traditionalist model.

CHAPTER NINE

SUMMARY AND CONCLUSION

The political-religious division between Progressives and Traditionalists is all-pervasive on Third Mesa. It largely determines where and how one lives. It determines the importance of pottery as a cash commodity and this, in turn, determines the percentage of a given class of vessels manufactured by a given potter and the way they are distributed. This division also determines the style in which a potter works—it may be innovative or may follow an established tradition. The two traditions of painted decoration, Style A and Style B, reflect not only earlier Traditionalist-Progressive divisions, but contemporary political and religious differences as well. These differences are part of two differing world views and concepts of space.

The significance of this study, I believe, is that it reveals the interrelationship of ceramic decoration and world view. The manufacturing process and the number of designs used, either discrete or as panels within a framed band design, reiterate the Hopi concept of natural order, and are common to both Style A and Style B potters. But the spatial relationship between designs is distinctively different in the ceramics decorated by Progressives and Traditionalists. This design structure is a material expression of how the two groups conceive of Hopi/Anglo-American relations. Ceramic decoration

simultaneously reinforces Hopi belief in how the world actually is ordered and how it ought to be ordered. The critical importance of world view is reinforced by the presence of structural principles of ceramic design in furniture placement. These reoccurring principles indicate that the two concepts of spatial organization associated with the differing Progressive and Traditionalist concepts of Hopi/Anglo-American relations have been internalized and are subconscious. At what point in the individual's development this takes place is difficult to determine, but these same structural principles also occur in children's drawings.

The interrelationship of ceramic decoration and world view reinforces Hodder's (1982) and Munn's (1973) argument that material culture does not reflect one cultural subsystem or another but is an active component within the web of culture. Style A and Style B decoration are active components of Hopi culture as they both reiterate and reinforce subcultural values. Ceramic decoration is an ever-present material expression of "the way things are and ought to be" according to two differing world views.

In this respect it is interesting to note that within the Hopi creation and emergence myths the duality of creation and destruction is resolved through reciprocity over time in that life leads to death which in turn renews life, but that differentiation and unification remain unresolved (see Fig. 3, Chapter 2), neither mediated nor one taking precedence over the other. These binary opposites perhaps parallel the two different approaches to Hopi/Anglo-American relations espoused by Progressives and Traditionalists and the differing structures of their designs.

The constant differentiation in the Progressive design process, as well as within the final design itself, contrasts markedly with the isolated discrete unit design preferred by Traditionalists. The units and motifs used are distinct and unified and, therefore, are like the Traditionalists' concept of the Hopi way— the communal Ant Hill of Hopi myth, separated from the space around it. Thus, if design structure is in fact the unconscious expression of world view, these two styles may also be a material expression of myth structure.

The goal of this study was to acquire an understanding of the relationship between the material culture of ceramics and the culture of the Hopi of Third Mesa, who produced it. To that end I examined the ceramic domain during 1979 and 1980. My examination includes a folk classification of Third Mesa pottery as well as stated and observed vessel use, a study of the role of ceramics as a cash-producing commodity and descriptions of methods of manufacture, the kinship and learning networks of the pottery producers, and both formal stylistic analysis and potters' own statements about each other's work.

Contemporary Third Mesa Hopi ceramics are decorated for religious, economic, and aesthetic reasons, and these are all intertwined. The only type of vessel that can be said to be painted specifically for

religious purposes is the *nahícaqapta,* or medicine bowl. Hopis commonly agreed that these "ought" to be decorated with specific motifs which symbolize various aspects of the Kachina cult.

Most Hopi pottery is decorated for economic and aesthetic reasons. Most small bowls and miniatures produced today are trade items, and most are decorated in a style known to appeal to Anglo buyers. Although economic gain motivates their production, their decoration is consonant with the potter's own aesthetic sense. Hopis appreciate a carefully made vessel and well-executed design, but Progressive and Traditional Hopi potters prefer different styles of painted decoration. Although both use motifs whose meanings are generally agreed upon, thus sharing a symbolic vocabulary, the styles in which this vocabulary is presented are vastly different.

At this level of analysis the style in which a vessel is painted is a material expression of a world view that Progressives and Traditionalists share in some respects. In addition to motifs, for example, some basic design subdivisions as well as the technology of construction are shared. But differences in their world views have developed over time, as have their ceramic stylistic traditions, because of their different histories and their diverse responses to the same historical events.

The kinship between potters and the teachers from whom they learned the craft may reinforce these differences. Kinship and place of residence clearly influence the Traditionalist preference for red clay. Moreover, access to clay sources and some specific designs, like those of Sikyatki Revival wares, are available to some potters only through marriage. Learning probably also accounts for the common use of a slip by Progressive potters and for some of the individual variations among potters. But although kinship and learning may reinforce variations in decoration, these influences are secondary compared to the impact of world views.

The two styles of painted decoration are an integral part of the Hopi world view and may have implications for archaeologists. Wobst (1977) and others have argued that material culture communicates information. Although true, as Hodder observed (1982), it is not always the case because stylistic variation between two ethnic groups can also occur in objects unobserved by the other group. Material culture can and does communicate information, but this does not explain why stylistic differences occur. As Renfrew (1983: 13) expressed it, "We need to know more of the concepts which are communicated, rather than merely the ability of a given channel to carry them." I propose that as an integral part of world view stylistic differences can and do communicate information, but as the by-product rather than end product of variations in style.

The fact that variation in the structure of ceramic decoration among Third Mesa potters occurs because of differences in their world views provides the archaeologist with an analogy that can be used to construct models or hypotheses. This study indicates how this model can be tested against the archaeological record. A group's world view contains its sense of order and structure and this should also be expressed in other material forms where spatial organization is preserved. Although a clear relationship can be seen between Hopi design structure and Hopi arrangement of furniture, further ethnographic research is needed to determine other areas of correlation. Essential to these investigations is the fundamental, and predominantly subconscious, material expression of world view.

Since among the Hopi of Third Mesa the two structural styles of painted pottery decoration are also found in furniture placement and in children's drawings, there is further support for the argument that material culture not only communicates cultural differences but serves also to reinforce them. The two styles also indicate the depth of the division currently existing between Progressives and Traditionalists. This division cannot and must not be interpreted solely as a conflict between political factions but rather as one involving two value systems.

POST SCRIPT

A cold March wind was blowing when I entered Oraibi. It had been nine years since I had first come here and read the sign forbidding white visitors. That sign, which had been taken down a year later, was now replaced with one that read "Old Oraibi Crafts," followed by a directional arrow. Although the sign has changed, little else has. Factionalism and the two styles of painted decoration associated with the Traditionalist and Progressive factions continue.

The small one-room craft shop is located next to Betty's house. Betty and her sister Terry are now the only Traditionalist Oraibi potters since their mother is no longer able to work due to advanced age. Betty's granddaughter, who was just learning to make pottery nine years ago, is now unable to pursue this craft because of the demands of her new baby. The only other Traditionalist potter who is still working is Vera from Hotevilla, her niece Elda having died from diabetes.

The two Progressive Raised Decoration potters have all but ceased making ceramics. Elizabeth White is now too ill to make pottery and lives in a nursing home in Flagstaff. Likewise, advancing years have made it impossible for Faith to do much more than make the occasional piece. In contrast, the three Progressive Style B potters, Lucy, Cindy and Loren, are maintaining their production and marketing of tourist trade pieces.

When I left seven years ago Betty had started selling small pieces made by her granddaughter and mother as well as pieces considered inferior made by her sister and herself. Betty's sales and the shop started by Betty's son Vaughn the following year had begun to provide two outlets, if limited, for Traditionalist Third Mesa ceramics.

During the last seven years Vaughn's shop, known as the Monongue Gallery, has expanded into a truly fine art gallery for which each piece has been chosen for the excellence of its workmanship and its beauty. This art gallery and its small "branch" in Tuba City, along with the Old Oraibi Crafts shop, occasionally sell Traditionalist pottery. The Old Oraibi shop has replaced Betty's direct sale and, as Betty used to do, mainly sells small pieces.

Traditionalist potters may sell their wares but still consider the income from pottery-making merely spending money, because subsistence farming remains chiefly important. Consequently, these outlets do not seem to have had a significant impact on the quantity of vessels produced by Traditionalist potters. The outlets do provide places for the sale of ceramics within the Traditionalist system so that the potters neither associate with the Tribal Council franchise on Second Mesa nor Anglo traders. Furthermore, Vaughn's shop serves to keep all profits within the Third

Mesa Traditionalist Corn Clan segment, although Betty still barters with the Santo Domingo trader.

As Traditionalist ceramic production continues to be limited and few are decorated it was impossible to determine during a brief visit the degree to which ceramic decoration may have changed. Most Style A vessels, like those made by Progressive Style B potters, were indistinguishable from those made seven to nine years earlier. The only exceptions were canteens made by Betty and Terry for sale in the Monongue Gallery. These vessels were decorated on their bulbous sides with large curvilinear discrete design units similar to the one on the Style B bowl illustrated in Figure 11. These new designs, however, were simpler and made with wide lines. The use of this kind of design clearly indicates that these vessels, like those made some years ago by Terry (see Appendix III), were made specifically for the Anglo market. Vessels decorated in this manner were not found within a Style A potter's house.

The new vessels I saw in use in both Traditionalist and Progressive potters' houses all remained in accord with Style A and Style B design precepts. These vessels were of the same types as those produced previously except that Terry is now decorating very large bowls. Terry uses these bowls, which are the same size and shape as piki bowls, as serving bowls when there is a large gathering. It appears, therefore, that Traditionalist and Progressive potters have remained faithful to their differing styles and that these styles remain in accord with their differing world views.

The fundamental differences between Progressives and Traditionalists still serve to sharply divide Hopis although the catalyst has changed. The division of the Joint-Use-Area remains a highly emotional issue but now the Moencopi Motel proposed by the Progressive Tribal Council is perhaps of more immediate concern. The motel is to be located at the junction of Arizona routes 160 and 264 and is to be built surrounding a central plaza area. Traditionalists oppose this motel because Kachina dances for tourists are to be held in the plaza, because it will also have a bar, and because they consider the motel site to be on their land. Thus, they see their rights ignored and religion denigrated. The Progressives see the construction of the motel as a way to increase employment and thereby raise the Hopi "standard of living." The "added attractions" of a bar and Kachina dances would serve to draw tourists and therefore allow the motel to compete successfully with the new Tuba City motel.

The conflict surrounding the construction of the Moencopi Motel is based on the two different views of what Progressives and Traditionalists believe is for the good of all. Both factions strive for what they hold to be "the way things ought to be" and these differences continue to be expressed in ceramic decoration.

March, 1988

APPENDIX I

METHODS OF CERAMIC MANUFACTURE

Clay Collection and Processing

Since potters do most of their work in the summer and autumn they usually do their large-scale clay collecting during one major outing in the spring. Children and male relatives lend a hand loading the clay into the family pickup. Lucy and Cindy, who make ceramics for sale to tourists, will collect over thirty buckets of clay in the spring. Other potters will collect considerably less. If a potter runs out of clay during the summer or fall, she and usually only her husband or brother will collect more as the need arises. The potter selects the actual clay she will use, and removes stones, sticks, and other visible impurities from it at the source.

All potters recognize two distinctly different clays: one that fires red and one that fires gray. The former is usually referred to as yellow clay (*sikácöqa*)[1] because of its color before firing, while the latter is called *cöqa* (clay) or *masícöqa* (*má·si* = dull, lacking color, gray).[2]

There are clay deposits throughout the Hopi mesas (Map 2), most frequently forming distinct layers toward the base of the mesa wall. At times they form a flat ridge along a lower section of the mesa before its descent to the Jeddito Valley.

Third Mesa potters dig from deposits which have proved to contain good ceramic clay.

All Third Mesa potters use red clay from a spot on Howell Mesa, seventeen miles west of Hotevilla, north of the Oraibi-Tuba City Road (Arizona State Road 264). They like this clay because it fires an unusually vivid red because of its high percentage of iron oxide. Third Mesa potters also exploit eight other clay sources.

Traditionalist potters from Oraibi and Hotevilla prefer to use red clay. This clay is also found at deposits near both of these villages (sources 1 and 3). Hotevilla potters, Vera and Amy, refer to their local red clay as *palácöqa*[3] (*palá* — red) instead of sikácöqa (*siká* = yellow). This clay is a pale yellowish gray before firing and turns a brownish red; it is sometimes mixed with Howell Mesa clay to increase its color. Vera uses this clay for 71.4 percent of her vessels and Amy for 60.9 percent of hers. The red clay used by Oraibi potters (source 3) fires redder than that from Hotevilla and, although less red than that from Howell Mesa, is likewise called *sikácöqa*.[4] Oraibi potters used this clay for almost three-quarters (72.7 percent) of their vessels. This deposit is also used by Lucy and her daughter Cindy, Progressives from New Oraibi. In contrast to Traditionalist potters they only use red clay for ten percent of their production.

Except for Loren from Lower Moencopi,

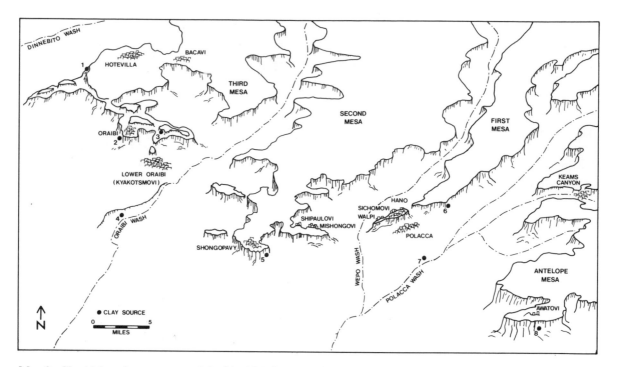

Map 2. Hopi Mesa clay sources exploited by Third Mesa and Moencopi potters. (The clay source at Howell Mesa, 17 miles west of Hotevilla, is also used.)

all the Third Mesa potters collect gray clay from a deposit below Oraibi (source 2). Amy from Hotevilla also sometimes collects gray clay from Second Mesa (source 5).

The three Progressive Style B potters who are related by marriage to First Mesa potters collect most of their gray clay from First Mesa. Lucy and her daughter Cindy used a deposit below Awatovi (source 8) for over eighty percent of their production between 1979 and 1980.[5] Loren not only collects her gray clay from below First Mesa (source 6) but also uses a First Mesa deposit (source 7) of kaolin for her white ceramic slip and paint.

Relatively pure kaolin, called *tí:ma*,[6] is used as a ceramic paint by the Traditionalist potters from Oraibi and the Progressive potters from New Oraibi. During my stay

none was used by Hotevilla potters although they said they had used it in the past. All of these potters collected it from the Oraibi Wash (source 4). It is *tí:ma* that is also used as a "whitewash" on the interior walls of some Hopi houses.

If a potter is looking for a new source she selects one by taste, preferring a clay that is "sweet." A potter frequently tastes her clay even if it is from a commonly used deposit. While "good clay" is not exactly sweet, it lacks the slightly salty and acidic taste of "bad clay."

When the potter brings the clay home, she breaks up large rock-hard lumps with a hatchet into pieces no larger than a quarter and removes smaller impurities. Then she puts the clay into a large metal or plastic container and covers it well with water.

After a day or so the clay has absorbed most of the water, and organic impurities (leaves, roots, etc.) float to the surface. She removes the remaining water and adds fresh water, repeating this process usually at least five times over the next ten days to a month. Some potters felt a longer period of soaking "made it cleaner"; others said it would "go bad if left too long." All potters agreed, however, that it took about ten days for the clay to "get really wet" and ready to use.

When the water above the clay appears clear of impurities, the clay is stirred and poured through cheesecloth to remove any pebbles or grit. (Lucy, whose clay appeared to be the finest, used a 100-mesh sieve she had purchased in Albuquerque.) The potter then places the clay in a cool, shady spot for twelve to twenty hours. After it changes from muddy to a rubbery consistency it is ready to use, and is wrapped in plastic until needed. The only potter who occasionally added temper to the clay was Betty, but she added temper only when making *wɨ:kosivɨ*. The temper was a coarse sand (Shepard 1956: 118) collected from the dry bottom of Dinnebito Wash.

Forming and Polishing the Vessel

When a potter is ready to work she examines the clay for consistency. If it is slightly dry, she cautiously adds water while she kneads the clay to remove any trapped air. The most common technique for forming the base is to pinch and press a ball of clay until it is flattened, and then mold it in the palm of the hand. Hotevilla and Oraibi potters occasionally use a basket as a mold for the base of a bowl. The potter then places the vessel base on a plate or a piece of wood, and pinches the edges upward. The pot itself is made of coils of clay, stacked one atop the other and then smoothed. Coils vary in size (from 1 cm to 2.5 cm), and the size of the coil is determined mainly by the size of the vessel. Most vessels are raised with either four or six coils. I never observed a vessel made with an odd number of coils. As each coil is added, it is attached to the one below by downward pressure of the fingers. This coil is then rubbed smooth outside and inside. A scraping tool is used to smooth the exterior and interior, and at the same time, the interior is pressed outward to create the desired curve of the vessel.

All the potters used pieces of gourd shell as a scraping tool, although Lucy also used a purchased wooden scraper, Betty the rubber end of a broken kitchen spatula, and Cindy a commercial metal-loop scraper. This coil method has been used for centuries and can be done virtually without tools. A somewhat different technique was used by Loren, who made disks and tiles for the tourist market. She first rolled the clay into a ball or tube and flattened it in her hand, and then used the interior of a bowl or a flat board as a mold. To ensure an even thickness of the clay for her tiles, she used a rolling pin and then cut them out with a rectangular form. The speed with which vessels were formed varied among potters. Cindy (apart from Betty's 11-year-old granddaughter) was the slowest, frequently spending an hour to form a miniature. By contrast, her mother Lucy would form a small bowl in 15 minutes and Betty a piki bowl in 45 minutes.

A very large vessel cannot be formed all at once because the clay is too soft; when it reaches about 18 cm in height it is left to dry until the clay is leathery, usually overnight. If the potter is busy and unable to complete the vessel at this point, the first section is dampened before construction continues.

When a vessel reaches the desired size and shape, the last coil is smoothed to form the rim. To check that the rim is even, the potter may place a plate, or some other round, commercially manufactured object such as a plastic lid, on the rim. This is evidently a very recent innovation not shared by the two elderly potters Anne and Vera. They lamented that due to fading ability and eyesight, their rims were not as even as they used to be. Should a younger potter discover that her rim is markedly uneven (more than half a centimeter off), she turns the entire rim inward until it is flat, cuts away the excess with a knife, and smooths the interior. Rims treated in this manner are more noticeably incurving.

Rapid drying is a problem in the arid Hopi area, and cracks frequently occur in works in progress. Damp towels may be placed over or around the drying vessels; Lucy and her daughter also covered their work with plastic to prevent this problem.

Once completed and dry, the vessels are finished by scraping, sanding, and occasionally by slipping and polishing. Scraping ensures uniform thickness of vessel walls. Small exterior bulges are moistened and then smoothed with a paring knife. The interior surface is scraped with a bent can lid, or a copper scouring pad. (Some potters omit this step, either because their work is very even or because they consider it unnecessary.)

The next step is to smooth the walls. Except for Vera from Hotevilla, who still used a coarse "sandstone" (quartz arenite cemented by limonite and calcite) for this purpose, all potters now use sandpaper (ranging from coarse to fine 30–40 gage).

The entire vessel is sanded, including the base.

Progressive Style B potters usually slip their pottery, but most of the Third Mesa potters did not slip their wares. Only five vessels made by Traditionalists were slipped during the course of a year. Lucy and Loren's slips were of red, gray, or white clay. Slipped vessels are not polished until the slip is quite dry, about half an hour after the slip has been applied with a sponge; some slipped vessels are not polished at all.

Vessels are polished with a smooth water-worn pebble often of jasper or chert. A section of the vessel is wetted, usually not larger than 3 by 6 cm, and then rubbed with the pebble to create a lustrous surface. Moistening a small section at a time prevents drying shrinkage from destroying the luster (Shepard 1956: 190–91). The luster that is achieved is attributed to the stone rather than to the pot. "Because it is shiny, it makes the pottery shiny," the potters say. A dull sheen can also be brought out by rubbing the dampened vessel with a cloth or a stocking. Potters did not consider this technique "polishing" but said it was to "make it smooth and pretty." Also during the polishing process a thin red wash is sometimes applied to the vessel surface by adding "a pinch" of red clay to the water used to dampen the surface.

Decoration

Although Hopi potters do not decorate most of the pots intended for Hopi use or interpueblo barter, approximately half the vessels in the study sample were decorated because most of them, specifically the miniatures and small bowls, were manufactured for sale. The most common decorative technique was painting. The only potters who did not use painted decoration were Faith and Elizabeth White from New Oraibi. These Progressive potters decorated their vessels by manipulating the clay itself. Faith's technique was to use a knife to lift the damp clay into peaks. Elizabeth White decorated some of her vessels with raised applique "corn maiden" or "flute player" figures (see Jacka and Gill 1976: 45).

All Third Mesa painted pottery designs are outlined in black. Before painting, potters usually mark their vessels in pencil to indicate the design itself or the general design area. Terry elaborated on this technique with cutout paper patterns around which she outlined the design. As one potter explained, "The hard part is to get the space just right." Band designs, or belts of decoration around a vessel, compared to framed bands were simple enough to be often painted directly, however. Lucy, who used the same framed-band designs again and again, could paint these directly onto the vessel as could other potters when "just putting a little bit [of design] on."

Framed-band designs, whether drawn or painted directly, are painted in a given order. The first lines always define the band area. Then, once the band is defined, the area within it is divided.

Third Mesa potters, as we have seen, work in two styles. Traditionalist potters used Style A derived from Polacca Polychrome, and Progressives use Style B from Sikyatki Revival wares. One of the important differences between these two can be seen in the way the potters construct the decoration (see Chapter 6). Cindy, her

mother Lucy, and Loren, who are Progressives and work in Style B, almost always divide the band into four or eight units by vertical lines to create a series of panels. These panels are then frequently further divided by diagonal lines (Fig. 5; Pls. 6, 8d, 9c, d). By contrast, when Style A potters Betty and Terry divide the band, they treat the pot as if it had a front and back, or four sides, thus creating a design on four or two "sides" rather than a continuous band. The order in which lines were applied on two vessels can be seen in Figures 16 and 17, Chapter 6. These lines were always applied from left to right, as the vessel is held at various angles to facilitate the drawing.

Once the design has been outlined in black, different sections may be filled in with a solid color, and then hatched or "stippled." Traditionalist Style A potters use the tip of a paintbrush for this purpose; Progressive Style B potters use the chewed end of a stick (usually a matchstick).

Paint

Black paint is made from *ti·mi,* which the Hopi call "wild spinach" (*Cleome serrulata;* Whiting 1939: 77), mixed with what is commonly called "ironstone," actually a hematite cement.[7] Both wild spinach and ironstone are capable of producing black paint, but all the potters agree that the ironstone produces the black color and the wild spinach "makes the liquid." Some potters argued that wild spinach was necessary to "make the black from the ironstone stick and not rub off after it's fired." According to Shepard (1956: 42) this is exactly the tendency of paint made from hematite; she explains further that one factor "which may prevent these colors from rubbing is the binding effect of impurities." As the stone used by Hopis contains calcite, this may act as the necessary impurity. It is also possible that the *tí·mi* may act chemically as a binder; however, the use of both *tí·mi* and hematite may reflect a cultural blending as opposed to a chemical binding.

Tí·mi is the source of the black paint used by the pueblo peoples of the Rio Grande area, specifically the Tewa (Robbins et al. 1916: 59). At Hano it is named with the three chief cultivated plants—corn, pumpkin, and cotton—which attests to its importance (ibid.). Mineral paint (hematite, iron oxide/manganese), on the other hand, was used for the black on prehistoric Hopi wares. Hence, it is not unreasonable to speculate that the Hopi used hematite for black paint and added the *tí·mi* after the Tewa introduced it at Hano. In order to prepare the *tí·mi,* which is usually collected in the spring when it is used for food, the stalk and leaves are boiled together until the water is reduced to a syrupy consistency. The stalks and leaves are then removed and about 30 cc (2 tablespoons) of the liquid is placed on a corn husk to dry. When cool, this concentrated juice becomes very hard. It is then wrapped in the corn husk until it is to be used. About a week before a potter needs it, she breaks off half a piece, places it in a plastic-capped pill jar with just enough water to completely cover it, and leaves it to dissolve into a greenish-black liquid of uneven consistency. A few drops of this extract are placed on a basalt palette (usually found at a nearby ruin) along with some of the hematite cement, and these are mixed and ground together to a desired consistency.

To apply the decoration the

Traditionalist potters of Oraibi and Hotevilla usually use commercial paintbrushes and only occasionally use a yucca brush. Progressive potters, on the other hand, only use commercial brushes for filling in design areas and use the narrow yucca brush for lines. Yucca brushes are made from a green yucca spike from the inner section of the plant (*Yucca angustessima;* Whiting 1939: 71). To prepare the brush, the yucca spike is first cut at both ends to a length of about 9 cm. One end (c. 1.5–2 cm long) is then chewed until it is frayed. Once frayed, the fiber strands are removed until the brush is the desired width. Traditionalist brushes range in width from 0.4 to 0.05 cm, although I never saw them use the narrower brush. This narrow brush is only a single yucca fiber. Because of its flexibility, the whole fiber is used as the brush; it is laid flat against the vessel and dragged along to create a thin line. This painting technique is illustrated by Chapman (1953: 27) in his discussion of Santo Domingo pottery. The use of the yucca brush is common to the Rio Grande pueblos (Chapman 1953; Lambert 1966).

Black-on-red, black-on-gray, and black-on-pink (the pink having been created by a thin wash at the time the vessel was polished) are the three most common color combinations for Third Mesa pottery. Most Traditionalist Style A pottery is black-on-red whereas Progressive Style B pottery is black-on-gray because of their preferences for either red or gray clay. Progressives also make more polychrome pieces.

Polychrome decoration was done by all the Style B potters, while Terry was the only Traditionalist Style A potter who consistently used this type of decoration. One polychrome vessel was made by Betty, the first time she had ever used a third color. The colors used on polychrome vessels are black, red, and white; both the red and white are clay paints. The clay from Howell Mesa is used for the red paint and white kaolin from the washes (sources 4 and 7) for the white paint. After the pottery has been painted it is fired.

Firing

Since the seventeenth century Hopis have used sheep dung piled around and on top of their ceramics for firing. This method of firing became common among pueblo peoples after the Spanish introduced livestock and is still the most common technique on Third Mesa, although the electric kiln has now become popular. The dung method is difficult and fraught with possibility for disaster, but can be done cheaply and close to home. To fire by this method a potter builds her dung kiln on a flat section of rock near her house. First she builds a rock circle and starts a fire of grass and twigs in its center. Then dried bark-like dung chips, broken up so as not to smother the fire, are added. Large (19.0 by 16.0 cm) sherds are placed over and in the fire and balanced on the stones to create a grate. She then places large pots to be fired on the grate upside down and fits smaller pieces around the edge. The number of pieces fired at one time varies according to the size of the vessels. The size of the actual mound of ceramics also varies, ranging from 50 by 50 cm with a height of 30 cm, to 60 by 60 cm, with a height of 50 cm. The entire mound of pottery is then covered with sheep dung.[8]

According to Shepard (1956: 78), dung will rapidly rise to a temperature of 900°C, then gradually rise to 940°C, creating a hotter open fire than wood or coal although of shorter duration. After about 30 minutes the temperature will begin to decrease rapidly because dung does not leave charcoal. Hopi potters frequently add lumps of coal to the fire, because this permits longer firing. Although smudging (fire clouding) is common on dung-fired pottery, the temperature obtained, coupled with the quality of the clay itself, makes this dung-fired pottery strong. Vessels are removed from the fire after about three hours when they are still warm but cool enough to handle. Dung firing usually takes place just after sunrise. The ground on which the pots are placed has begun to warm, but the air is usually calm and likely to remain so until the winds begin in the afternoon.

All Third Mesa potters are extremely concerned about the wind, which causes uneven firing and breakage. Oraibi and Hotevilla potters also say, "You should never fire when there are clouds for they [the pottery] will take up the water, then there is no rain." High cirrus clouds are also associated with rising winds. Vera from Hotevilla adds to her firing a small miniature as an offering to Spider Grandmother to prevent breakage. Lucy and her daughter warm their pottery in their electric stove before firing, "to help get it hot evenly so it won't crack." This is a very important step, as warming the pottery allows for the slow release of moisture trapped in the clay, which will cause breakage if forced out by too rapid firing. No dung firing takes place in the winter when the ground may be cold or damp.

Today, throughout the Hopi mesas, the electric kiln is used as widely as the sheep-dung fired oven. The occupants of Moencopi have access to the various kilns in

Tuba City. Terry owns an electric kiln at Oraibi and fires pottery for anyone in the area for a fee of twenty-five cents to one dollar per vessel.[9] She does not charge her mother, but expects some form of reimbursement from her sister. Although expensive, the appeal of Terry's kiln is that breakage is unlikely. Dung firing, by contrast, is extremely risky. The knowledge that hours of labor can be lost makes the firing stage a very anxious one.

Smudging and Sealing

Most ceramics intended for sale to tourists are ready for the market after firing. This, however, is not the case for most vessels used by the Hopi, or for most of their pipes.

These receive the most elaborate post-firing treatment. To smudge new pipes after firing, they are rubbed with crushed sunflower seeds while they are still warm from the kiln until they are shiny from the oil. The pipes are then placed in a small pit with smoldering corncobs, flakes of *píki* left after the bread has been cooked, or both, and the pit covered with a large pot or sherds.

Like the pipes, the *wikóro* are coated, while still warm from the kiln. Potters use "piñon gum" (sap) on them. During the late spring or summer, the sap is collected from *Pinus edulis* (Whiting 1939: 63). At this season, large lumps of sap form on the tree wherever the bark has been penetrated. A lump about 2.5 cm square will coat an area about 28 by 16 cm as it softens on contact with the warm vessel. Although the surface may remain somewhat tacky when the pot has cooled, piñon gum is a surface sealer that renders the vessel comparatively watertight.

Píki bowls, stew bowls, and some serving bowls are also treated to increase their impermeability. These vessels are covered with fat on the interior and on the exterior if there is no painted decoration. Most potters use sheep fat, although commercially prepared lard is also popular. The pots are rubbed with fat until they are greasy but with no visible excess, then placed in a gas or electric stove set at 148.9 to 176.7°C for at least four hours, preferably overnight. When they are removed, the vessels may look slightly darker. Cushing (1920) describes a similar process practiced by Zuni potters who reheated cooking vessels that had been treated with piñon sap. Fat appears to be, however, an equally effective sealer. I observed during a six-day period vessels so treated that showed no liquid absorption. When Hopis were asked about their preference for fat as a sealer as opposed to piñon sap, the unanimous response was that fat tasted better!

Commercial glazes are also used on pottery the Hopi intend to use themselves but these must be applied in Terry's electric kiln because dung does not fire hot enough. Terry uses a clear glaze, for instance, which must be fired at between 999 and 1023.8°C. Terry said she glazed her vessels because it made them easier to wash and stronger. Faith, who uses the same glaze as Terry but has her pieces fired in Winslow, said she glazed the interior of her serving bowls because it prevented liquid absorption. Using a commercial glaze can also repair a vessel cracked in a dung kiln. Betty did this with one of her piki bowls. Both she and Terry agreed that "it was better to use glaze than to have a vessel you couldn't use."

APPENDIX I NOTES

1. *Sikya'chka* (Stephen 1936: 497–98); *sika'tska* (Whorf *in* Stephen 1936: 1294).

2. Clays, red or gray, may also be qualified according to their place of origin, for example *awátpicöqa* (clay from Awatovi).

3. *Pala'chka* (Stephen 1936: 1194).

4. Stephen (1936) states that *sikya'chka* is a "yellow brown ocher pigment, obtained in a spring in the bottom of the Grand Canyon" (497–98). This particular clay, used as Kachina mask or body paint, was termed *sŕ·ta* and not *sikácöqa* by the Hopis I spoke with. Voegelin and Voegelin (1957: 14) simply gloss *sŕ·ta* as "ocher." Stephen also describes the use of *sŕ·ta* (*Chü'ka,* Stephen 1936: 1213; *tsö·'ka,* Whorf *in* Stephen 1936: 1214) to make *"pala'chka"* as Kachina body and mask paint but adds that a "true *pala'chka*" is found locally. The latter was probably used for ceramics.

5. During this period (Summer 1979), Lucy's husband became ill and, to save time, Lucy purchased commercial clay in order to maintain her heavy tourist market production. She mixed it with gray clay from Awatovi, but unfortunately, during firing, most of these vessels cracked. Commercial clay was also bought by Loren for mold-made plates.

6. *Tü'ma* (Stephen 1936: 1310); *te'ma* (Whorf *in* Stephen 1936: 1310).

7. A thin section of this rock was taken by Wallace Phelps and examined by Kevin Shelton (Yale University Department of Geology) and was identified as a hematite cement containing hematite, calcite, and quartz.

8. This method of firing has been described for First Mesa (Colton 1939); for San Ildefonso (Shepard 1956); for Santo Domingo (Chapman 1953); and for Rio Grande pueblos generally (Lambert 1966).

9. Terry regularly uses a 0.05 firing cone (between 1046.11 and 1062.2°C).

APPENDIX II

FOLK CLASSIFICATION OF VESSELS (DOMESTIC WARES) AND THEIR PARTS

This folk classification is based on a sample of 115 vessels. The sample represents virtually the entire year-long production of most Third Mesa potters and seventeen vessels from the collection of the Museum of Northern Arizona (M.N.A.) which were included to increase the sample of a specific class or to balance the samples so that each potter was adequately represented. All sample vessels, including those from the Museum, were identified by the maker and other potters, and by no fewer than five male and female non-potters from Third Mesa.

Apart from miniatures (see Chapter 6) every vessel was readily classified with a Hopi term. Identification was based on an examination of the piece itself, except for a few large vessels and those at the M.N.A. identified from photographs. There was no discernible distinction between terms used by male and female non-potters.

Potters were more inclined to use terms based on shape rather than function when referring to vessels they planned to sell or give away. One potter said, when pressed for a more specific term, "I don't know—it depends on what they will use it for." In contrast, non-potters were inclined to identify vessels according to their intended use; as one woman said, "That is how I'd use it, anyway."

The more general terms based on shape are *wikóro, caqápta,* or *sí·vɨ.* All domestic wares were classified according to one of these categories. A *wikóro* was called a canteen, bottle, or sometimes an olla in English. Hopi informants most commonly translated *caqápta* as a "bowl." On occasion they would simply translate it as "pottery." The *sí·vɨ* was usually glossed a "jar," although frequently it was called a "pot."

The informants' readiness to call vessels *caqápta, sí·vɨ,* or *wikóro* is in marked contrast to their frequent hesitancy to add qualifiers, perhaps reflecting the vessel's unknown use. Consequently, many vessels that might have been given qualifiers to indicate function such as stew bowls (*nöqkʷíscaqapta*), are simply classed as bowls (*caqápta*) or jars (*sí·vɨ*). Qualifiers of size, large or small, were more readily given than qualifiers of function. In an attempt to overcome the problem of functionally specific terms, both potters and non-potters were asked: (1) what they would term the vessel; (2) how they would use the vessel; (3) what they would call the vessel if they were using it that way; (4) whether that was the only way they could use the vessel; (5) if there were other uses, what the term for the vessel would be.

Caqápta

The most commonly used vessel today is a *caqápta*. It has been classed as a dish and a food basin (Stephen 1936: 538, 1021);[1] as a dish, pot, or vessel (Whorf *in* Glossary of Stephen 1936: 1207);[2] as a dishpan and a pot (Voegelin and Voegelin 1957: 57); and as a bowl (Owen *in* B. Wright 1979: 65).[3] Wright (72) concludes that this term "is reserved for any low walled container." Quantification reveals, however, that a *caqápta* is shallow only in relation to the size of the rim diameter (Fig. 36). In a sample of 88 *caqápta* including the miniatures that were consistently termed either *caqápta* or *caqáphoya* (*hoya* = small), it was found that although their height ranged from 1.6 to 17.5 cm, the average height/rim ratio was 0.6. That the height/rim ratio is a distinctive *caqápta* attribute is not only indicated statistically (see Fig. 36) but also linguistically. When identified in Hopi, it was this container term that was used for the lidless boxes which, had they been round, would have had a height/rim ratio of 0.4. This is the term that also was first given for the free-form vessels. Like the boxes, their height/rim ratio (0.3) was consistent with *caqápta* proportions, i.e., wider than high.

Within the study sample only one group of *caqápta* was qualified according to shape. These vessels are the *pá:wik^wocaqapta* (*pá:wika* = duck), sometimes referred to as *pá:wikcaqapta*. The fact that these are defined by shape, whereas boxes and free-form vessels are not, may reflect that they have long been manufactured. Smith (1971: 243) notes that "bird figurines" were found during all periods of occupation at Awatovi (c. 1200–1700 of this era). These vessels may originally have had a specific

function but this seems doubtful as they are not qualified according to their intended use. One rather large (c. 24 cm) *pá:wik^wocaqapta*, as well as one of the smaller sample vessels, was observed in a Hopi house. Others were filled with Easter eggs and given out by the Kachina at First Mesa on Easter weekend. Rabbit-shaped vessels were also given out at this time. These vessels were referred to as *caqápta*, or "rabbit bowl" in English.

These *pá:wik^wocaqapta* conform to the *caqápta* height/rim requirement with an average ratio of 0.5. They are all small, ranging from 13.0 to 15.2 cm from the tip of the beak to the end of the tail and are decorated in black on either red or gray clay.

According to Stephen (1936: 328) *caqápta* in the 1890s were qualified according to size, being either large, *wí:kocaqapta*[4] or small, *caqáphoya*. The *wí:kocaqapta* he glossed as a "large basin." Although these vessels were remembered, they have evidently not been produced for the last thirty years, and so none have been included in this sample. Stephen termed a "small food basin" as a *caqáphoya* (1936: 1021)[5] and he describes it as a salt container (1036). Likewise, Whorf (Glossary *in* Stephen 1936: 1207) refers to this container as a small dish[6] as does Voth (1967: 11); however, Voegelin and Voegelin (1957: 57) gloss it as "cup." Containers that were termed *caqáphoya* ranged from miniatures used as children's toys, regardless of shape; bowls of ceramic, glass, or paper; saucers containing food (none was ever seen with an accompanying cup); and mugs, ceramic or glass. Clearly, varieties of sizes and shapes are represented.

The *caqápta* attribute of the vessel height being less than the rim diameter is not so

Folk Classification	No. of Vessels		Ht (cm)	Diam. (cm)	Ht. Diam. Ratio	Capacity (cc)	% of Vessels with following attributes					
							Decor.	Polished interior	Polished exterior	Incurving rim	Straight rim	Everted rim
caqápta	88	mean	7.6	14.9	.6	1,559.5	57.9	67	59	63.6	36.4	0
		range	1.6–17.5	2.3–37.0	.1–2.0	5.0–14,500.0						
		std. dev.	3.5	8.4	.3	2,341.0						
miniatures	11	mean	3.4	3.9	.1	48.0	100	45	100	45	55	0
		range	1.6–5.3	2.3–8.0	.5–2.0	5.0–125.0						
		std. dev.	1.1	1.7	.5	39.1						
pá·wikʷocaqapta	4	mean	3.6	7.6	.5	82.5	100	75	75	50	50	0
		range	3.3–4.2	6.6–9.0	.4–.6	60.0–125.0						
		std. dev.	0.4	1.0	.1	30.2						
caqáphoya	28	mean	6.0	9.8	.6	367.7	75	64	29	57	43	0
		range	3.1–10.0	4.0–16.2	.3–1.6	83.0–875.0						
		std. dev.	1.6	2.5	.3	213.1						
homɨcaqaphoya	3	mean	7.2	8.3	.9	263.3	0	0	0	0	100	0
		range	6.7–7.5	6.8–10.5	.6–1.1	165.0–375.0						
		std. dev.	0.4	1.9	.2	105.6						
paqwɨscaqapta	15	mean	12.6	26.9	.5	5,190.9	0	100	0	100	0	0
		range	10.0–17.5	24.0–30.0	.4–.7	3,500.0–6,500.0						
		std. dev.	2.1	1.5	.1	835.6						
wɨ·kopaqwɨscaqapta	1		17.0	37.0	.5	14,500.0	0	100	100	100	0	0
nöqkʷɨscaqapta	8	mean	9.7	22.1	.4	2,725.0	12.5	100	12.5	100	0	0
		range	7.7–12.0	18.7–25.0	.3–.6	2,500.0–3,000.0						
		std. dev.	1.3	2.4	.1	253.7						
nöqkʷɨscaqapta or *oyâ·pi*	8	mean	10.3	17.7	.6	1,825.4	75	50	50	62.5	37.5	0
		range	9.2–13.5	14.3–20.8	.5–.8	1,500.0–2,416.0						
		std. dev.	1.5	2.0	.1	319.5						
oyâ:pi	6	mean	6.2	21.3	.3	1,174.0	100	100	50	50	50	0
		range	4.5–7.4	19.3–27.6	.2–.3	233.0–1,875.0						
		std. dev.	1.1	3.1	.0	625.8						
sí·vɨ	23	mean	15.2	11.2	1.8	2,635.2	60	30	70	34.8	39.2	26
		range	4.2–37.3	2.5–35.0	.5–8.7	20.0–20,250.0						
		std. dev.	8.4	7.6	1.6	5,153.0						
sivɨhoya	5	mean	6.4	4.8	1.5	103.0	80	20	80	60	20	20
		range	4.2–9.3	2.5–9.2	1.0–1.9	20.0–250.0						
		std. dev.	1.8	2.6	.4	89.0						
wɨ·kosivɨ	2	mean	24.9	28.1	1.0	18,125.0	0	0	0	0	50	50
		range	22.4–27.5	21.3–35.0	.6–1.3	6,000.0–20,250.0						
		std. dev.	3.6	9.7	.5	3,005.2						
pashɨmsivɨ	6	mean	11.8	7.3	1.8	453.1	83	0	83	50	33	17
		range	10.0–15.2	5.2–10.0	1.0–2.3	116.0–750.0						
		std. dev.	1.9	2.3	.7	245.5						
wikóro	4	mean	19.1	3.8	4.8	2,731.0	0	0	0	0	100	0
		range	12.2–29.0	3.1–4.7	3.8–6.2	187.0–7,000.0						
		std. dev.	8.9	0.8	1.0	3,110.0						
wikórohoya	2	mean	12.6	3.1	4.0	275.0	0	0	0	0	100	0
		range	12.2–13.1	3.1–3.2	3.8–4.2	187.0–363.0						
		std. dev.	0.6	0.0	.3	124.5						

Figure 36. Quantification of vessels grouped according to their folk classification.

strictly applied as vessels decrease in size. Miniatures are the most diverse, with a height/rim ratio ranging from 0.5 to 2.0. That this group does not conform is evident when they are removed from the *caqápta* sample: the height/rim ratio drops to 0.5 instead of 0.6.

Caqáphoya was termed for both cups and bowls. If there was a need to distinguish the two, *homícaqaphoya* was used, translated for me as "a cup with a handle." Voegelin and Voegelin (1957: 21) cite the use of *ho:mi* as a suffix in the Hopi term for pear, *"mansá:na-homi:taqa." Mansá:na* is an apple; *ta:qa* is a man or male being, e.g., *taqáca:yri* = buck. Thus, perhaps a *mansá:na-homi:taqa* could be translated as an apple with a male type of protrusion and a *homícaqaphoya* as a small vessel, preferably with a rim greater than its height, with a protruding lug or handle. In this case *ho:mi* could have been used as a prefix, since *hoya* is a final position suffix.

Twenty-eight vessels were defined as *caqáphoya,* and of these, 75 percent are decorated. Although specific examples are different, there is a statistically defined norm. Excluding three atypical examples (vessels 23, 41 and P.M. 249053), all of the *caqáphoya* adhere to the *caqápta* height/rim ratio.

Paqwíscaqapta are commonly called "piki bowls" in English but Hopis are quick to tell you, "That's not what they really are; they are for mixing any kind of batter in—cakes, piki, bread, anything like that." Indeed these vessels are qualified as such: *páqwri* refers to batter or dough. In spite of this, although modern plastic bowls were occasionally seen containing piki batter, only once did I see a *paqwíscaqapta* being used for any other type of batter or dough. Unlike most *caqápta,* these vessels were

immediately qualified. Specificity of term is paralleled by specificity of attributes. The vessels are remarkably uniform (Fig. 36). They all have stone-polished interiors and inverted rims, are red (either manufactured from red clay or, if from gray clay, are slipped or washed with red clay), are not decorated, and they are about twice as wide as high (height/rim ratio: 0.4–0.7, mean 0.5, std. dev. 0.1). Although this ceramic type is clearly standardized, there was a considerable range in capacity. When asked about this, Hopi women told me that this range was necessary, as *paqwíscaqapta* of different sizes were needed according to "how much you want to make. You fill it up [with piki flour] to here [about half full] and then add water to just about fill it up." These are therefore measuring bowls as well as mixing bowls, which would reinforce the need for conformity of shape.

Only one *wí:kopaqwíscaqapta* (large batter bowl) is included in this study sample. It had been made nearly twenty years earlier by Anne, one of the potters from Oraibi. It is included in the sample because it clearly conveys the Hopi concept of a large vessel. This container has recently been used only for mixing bread dough in preparation for a wedding feast. Its attributes are the same as for other *paqwíscaqapta* except that it is also polished on the exterior. According to every Hopi with whom I discussed their attributes, a *paqwíscaqapta* had to be polished on the interior "so that batter will slip." When asked about rim shape, I was told that they had to be incurving "so you can scrape the edge of your hand on them." Scraping the hand on the edge of the vessel was an absolutely routine movement in piki making: the woman sat in front of the piki stone, under which there was a fire, with the *paqwíscaqapta* next to her; she would put her hand into the bowl, mix the batter a couple of times, fill her hand with the batter, scrape the edge of her hand against the rim to remove any excess, and then with her hand spread it across the hot stone. It is interesting, however, that the incurving rim is maintained on the *wí:kopaqwíscaqapta* which, according to family members, was used only for fry-bread dough. This vessel was too large to carry around but anyone not living in Oraibi always immediately identified it from a photograph as a *wí :kopaqwíscaqapta.*

In spite of the prompt identification of all *paqwíscaqapta* as such, they were not always used as batter bowls. Occasionally during ceremonies, when a large number of people gathered in a single house, the bowls were used to contain stew and were then called *nöqk"íscaqapta*[7] (*nöqk"ivi* = stew of corn, hominy, and meat). When washed and returned to the shelf they were once again *paqwíscaqapta.* Usually, smaller vessels termed *nöqk"íscaqapta* were used to contain stew.

Like the *paqwíscaqapta,* these vessels form a quantitatively uniform class and none were produced for sale. Unlike the *paqwíscaqapta, nöqk"íscaqapta* were occasionally polished on the exterior and decorated.

Sometimes these same bowls were called *oyâ:pi.* This term, which was translated by Hopis as "serving bowl," was used when the bowl contained something other than stew, fried chicken for example. This same vessel could also be used as "*paqwíscaqapta* if you just wanted to make a little." As one potter finally said to me at the end of a long day, "You can use this bowl for a *nöqk"íscaqapta, oyâ:pi, paqwíscaqapta;* you can use it as anything you want!"

Except for one vessel (no. 35), which had been used only as an *oyâ:pi* containing fruit, all of these pots were used as *nöqk"íscaqapta.* It is interesting to note that they all have polished interiors and inverted rims, and a capacity of between 2,500 and 3,000 cc, and that 12.5 percent of them are decorated and/or polished or, in one case, commercially glazed on the exterior.

Another group of vessels was likewise classed as *nöqk"íscaqapta* but could not serve as *paqwíscaqapta;* the reason given was always that they were too small, ranging between 1,500 and 2,416 cc capacity. Again there is no capacity overlap between these vessels and those that could function as *nöqk"íscaqapta, oyâ:pi,* or *paqwíscaqapta.* Moreover, only 50 percent of them had stone-polished interiors and only 62.5 percent had incurving rims; 75 percent were decorated.

When informants were asked to term these vessels, they first classified them simply as *caqápta.* When they were asked to be more specific, they called them *nöqk"íscaqapta* and/or *oyâ:pi.* Everyone who said they were *noqk"íscaqapta* readily said they could also be *oyâ:pi,* but some of the people felt that although they could be used as *nöqk"íscaqapta* they were too small and therefore were unlikely to be used as such. Only four of these vessels were seen in use; three of them contained stew. These same three containers were also used as serving bowls for wild spinach (*tí:mi*) but the other one was used only for fruit. These vessels, therefore, are not like the previous group (*nöqk"íscaqapta*) that can also be used as *oyâ:pi* or *paqwíscaqapta,* but are either *nöqk"íscaqapta* or *oyâ:pi* depending upon their use at the time. Thus, when informants were asked only to classify the vessels, they were termed according to shape as indicated by the height/rim diameter ratio.

Six vessels were termed *oyâ:pi* or, in the case of one potter, *óyoypi*. As mentioned, Hopis translated oyâ:pi as "serving bowl." However, the container morpheme *caqápta*, which can be glossed as "bowl," is not used; *oyâ:pi* is derived from a verb. Whorf (*in* Stephen 1936: 1204) and Voegelin and Voegelin (1957: 37) have glossed *ʔóya* as "it moves, places, transfers them." Whorf (1946: 176) considers *pi* as both a verb and noun suffix; it is a verb suffix for "verb-derived nouns of place and instrument" and a "quasilocative" noun suffix; however, "its locative sense is so weak that it can be used as a nominative or objective noun" (1953: 202).

As a verb nominalizer the suffix *pi* is also used with the verb *in*—to put into a receptacle or container (Whorf *in* Stephen 1936: 1264); containers termed *ʔín·pi* were only used for solids which Whorf glosses as a "receptacle, dish, pan, and jar."

Stephen notes the use of this term for a "meal jar" *nomán ʔinpi*[8] (1936: 1264). Voegelin and Voegelin (1957: 57) likewise gloss *ʔín·pi* as a dish or pan and also as "scoop shovel." None of the sample vessels was termed *ʔín·pi*, which was used for wicker containers qualified by their contents. These two terms are *pikín·pi*, the flat tray made from *sívi* (su:vi, Sumac, *Rhus trilobata;* Whiting 1939: 84) on which the piki bread was placed and carried to the house; and *sipálainpi*, a loop-handled basket which was also made from *sívi*. The basket was used to carry peaches (*sipála* = peach) while they were being picked and then to take them home. These two terms were also cited by B. Wright (1979: 60–61).

Owen (1911) records the use of *ʔóypi* in the term *"wutak'-uvaluoi'pi"*: this is a small coiled plaque on which mush is brought into the kiva for the Wuwuchim initiates (Wright 1979: 66). *ʔÓypi* is the expected form given the pattern established by *ʔín·pi;* one would anticipate this term as opposed to *oyâ:pi*.

The noun suffix *pi* is widely used for such vessels as *kíy·pi*[9] = water/liquid container; *nahíkiypi*[10] = medicine/liquid container; *kiyápi*[11] = dipper; and *sivákiyapi* = silver/metal dipper (bucket). The noun suffix *pi* is also used for *"kutukchaiyánpi"* (Wright 1979: 60–61) which is the basket that is used to remove parched corn (*kitíki*) from the fire.

This brief summary of container terms that have the suffix *pi* points to a critical difference from those, for example, termed *caqápta,* which are defined by shape, which then may be qualified by size or function or in the case of the duck bowls by shape. The *pi* suffix defines a vessel exclusively according to its function: *kíy·pi* is a water container, *ʔín:pi* a container for solids. Where the specific use is known, these containers transport either liquids or solids. Whorf glosses a *kíy·pi* as a water jar and states that it is the same thing as *ke:ysive* (*in* Stephen 1936: 1237). I suggest that even if the same vessel is a *kíysívi,* it becomes a *kíy·pi* only when it is used to transport water. Today this term is used for the cans that are taken to and from the spring and into which the water is siphoned. Likewise, Stephen[12] refers to *nahíkiypi* as a "crenellate ceremonial bowl." A better translation would be "medicine/water container," as when this bowl is not in use it is called a *nahícaqapta* = medicine bowl. In the former, the container morpheme indicates process, whereas the *caqápta* morpheme refers to shape. On four sides the rim of the bowl is shaped to form a four-step "pyramid" which represents clouds. If the rim below the crenellation is considered the height, these vessels follow the height/rim diameter ratio of the *caqápta* class. They are usually painted and may frequently have a loop handle.

A serving bowl to transfer food from a cooking vessel to the table and from which food is again transferred to individual plates is a modern innovation. Since this vessel is not used in the traditional manner it is not surprising that its use is emphasized, as opposed to its shape. The potter who made a number of these bowls for herself as well as for sale termed them *oyóypi*. The reduplication of the verb stem was needed, she explained, because "food is put in and out"; in other words, the transfer is repetitive. (That verbal initial reduplication may be used to indicate progressive aspect is in accord with Voegelin et al. 1979.) This same potter insisted that her vessels were not and could not be called *caqápta*. All other potters and non-potters alike agreed that the name depended on the function of the vessel. However, non-potters, before they learned the function of these bowls, had classified them as *caqápta*. Although these vessels are classified according to use, they form a quantitative, definable class. Their rim diameter is greater than that of other vessels of comparable height and they all have polished interiors. The capacity ranges between 233 and 1,875 cc; thus there is some overlap between this group and the vessels that can serve as *oyâ:pi* or *nöqk*ʷ*íscaqapta*.

Sí·vɨ

Like the term *caqápta*, *sí·vɨ* refers to a container or a specific shape; it is glossed as a pot by Kalectaca[13] (1978: 205). Whorf (*in* Stephen 1936: 1293)[14] glosses it as a hollow

object, receptacle, container, or can. Stephen (1936: 1182) notes that an undecorated cooking vessel as well as a "box, jar, almost any receptacle, is called *sibvu*"; he does, however, provide specific examples and illustrations of such containers. According to Stephen (1936: 1182),[15] and Voegelin and Voegelin (1957: 22), *soŋó:sivɨ* is the term for the oblong reed wedding-robe case (*soŋóko* = *reed*, *sí·vɨ* = container). Stephen also illustrates four containers that have the *sí·vɨ* container morpheme. These are "a honey jar" (Fig. 58), "wooden cones used by clowns" (Fig. 101), "water jar for snakes" (Fig. 340), and "ollas containing snakes" (Fig. 392). All are taller than their rim diameter.

That wall height is associated with the *sí·vɨ* container term is indicated by Voegelin and Voegelin (1957: 58), who have glossed the term *potásivɨ* (*pó:ta* = coiled plaque, flat basket, *sí·vɨ* = container) as a "basket shaped like a pot"; and the term glossed as a wicker (rabbitbrush?) plaque, flat basket, is *yɨŋʔápi*, which is a noun derived from the verb *yɨŋʔáplaw* (weave a basket) and the suffix *pi*. When the shape changes from a flat basket or wicker plaque to a deeper basket, although it may still remain "shallow," (ibid.) the container morpheme is *sí·vɨ*, thus *yɨnápsivɨ*. This basket may still remain shallow, presumably in relation to its diameter, which reflects the increased relative depth of the basket. The concept of relative depth may be seen in the diversity in the height/diameter ratio within this class (Fig. 27). In discriminant-function analysis, using height, rim diameter, height/rim ratio, and capacity as variables, the height/rim ratio was shown to be of primary importance. However, group membership, based on a sample of 23 *sí·vɨ*, was 72.7 percent in contrast to the *caqápta* which had a membership of 96.2 percent. The quantitative diversity within this class can also be seen in eight ceramic vessels which, according to Voth, were termed "*hisháto sivu* = old containers" (Wright 1979: 74–75). In contrast to the other vessels, three of these are approximately 8.0 cm high, with diameters approximately equal.

Two vessels (which have not been included in this sample because of lack of classification agreement) indicate perhaps another factor involved in the heterogeneous nature of the *sí·vɨ* class; these were termed *kɨtɨksivɨ* (*kɨtɨki* = parched corn) by the maker because that is what she used them for. They were 10.4 and 11.0 cm in height with a rim diameter of 12.7 and 12.2 cm respectively. The height/rim diameter ratios were therefore 0.8 and 0.9, within the upper limits of the *caqápta* class. They were in fact termed *caqápta* or *caqáphoya* by other potters and non-potters alike, but when ten Hopis were asked the term for this kind of vessel when it was used to contain parched corn, four called it *kɨtɨksivɨ*. The others insisted it was a *caqápta* or *caqáphoya* or said they didn't know. It appears then that in this case parched corn is kept in a *sí·vɨ* even if at times it fails to meet the general concept of the height/rim diameter ratio of the vessel. This situation may be analogous to the "jam jar" in English which frequently fails to have attributes commonly associated with a jar. This may also be the case with vessels termed "*hisháto sivu.*"

A greater diversity of rim shape as well as height/rim ratio is permitted in the *sí·vɨ* class. Although 39.2 percent of the *sí·vɨ* rims were straight, 34.8 percent were incurving and 26.0 percent were everted, which is permitted in this class, whereas

they do not occur in *caqápta*. Likewise, handles were found only on *homícacaphoya*, whereas 26.0 percent of the *sí·vɨ* had either handles or lugs. This attribute, although variable, is not considered critical by Hopis since none of these vessels was so qualified. When specifically asked about this attribute, I was told, "You can call it a *homísivɨ* but nobody does. We used to make more that way {with lugs} when we used them for cooking." Not including the *kɨtɨksivɨ* which have not been included in this sample, five vessels (nos. 62, 65, 124, 133, 155) were used or intended to be used for cooking or as food or water containers; all were undecorated. Two were used also to contain prayer sticks and feathers. These vessels were not, however, qualified according to use.

Like the *caqápta*, the *sí·vɨ* class was linguistically qualified according to size, the *sivɨhoya* being shorter. There is no overlap between this class, which ranges from 4.2 to 9.3 cm in height, and any other members of the *sí·vɨ* class; 80 percent of these vessels are decorated and polished on the exterior, and because of that, 60 percent were produced for sale. The remaining *sivɨhoya* were used as children's toys. In contrast, the two vessels termed *wɨ:kosivɨ* were intended for household use. One of these was termed by the daughter of the maker *lóloqinsivɨ* (*ló:qökna* = he married her; Voegelin and Voegelin 1957: 49). She explained, "This was how we have all used it—our hair was washed in it at our weddings." Nonetheless, she also stated it was a *wɨkosivɨ* (*wɨ:ko* = big). The other *wɨ:kosivɨ* was frequently termed a "storage jar" in English. It was not qualified further in Hopi.

The only *sí·vɨ* that were qualified according to their use, apart from the *kitíksivi*, were *poshímisivi* (*pó:si* = seed; *hí:mi* = she shells corn). One female non-potter called it a *poshímisivi*[16] but said it could also be called a *poshímsivi* because "It's the same thing." These jars were used to hold seeds given out by the Kachina dancers, later to be placed in the fields as an offering. Of the six containers in this study sample, two had a single central loop handle and the remainder had, or originally had, lids. Two of these, made by Terry, were topped by a Koyemsi effigy head; five were decorated and polished on the exterior. These vessels shared with the *sí·vi* class in general a variety of rim shapes. All were made from red clay.

Wikóro.

The last group of containers within this sample are *wikóro*. Voegelin and Voegelin (1957: 57) have glossed this term as "jar, bottle—as milk bottle." Whorf (*in* Stephen 1936: 1317) likewise calls it a "jug or bottle" or a "vase with a narrow neck." Stephen[17] (1023) calls it a "water bottle" or "decorated pilgrim bottle." Owen[18] (1911) uses this term for a gourd container which he calls a "canteen." Voth (Wright 1979: 77) states that the narrow-necked gourd vessels used by the priests were termed *moŋʷikoro*[19] (*moŋʷi* = priest), whereas Voegelin and Voegelin simply gloss it as "gourd" (21). (This is apparently a different gourd from the one termed *tawíya*, *Lagenaria vulgaris*, which is inedible and is used for rattles and Kachina masks.) These pots are probably ceramic versions of the gourd water containers that used to be carried as canteens. They are rounded, with one flat side, a short neck, and a loop handle on each side of the vessel. All but one, which was made either as a child's toy

or for sale, were treated with "piñon gum" (piñon sap) to render them water resistant. Even when not treated with sap there was never any question about their classification. The flat side goes against the body or the horse because "It's easier to carry that way." The rim diameter is small to accommodate a corncob cork and prevent spilling, and the loop handles hold the carrying strap. It is therefore primarily shape that defines this vessel class, specifically the constricted neck and rim in relation to the width and height of the body. Whorf recognizes this when he glosses *wikóro* as a "vase with a narrow neck." This is an important attribute for Hopi classification; four Hopis identified a bottle-shaped container as a *wikorsivi* (no. 107). According to them, this term was used "because it's tall but little on top." The vessel was 37.3 cm tall with a rim diameter of 4.3 cm; it was 7.7 cm higher than the maximum sample *wikóro* height and had a round globular body and flat base. The rim diameter, however, was within the *wikóro* range (3.1 to 4.7 cm). Thus by calling this vessel a *wikorsivi*, the Hopis were indeed defining its shape as a deep container (*sí·vi*) with a gourdlike restricted neck terminating in a narrow opening (*wikóro*). The height/rim ratio of this vessel was 8.7 whereas that of the average *wikóro* was 4.8. This one, like the entire *wikóro* class, had a straight rim. No Hopis stated that a narrow neck and rim were critical for class inclusion, but when that was pointed out they said, "These are for water," indicating that this rim shape was the most practical for pouring from or drinking from.

The *wikóro* class was qualified also according to size. The two *wikórohoya* vessels were 12.2 and 13.1 cm in height with rim diameters of 3.2 and 3.1 cm respectively. Vessel 73, however, was not only lower but narrower than the other, having a capacity of 187 cc as opposed to 363 cc (the vessel that was not treated with piñon sap). None of the sample *wikóro* was identified as large. When Hopis were asked about this they said (in reference to vessel 26), "You could not have a big one because it would be too heavy to carry. This is as big as you can make it" (this vessel was 29.0 cm in height, rim diameter 4.7 cm, and 617 cc capacity).

Except for Loren from Upper Moencopi, who made disks for sale, disks and pipes were made by Hopi potters only on request, for these are religious as opposed to household items. *Nahícaqapta* were also only made to order. During my stay on Third Mesa, Lucy was the only potter who was asked to make what I have termed disks. These were used as weights for the long string of prayer feathers attached to the back of the Long-Haired Kachina (*aŋáqcina*) masks. The term for them is *ʔátkahapiʔala*[20] (*ʔátkhaʔa* = down below, deep; *piʔála* = hip bone). This term therefore indicates the disk placement, regardless of material. Since these ceramics are not containers, and since stones, small sticks, ceramic miniatures, miniature rabbitbrush, and coil plaques may all be used for this purpose, it is not surprising that a container morpheme is not used. If *aŋáqcina* were the last Kachinas to leave the village prior to their return to the San Francisco Peaks, the *ʔátkahapiʔala* were removed by the dancers' "aunts" (either their fathers' or mothers' sisters) who had provided the food for the dancers' kiva before the public dance. These objects were occasionally kept, but were more commonly used as offerings. The disks

averaged 6.0 cm in diameter and were concave on one side and decorated on the other; both sides were polished. They had two suspension holes (0.3 cm diameter) approximately 1.0 cm from the top. The sole difference between those made by Lucy and by Loren was that some made by the latter for sale were larger (7.9 cm).

Pipes of the elbow type with *pá:qavi* (reed = *Arundo dono;* Whiting 1939: 64) stems were most common; they were commissioned by men for use in the kiva. All of them were termed *có:ŋo*.[21] Globular or rain cloud projections were commonly applied as handles because the pipes become hot and are uncomfortable to hold. Apart from the religious significance of the four-corner square pipe, there was no practical reason for this shape. According to the Hopis, except for religious occasions only a few old men smoke pipes, cigarettes having replaced pipes for social use. When the pipe is smoked in the kiva, it is referred to as a *ná:wanpi* (*ná:wakna* = he tries, tests, attempts to determine the future, concentrates mentally on a hope to bring it to pass through meditative prayer, prays for something, with place or instrument suffix *pi*).[22] Thus pipes, like the ceremonial bowls, are given different terms depending on their immediate use and on the changing emphasis from the pipe as object to its use in a religious act.

Pipes are the only ceramic production that the men are known to have participated in. Cindy's husband did everything but fire the pipe. Two other men molded the pipes "so they felt good," and the women carved the decoration and finished and fired them. Pipes varied considerably in wall thickness (1.0 to 2.5 cm) and total length (5.2 to 8.5 cm) which were dictated by handles and decoration.

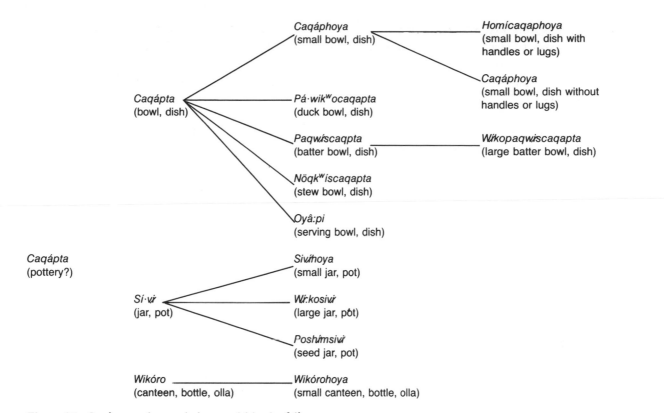

Figure 37. Study sample vessel classes within the folk taxonomy.

The height and interior bowl diameter were quite uniform, with an average of 5.2 and 2.0 cm, respectively.

The folk classes of the vessels in the study sample indicate a taxonomy as diagramed in Figure 37. Further research is needed to verify this taxonomy and to determine if, in fact, *caqápta* is a general term for "pottery" as well as the more specific reference to "dish or bowl."

FOLK CLASSIFICATION OF VESSEL PARTS

In defining areas of vessels, there was agreement that the rim was *móʔa* (mouth) and the vessel body the *póno* (stomach). As Hopis use the term *móʔa* it must be realized that it cannot be simply glossed as a rim but is reserved for rims of objects into which things are placed. Thus the rim of a disk is not called a *móʔa,* whereas the rim of a pipe is. *Póno* is also used for the excave, central section of an *ʔátkahapiʔala,* a dish used as a weight for Long-Haired Kachina hair feathers, even though it is not a container.

Unlike the terms for the rim and body of the vessel, terms for the base of a vessel were not agreed upon. Two potters told me that the term was $k^w ák^w spi$ ($k^w ák^w si$ = penis with locative suffix *pi*). In both cases I was not given the body reference in English, and it was told to me with great embarrassment. One potter even said, "Some people say *kíkri*, but that's not really the right word." In fact this term was given by two other Hopi women. One did not seem to know what I was asking, and I inadvertently used the term "bottom" which may have caused her use of *kíkri* (kíri

= buttocks; plural, *kíkri* = seat). I was unable to elicit a term for the base of a vessel from any Hopi men, who frequently claimed not to know it in Hopi.

As previously discussed, the term *hó:mi* was used for vessel handles, and pertained not only to *homícaqaphoya* but also to the loop handles and lugs on *sí·vi*.

NOTES

1. Chaka'pta.
2. Tasaka'fta.
3. Tcakafta.
4. Wuko'chkapta.
5. Chakap'hoya.
6. Tsaka'fthoya.
7. B. Wright (1979: 72) terms these vessels *nukwif'chakapta* or *nukwip'chakapta*. He also notes that on First Mesa they are termed *neki'chakapta*.
8. *Numa'ninpi* (Stephen 1936: 1264); *nöma'n'iñpi* (Whorf *in* Stephen 1936: 1264).
9. *Kü'yipi* (Stephen 1936: 1237); *ke'ypi* (Whorf *in* Stephen 1936: 1237).
10. *Na'küyipi* (Stephen 1936: 1257).
11. *Küya'pi* (Stephen 1936: 1237); *keyápi* (Whorf *in* Stephen, 1237).
12. *Na'küyipi* (Stephen 1936: 1021).

13. *Suvu.*
14. *Si've.*
15. *Shuno'sibvu* (Whorf *in* Stephen 1936: 1292, *sono'sive*).
16. Voegelin and Voegelin (1957: 20) gloss *póshimi* as "seed = belonging to a specified plant." In this instance the plants are not specified but all are cultivated.
17. *Wiko'zrü.*
18. *Wikuru.*
19. *Mongwikuru.*
20. *At'kyakabiadta* (Stephen 1936: 400).
21. *Chono* (Stephen 1936: 75, 968); *tso:no* (Whorf *in* Stephen 1936: 1210); *chongo* (Voth *in* B. Wright 1979: 56).
22. See Whorf *in* Stephen (1936: 1261).

APPENDIX III

DESIGN TYPE, COMPOSITIONAL SYMMETRY AND MOTIF USE IN RELATION TO VESSEL CLASS

In order to determine the relationship between Style A and Style B and vessel class, vessels in each folk class were examined. This sample only includes vessels that were identified by at least sixteen Hopis unless otherwise stated. Design type and compositional symmetry assigned to some of these designs, however, are my own analytical constructs generally in accord with common academic usage.

Caqápta

Vessels termed *caqápta* are, excepting two, painted only on the exterior. The only *caqápta* with painted decorations which were not linguistically qualified according to shape, size, or intended use were a bowl and an effigy vessel in the shape of a rabbit. The black-on-white rabbit effigy has a painted face and a band encircling the body. The black-on-red bowl (vessel 68) was decorated with a framed band around the body of the vessel. The rabbit bowl was given the term *caqápta* and not qualified because of its atypical shape. When qualified, the bowl was referred to as a *caqáphoya* (small bowl). A framed band encircling the exterior of the vessel was the type of design used on 77.8 percent of all *caqápta* except for duck bowls and ceremonial bowls. The beak and eyes as well as wing and tail feathers were painted in black on the duck bowls (Pl. 5).

Nahícaqapta (Ceremonial Bowls)

The exterior of the ceremonial bowls is decorated either with discrete or hanging discrete units. The rim is always in the shape of rain clouds motif 1b or g (Chapter 6, Fig. 18) on four sides, and, of the eleven seen in use, only one, which was at Hotevilla, is unpainted. The other ten vessels were painted on the exterior, but it appears that none had interior decoration. Five had a black band approximately 0.5 cm wide which encircled the bowl either on the rim or 1 to 2 cm below the flat portion of the rim. If below the rim, it did not follow the rim line but encircled the vessel. Motif 5, water, was used on one vessel instead of the plain black band; it encircled the top of the pot with scrolls extended down onto the body. Motif 4, a different form of rain clouds with lightning, was always painted on at least two sides of a ceremonial bowl as a discrete unit, occasionally as the sole decoration. Motifs 9, tadpole, and 10, corn plant (Chapter 6, Fig. 19) were frequently seen on two sides, as hanging discrete units within a semicircle where both ends were connected to a plain encircling band. Motif 9 was never seen as a single tadpole but as three tadpoles with their tails toward the base. Motif 10 was depicted growing upward from base to rim.

The undecorated vessel and two others were red, the remaining vessels whitish. The encircling band and motifs were painted in black. Two ceremonial bowls, one at Shongopavi and one at Hotevilla, were decorated with commercial ceramic paints. In one, yellow was used to fill in the semicircle in which there were three black tadpoles; in the second vessel the three rain clouds (motif 4) were painted in with blue, yellow, and red from left to right. The illustrative nature of these motifs as well as their actual composition lends to the discrete-unit design type.

Apart from the encircling black band, for which I was unable to obtain an identification, and the black semicircle enclosing motifs, no independent elements, design units, or Sikyatki Revival designs were used on these bowls. Only motifs are painted on ceremonial bowls, in accord with the ceremonial function of the vessel.

In contrast to *nahícaqapta,* only five *caqápta* intended for secular use were so decorated. These vessels used motifs, elements, design units, and Sikyatki Revival designs as well as motifs.

Miniatures

Three of the five *caqápta* decorated with discrete units were "miniatures" (see Fig. 38). Simple black bands, and occasionally bands to which were attached elements without change in their directional orientation (as seen in motif 5), are the type of design preferred on miniatures because of their small size. This is also probably why discrete units were used. In all three cases a discrete unit was placed on two sides. The fact that two (90, 198) of the four vessels with motifs were produced for sale clearly indicates that motifs were painted solely according to the potter's interest. The choice of a motif for vessel 90 (Fig. 10), the only miniature which is a jar rather than a bowl, may in part be due to the vessel's shape. Of particular interest here, however, is that again motifs are used as discrete units, but in contrast to the use of motifs on the ceremonial bowls, the primary motivation was to create a design within a small area.

Miniature vessel 141 was painted with a framed band by Loren and is similar to its larger counterpart, the small bowl illustrated in Plate 9d: like the latter and the miniature jar (vessel 90), there is a band below and following the rim. As the framed band is the dominant design, however, it has been so classified.

Caqáphoya (Small Bowls)

Of the twenty-one small bowls which were painted, simple black bands were placed approximately 0.5 cm below the rim on fifteen vessels. This form of banding constitutes the sole decoration on two vessels (M.N.A.—Museum of Northern Arizona—E200). Bands, to which were attached Sikyatki designs, were used to decorate a lozenge-shaped pot (Fig. 7: upper). This was the only vessel made in this shape that was seen on Third Mesa during the period of this research, and no other vessels were seen which used this form of triple banding. The framed band is in contrast to the unique design on this vessel.

Framed-band designs were used on 76.1 percent of the painted *caqáphoya.* These bands are strips of decoration encircling the

Folk Classification	Vessel #	Maker/ Decorator	Motifs	Design Type
Caqápta (not qualified)	68	Betty	—	Framed band—B, 1
Miniatures	60	Faith/Lucy	—	Band
	135	Terry	—	Band
	139	Loren	—	Band
	148	Lucy	#5	Band
	149	Lucy	#5	Band
	601	Faith/Lucy	—	Band
	602	Faith/Lucy	—	Band
	141	Loren	—	Framed band—B, 3^2, 4^2
	90	Cindy	#7, 11	Discrete unit
	136	Terry	#7	Discrete unit
	603	Faith/Lucy	—	Discrete unit
Caqáphoya	23	Lucy	—	Band
	M.N.A.E200	Amy	—	Band
	M.N.A.E200	Amy	—	Band
	11	Betty	#2, 5	Framed band—A, 1
	12	Betty	#1, 5	Framed band—A, 5
	30	Diana/Betty	—	Framed band—A, 1
	34	Diana/Betty	#7	Framed band—A, 1
	97	Terry	#5	Framed band—A, 1
	17	Lucy	#11	Framed band—B, 4
	20	Lucy	—	Framed band—B, 2
	28	Cindy	#1	Framed band—B, 2^3, 6^1
	31	Lucy	#1	Framed band—B, 2
	41	Lucy	—	Framed band—B, 2
	54	Cindy	#1	Framed band—B, 2^2, 4^2
	78	Terry	#1	Framed band—B, 1^2, 2^2
	85	Betty	—	Framed band—B, 1
	92	Terry	—	Framed band—B, 1
	142	Loren	—	Framed band—B, 2^4, 4^2, asymmetrical^2
	143	Loren	—	Framed band—B, 4
	P.M.249053	Lucy	#1	Framed band—B, 4
	P.M.248952	Terry	#1, 11	Discrete unit
Nöqk^{w}íscaqapta/ Paqwíscaqapta	80	Terry	#1	Framed band—B, 1
Nöqk^{w}íscaqapta/ Oyâ:pi	P.M.248946	Betty	#1	Framed band—A, 2
	32	Loren	—	Framed band—B, 2^6, 4^2
	35	Loren	—	Framed band—B, 2^6, 4^2
	29	Betty	#4, 7, 12	Hanging/discrete units
Oyâ:pi	91	Lucy	#1	Framed band—B, 1^2, 2^4, 4^2
	P.M.248945	Terry	#5, 9	Framed band—B, 4

Figure 38. Design type and symmetry in relation to motifs used and maker of exterior-painted *caqápta* excluding duck and rabbit bowls.

vessel and they have greater length than width. Motifs, elements, design units, and Sikyatki Revival designs are painted within the framing lines in a wide variety of compositions (see Pls. 8, 9; Figs. 5, 7, 13, 14). These compositions can be classified according to the symmetrical arrangement of the figures within the framed band (Shepard 1948, 1956; Washburn 1977).

Shepard (1948: 219–20) lists seven classes of one-dimensional infinite designs: (1) translation, also sometimes referred to as serial repetition because the design is repeated without change in directional orientation; (2) longitudinal or horizontal reflection along the central axis of the band; (3) vertical reflection along equally spaced transverse axes; (4) bifold rotation about a series of point axes; (5) intercepting horizontal and vertical reflection; (6) slide reflection in which the reflected parts are moved along the axis into the succeeding position; (7) vertical reflection and bifold rotation. It was found that all but class 7 were used by Third Mesa potters.

As many of these symmetries are not the same in different panels within the same framed band and some panels are asymmetrical, these framed bands cannot be considered to belong to a structural class in their entirety. In Figure 38, each vessel with painted exterior decoration within the *caqápta* folk class has been listed, along with the type of design. The framed bands, however, are followed by a class number. Vessels that have a series of panels with different symmetries are numbered by class and panel number.

One small bowl (Pl. 9b, vessel P.M. 248952), which was painted by Terry, has two discrete units. One consists of two birds; the other is a rain cloud. Once again discrete units are motifs.

Motifs were used on eleven *caqáphoya* (Fig. 38). Motif 1, rain clouds, was most common and is represented on seven vessels (Pl. 8a, c, d, and Pl. 9c). Motif 2 (rain cloud) is found on vessel 11 (Fig. 7: lower) as is motif 5 (water). Motif 5 is likewise used in connection with the motif 1 rain cloud on vessel 12 (Pl. 8a). The bird motif is found on vessel 167 (Fig. 5) and again in association with motif 1 (P.M. 248952). The use of motifs painted on small bowls (primarily produced for sale or barter) is in striking contrast to the ceremonial bowls. It is not simply that motifs are not used on some small bowls but that if used, they are commonly overshadowed by elements, design units, and/or Sikyatki designs. The only exceptions are the three vessels (11, 12, and P.M. 248952) on which two motifs are depicted. Elements, apart from band lines, are used on only one of these (Fig. 7: lower), and none of them uses design units or Sikyatki designs.

In conclusion, the framed band is the preferred type of design used on *caqáphoya,* probably because it lends itself to the *caqápta* shape. However, when more than one differently termed motif is used, either the design changes to that of discrete units or the motifs are surrounded by sufficient space so that they can be seen in isolation. As this is true for all *caqápta* with exterior decoration, motifs and design type or style are clearly interdependent.

Nöqk* w*íscaqapta (Stew Bowls)

The only *nöqk*w*íscaqapta,* that could be used as a *paqwíscaqapta,* was vessel 80 (Fig. 14: upper), painted with a framed band containing six panels. Within these panels motif 1f is translated along the base line and a triangular element is translated along the upper line.

Four *nöqkʷíscaqapta* or *oyâ:pi* were painted. Three of these were decorated with framed bands (vessels 32, 35, P.M. 248946).

Vessel 29 was painted with four discrete units. Three of these are hanging; one is design unit 1 (Fig. 20); the other two are motif 4a (rain clouds with lightning) and the same motif with the addition of prayer feathers and a single scroll (Fig. 8: lower). These motifs were referred to as "wet earth." The potter who made and decorated the vessel also gave this term to design unit 1; however, since this was commonly considered "just a design" by other Hopis, it has been so classified. The only discrete unit was of a Sun Kachina (motif 12). In view of the number of motifs on this vessel, it is not surprising that discrete units have been used either attached to or detached from the top framing band.

Oyâ:pi (Serving Bowls)

Two serving bowls were painted on the exterior; one of them (P.M. 248945) was also painted on the interior. Vessel 27 was painted only on the interior. Painting on the inside is no doubt preferred because these vessels are low (average height of all *oyâ:pi*, 6.2 cm) and wide (average rim diameter, 21.3 cm). Vessel 91, painted only on the exterior, has a framed band design (Fig. 9) consisting of two alternating groups of four panels (eight in all).

The only termed motif on this vessel (Fig. 9) is motif 1. In contrast, the serving bowls painted on the interior use two motifs. One of these (P.M. 24945) is also painted on the exterior: a framed band consisting of two bands along which scrolls are translated as in motif 5, water. As these bands move in opposite directions the scrolls are in bifold rotation. The area

between them, however, is so great that tadpoles are placed diagonally across the space.

This vessel also has interior decoration: the *hoysícvi* or Four Corners motif is painted in the center, surrounded by four tadpoles (Fig. 11: upper). The other *oyâ:pi* (Fig. 11: lower) has motifs 1 (rain clouds) and 7 (feathers) on the interior.

Sí·vi

In contrast to the *oyâ:pi* (a low bowl with a large rim diameter) is the *sí·vi*, the height of which is approximately 1.5 times greater than the rim diameter. This shape has clearly influenced decoration of the vessel in that designs are found only on the exterior where they are clearly visible, and shape may also have influenced the type of design. In contrast to the *caqápta* (excluding the duck bowls), of which 87.5 percent are decorated with either bands or framed bands, these design types are used only on 50 percent of the *sí·vi*. The remaining 50 percent are painted with designs which are either discrete or hanging discrete units (Fig. 39).

No jars are decorated solely with simple black bands; four had bands with attached elements, or Sikyatki designs and/or motifs, as the only decoration. Vessels 61 and 93 are *sivíhoya* (small jars). Sikyatki design o (Fig. 21) is attached to the rim band on vessel 61, and scrolls are attached to both the rim band and body band of vessel 93. Vessels 94 and 95 are *poshímsivi* (seed jars), and they have lids bearing Koyemsi head effigies. There are four bands or areas of band designs on the jars themselves. Vessel 94 bears two simple black bands, one below the rim and the other at the base of the neck. Just above the point of maximum circumference there is a

Folk Classification	Vessel #	Maker/ Decorator	Motifs	Design Types	Vessel Shape
Sí·vi	36	Terry	#5, 14, 16	Discrete units	Necked jar
	86	Terry	#5, 14, 15	Discrete units	Necked jar
	99	Terry	#5, 6	Discrete units	Necked jar
	200	Terry/Cindy	#1, 13	Band	Necked jar
	M.N.A.E6259	Terry	—	Framed band—B, 4, 3, 6	Necked jar
Sivíhoya	61	Faith/Lucy	—	Band	Globular pot with lugs
	87	Cindy	#7	Discrete units	Necked jar
	93	Terry	#5	Band	Pot with inverted rim
	96	Terry	#1, 7	Framed band—A, 1^2 asymmetric[2]	Pot with out-flaring rim
Poshímsivi	94	Terry	#5, 11	Band	Necked jar with lid
	95	Terry	#5	Band	Necked jar with lid
	98	Terry	#5, 7	Hanging discrete units	Loop-handled pot
	M.N.A.E6249	Betty	#1, 5, 10, 12	Hanging discrete units	Necked jar
	P.M.248951	Terry	#1, 4, 13	Discrete units	Loop-handled pot

Figure 39. Design type and symmetry of *sí·vi* in relation to shape motifs used, and maker.

hatched band. Along the baseline band four large scrolls are translated; they extend up the body to just below the point of maximum circumference. On vessel 95, in the same four positions as the bands on vessel 94, are two black bands. Scrolls are translated along the second black band in all four band areas.

The only other container with a design that is a band is vessel 200 (Pl. 7). Like vessel 94, it has a simple black band below the rim and at the base of the neck. On this jar the area between the bands is not polished, which creates a band different in color and tactile quality. Following the black band at the base of the neck is a band to which Long-Haired Kachina masks and a slightly modified version of Sikyatki design p have been attached and alternately translated. This vessel was made by Terry and decorated by Cindy (Pl. 7: left); Terry later added the commercial paint (right).

Framed bands are painted on two jars (96 and M.N.A. 6259). Vessel 96 is a *sivíhoya*,

a small neckless pot (height 6.8 cm) with a black band below the rim and a four-paneled framed band covering the body, beginning approximately 0.5 cm below the band. The other framed band is on a vessel commissioned by the Museum of Northern Arizona in 1973. According to Terry, "The Museum people came around and asked me to make a decorated piece for them in the spring . . . for the Hopi Show. I made them a water bottle the way they like." Evidently Terry decided the decoration the Museum wanted was in the "Nampeyo style"; it consists of two bands, one on the neck and the other adjacent on the upper body. The bands consist of "bat wings," which are bifold figures that rotate along horizontal axes and are in slide reflection along the vertical axes. Michael Stanislawski noted the unusual use of bat wings by a Third Mesa potter on the Museum of Northern Arizona acquisition card. He stated that the design "is commonly used by the Nampeyo family,

Garnet Pavatea, and others on First Mesa who resent its being used by others, especially those on Third Mesa."

Five jars were decorated with discrete units. Three of these are similar in that they have two or more black bands on the neck, and scrolls are translated along the band at the base of the neck so that they extend onto the vessel body. In addition, they all have bands with attached scrolls at the base of the body, with the scrolls extending upward.

Different motifs are shown on the bodies of these jars. On vessel 36 (Pl. 5: left) two Humpbacked Flute Players alternate with the Bear's Paw. On vessel 86 (Fig. 10: lower) Humpbacked Flute Players alternate with One-Horned Flute Players, and on vessel 99 there are four suns.

The other two vessels are dissimilar. One is a seed jar (P.M. 248951) and is less a jar than a loop-handled pot (Fig. 12: right). Rain clouds with lightning (motif 4c) are painted on both sides of the handle with the "rain" forming part of the rim bands at the handle. Below this band Long-Haired Kachinas as discrete units alternate with scrolls similar to Sikyatki design p (motif 1 rain clouds attached) which extend down from the lower rim band and become hanging discrete units.

The other vessel (87) has two bands on the neck, below which there are only two discrete units, as opposed to four, probably because of its size (height 6 cm).

Two *poshímsivi* are painted with hanging discrete units. Vessel 98 is a loop-handled pot approximately the same size and shape as vessel P.M. 248951. Vessel M.N.A. E6249 is a necked jar; this one was also commissioned by the Museum of Northern Arizona in 1973. The potter recalled the request and the difficulty she had: "I don't know what they wanted. Painting is so hard. Finally, I just made a *poshímsivi*." On the neck of this vessel there is a line forming three scrolls which are not attached to a band, nor is there a band below the rim. Joined to this line between the scrolls are three discrete ovoid units. Within one oval is motif 10 (the corn plant); the second is a design unit; in the last oval, motif 1 rain cloud is seen on one side and a scroll on the other. An undulating line also encircles the vessel at its greatest width. Attached to it are the Sun Kachina and two circles which are design units 2 and 3.

More *sí·vi* proportionately display motifs (85.7 percent) than do *caqápta* (55.2) or miniatures (36.4). Motifs were painted on all but two *sí·vi* (Fig. 39). Two or more motifs were painted on eight *sí·vi*; on six of these, discrete or hanging discrete units were used. When more than one motif is used, the design type chosen is likely to be that of discrete units, in accord with the *caqápta* data; 64.3 percent of the total number of vessels on which there were two or more motifs display the discrete or hanging discrete unit type of design. In contrast, only one band uses two motifs and, of the twenty-six framed bands, only four contain two or more motifs. Although nine of the twelve vessels decorated with either discrete or hanging discrete units use two or more motifs, six of these are by Terry, who is also responsible for 69.2 percent of the small *sí·vi* sample. Because this sample is so skewed by a single potter, it is difficult to determine the relative influence of function or shape on the choice of motifs used and on the design type. The intended or actual use of the *poshímsivi* may have influenced the use of motifs. These containers of seeds given by the Kachina are painted with two or more motifs and/or have lids in the form of a Koyimsi head.

The wide use of motifs on *sí·vi* could also be affected by the shape of the vessel. Of the fourteen decorated *sí·vi*, nine were necked jars. Shepard (1956: 261) notes, regarding a Greek amphora of similar shape, that the neck forms a separate design field from the body: "Ordinarily, realistic figures are not painted across an angle in the profile where they cannot be seen from one position without distortion." Motifs 6 and 11–16 could certainly be considered "realistic figures"; they are all used on jar bodies. Motif 11, as well as "the bird" itself, is found on a miniature jar (vessel 90, Fig. 10, upper, was commonly termed a miniature and is so classified). Motif 12, like motif 11, is depicted on both jars and *caqápta*. Motifs 6 and 14–16, however, are found only on the body of jars (36, 86, 99). Partly because of the use of these motifs, 60 percent of the jars (including the miniature) bear discrete or hanging discrete unit designs.

APPENDIX IV

INDIVIDUAL VARIATION IN DESIGN

Some potters produce more of one class of vessel than others do (Fig. 40). As will be discussed, the potter's decision to make a specific class of vessel is based on several factors. The painted vessels within the quantified sample, however, represent the degree to which different potters choose different vessel classes, although the sample does not reflect the number produced by different potters during the study period.

Different potters also use different organizational techniques in their framed bands and frequently in different panels within the same band. The different symmetry classes (see Appendix III) used have also been listed in Figure 40. When different panels use different symmetries the symmetry class number is followed by the number of panels within this class.

Added to the striking differences in motif and design use as well as in design structure and symmetry, is the variety in the width of line. Mean line width varies from the heavier line of Betty and Vera (0.15 cm), Terry (0.13 cm) and Amy (0.11 cm) to that of Loren (0.06 cm), Cindy (0.03 cm), and Lucy (0.03 cm). This variation reflects the fact that both Betty and Terry use either a commercial or a wide (0.4 cm) yucca brush. The narrow (0.05 cm) yucca brush is used by Loren, Lucy, and Cindy who only use a commercial brush to fill in a figure. Loren's line is consistently wider than Cindy's. This may indicate individual mechanical differences or that a wider brush is used. Cindy uses the same brushes as her mother Lucy. These two potters are therefore technically capable of creating the same line. This in fact occurs; however, using line width as a sole attribute, vessels painted by the two potters would be classed together and rated according to the care with which a pot was made. The lines painted by these potters range from a width of 0.06 cm to 0.02 cm. Among Third Mesa potters therefore, line width, angles, and the shape of elements are not individually distinctive, as suggested by Hill (1977).

	Vessels	Rim Band: on rim	Rim Band: below rim	Design Type: band	Design Type: framed band	discrete unit	hanging d.u.	Framed Band Group: A	Framed Band Group: B	Symmetry Class: 1	Symmetry Class: 2	Symmetry Class: 4	Symmetry Class: 5	$1^2, 2^2$	$2^{6/2}, 4^2$	$2^4, 4^2, 1/a$	$2^3, 6^1$	$3^2, 4^2$	Design Units	Sikyatki Designs	Motifs Used	2 Motifs or More Used
Terry	2 miniatures		1	1		1																1
	6 caqápta	1	6	0	5	1		1	4	3		1		1					2	1	3	2
	10 sí·vi	0	8	3	2	4	1	1	1	1		1		0					0	3	2	7
Total	18	1	15	4	7	6	1	2	5	4	0	2	0	1	0	0	0	0	2	4	6	9
Betty	0 miniatures																					
	8 caqápta		1		7		1	5	2	5	1		1						5		2	3
	1 sí·vi		0		0		1	0	0	0	0		0						1	1	0	1
Total	9	0	1	0	7	0	2	5	2	5	1	0	1	0	0	0	0	0	6	1	2	4
Loren	2 miniatures		1	1	1				1									1		1		
	4 caqápta	2	4	0	4				4			1			2	1	0		3	3		
	0 sí·vi	0	0	0	0				0		0				0	0		0	0	0		
Total	6	2	5	1	5	0	0	0	5	0	0	1	0	0	2	1	0	1	3	4	0	0
Lucy	6 miniatures		3	5		1														2	2	
	7 caqápta		6	1	6	0			6		3	2				1				6	4	
	1 sí·vi		1	1	0	0			0		0	0				0				1	0	
Total	14	0	10	7	6	1	0	0	6	0	3	2	0	0	0	1	0	0	0	9	6	0
Cindy	1 miniature		1			1																1
	2 caqápta		0		2	0			2						1					2	2	0
	2 sí·vi		2	1	0	1			0								1		1	2	1	1
Total	5	0	3	1	2	2	0	0	2	0	0	0	0	0	1	0	1	0	1	4	3	2
Amy	0 miniatures																					
	2 caqápta		2	2					2													
	0 sí·vi		0	0					0													
Total	2	0	2	2	0	0	0	0	2	0	0	0	0	0	0	0	0	0	0	0	0	0

Figure 40. Quantification of design type, symmetry, and use of motifs according to individual potters. (Duck bowls made by Amy and Vera and rabbit bowls made by Lucy are not included.)

Appendix V

QUANTIFIED VESSELS LISTED ACCORDING TO THEIR FOLK CLASSIFICATION

Vessel	Height (cm)	Rim Diameter (cm)	Height/ Rim Ratio	Capacity (cc)	Painted	Maker/ Decorator
			Caqápta (unqualified)			
50	7.8	15.5	.5	937		Vera
66	5.2	10.5	.5	312		Lucy
68	4.9	14.6	.3	500	*1	Betty
M.N.A.E1505	8.0	16.7	.5	2062		Elizabeth
			"Miniatures"			
60	4.7	8.0	.6	125	*1	Faith/Lucy
90	4.7	2.3	2.0	30	*1	Cindy
135	3.5	3.1	1.1	75	*1	Terry
136	3.5	5.3	.7	90	*1	Terry
139	3.5	2.3	1.5	30	*1	Loren
141	5.3	5.4	1.0	30	*1	Loren
148	3.0	4.0	.7	67	*1	Lucy
149	3.1	3.1	1.0	67	*1	Lucy
601	1.6	3.2	.5	5	*1	Faith/Lucy
602	2.0	3.6	.6	7	*1	Faith/Lucy
603	2.5	3.2	.8	7	*1	Faith/Lucy
			Pá·wik^wocaqapta			
67	3.3	6.6	.5	83	*	Diana
77	3.5	9.0	.4	125	*	Anne
P.M.248953	3.4	7.6	.5	60	*	Anne
P.M.248958	4.2	7.2	.6	62	*	Vera
			Caqáphoya			
11	7.0	16.2	.4	875	*1	Betty
12	7.0	10.5	.7	325	*1	Diana
17	5.8	7.0	.8		*1	Lucy
20	6.2	8.2	.8		*1	Lucy
23	10.0	6.4	1.6	625	*1	Lucy
28	4.9	10.5	.5	250	*1	Cindy
30	4.1	9.6	.4	187	*1	Diana/Betty
31	6.0	9.5	.6	250	*1	Lucy
34	6.5	8.4	.8	312	*1	Diana/Betty
41	5.0	11.3	1.1	219	*1	Lucy

*Vessels marked with an asterisk are painted.
1. For a listing of decorator, design class, and motifs used, see Fig. 38, Appendix III.
2. For a listing of decorator, design class, and motifs used, see Fig. 39, Appendix III.

Vessel	Height (cm)	Rim Diameter (cm)	Height/ Rim Ratio	Capacity (cc)	Painted	Maker/ Decorator
54	3.3	10.6	.4	166	*1	Cindy
72	7.0	10.0	.3	375		Anne
74	7.3	9.6	.7	375		Anne
78	7.0	10.3	.8	375	*1	Terry
85	8.2	12.7	.7	750	*1	Betty
92	6.9	8.8	.7	310	*1	Terry
97	6.3	7.4	.6	166	*1	Terry
142	5.7	13.2	.4	500	*1	Loren
143	6.6	12.6	.5	562	*1	Loren
M.N.A.E200	6.6	10.5	.6	375		Amy
M.N.A.E200	3.1	10.1	.3	83	*1	Amy
M.N.A.E200	4.4	9.7	.4	125	*1	Amy
M.N.A.E1072	8.0	9.1	.9	375		Anne
M.N.A.E1299	4.5	10.7	.4	250		Terry
M.N.A.E1300	4.8	13.4	.4	325		Terry
M.N.A.E8154	3.3	4.0	.8	875		Vera
P.M.248952	6.9	9.4	.7	312	*1	Terry
P.M.249053	6.5	5.8	1.1	219	*1	Lucy

Homícaqaphoya

Vessel	Height (cm)	Rim Diameter (cm)	Height/ Rim Ratio	Capacity (cc)	Painted	Maker/ Decorator
71	7.5	7.7	1.0	250		Anne
M.N.A.E4160	6.7	10.5	.6	375		Betty
P.M.248950	7.4	6.8	1.1	165		Anne

Paqwiscaqapta

Vessel	Height (cm)	Rim Diameter (cm)	Height/ Rim Ratio	Capacity (cc)	Painted	Maker/ Decorator
3	10.7	28.3	.4			Betty
4	10.7	25.8	.4			Betty
5	10.3	27.2	.4			Betty
13	14.5	26.5	.5	5125		Lucy
14	17.5	25.5	.7	5750		Lucy
15	15.0	27.0	.5	5250		Lucy
25	13.1	27.5	.5	6000		Vera
46	13.3	30.0	.4	6500		Vera
47	11.0	26.3	.4	3500		Vera
138	10.4	28.3	.4	4875		Betty
146	12.4	28.7	.4	5750		Betty
147	13.0	26.0	.5	5250		Betty
P.M.248949	13.5	26.0	.5	5625		Anne
P.M.248948	14.3	24.0	.6	4500		Anne
P.M.248947	10.0	26.0	.4	4166		Betty

Wi:kopaqwiscaqapta

Vessel	Height (cm)	Rim Diameter (cm)	Height/ Rim Ratio	Capacity (cc)	Painted	Maker/ Decorator
144	17.0	37.0	.5	14500		Anne

Nöqkʷíscaqapta

Vessel	Height (cm)	Rim Diameter (cm)	Height/ Rim Ratio	Capacity (cc)	Painted	Maker/ Decorator
6	8.7	24.8	.3			Betty
7	9.0	22.5	.4			Betty
8	10.4	22.3	.5			Betty
9	10.6	18.7	.6			Betty
10	9.5	19.8	.5			Betty
48	9.4	23.8	.4	2500		Vera
80	12.0	20.2	.6	3000	*1	Terry
150	7.7	25.0	.3	2675		Amy

Nögkʷíscaqapta or Oyâ:pi

Vessel	Height (cm)	Rim Diameter (cm)	Height/ Rim Ratio	Capacity (cc)	Painted	Maker/ Decorator
2	9.5	18.5	.5	1875		Betty
29	11.4	14.3	.8	1875	*1	Betty

APPENDIX V

Vessel	Height (cm)	Rim Diameter (cm)	Height/Rim Ratio	Capacity (cc)	Painted	Maker/Decorator
32	10.0	20.8	.5	2125	*1	Loren
35	9.2	19.8	.5	1500	*1	Loren
49	9.4	16.0	.6	1687		Vera
79	9.4	17.7	.5	1500		Anne
M.N.A.E3315	13.5	17.5	.8	2416		Vera
P.M.248946	9.9	17.4	.6	1625	*1	Betty

Oyâ:pi

Vessel	Height (cm)	Rim Diameter (cm)	Height/Rim Ratio	Capacity (cc)	Painted	Maker/Decorator
27	4.5	27.6	.2	1250	*	Lucy
57	7.4	20.7	.4	1875		Faith
58	7.0	20.3	.3	233		Faith
91	6.6	20.4	.3	1750	*1	Lucy
M.N.A.E3319	5.0	19.7	.2	686		Faith
P.M.248945	6.4	19.3	.3	1250	*1	Terry

Si·vi (unqualified)

Vessel	Height (cm)	Rim Diameter (cm)	Height/Rim Ratio	Capacity (cc)	Painted	Maker/Decorator
36	19.1	11.2	1.7	2375	*2	Terry
81	19.8	10.5	1.9	1500		Anne
86	20.0	13.6	1.5	2812	*2	Terry
99	18.8	11.6	1.6	2750	*2	Terry
200	32.0	11.5	2.8	1300	*2	Terry/Cindy
M.N.A.E6259	37.3	4.3	8.8		*2	Terry
M.N.A.E6387	14.5	16.7	.9	2750		Vera
P.M.248954	15.3	20.7	.7	2750		Lucy
P.M.248956	10.0	20.4	.5	1000		Vera
P.M.248960	10.2	13.1	.8	1250		Amy

Sivíhoya

Vessel	Height (cm)	Rim Diameter (cm)	Height/Rim Ratio	Capacity (cc)	Painted	Maker/Decorator
61	4.2	2.5	1.7	20	*2	Faith/Lucy
75	6.1	5.1	1.2	125		Anne
87	6.0	3.6	1.7	62	*2	Cindy
93	9.3	9.2	1.0	250	*2	Terry
96	6.8	3.7	1.9	62	*2	Terry

Wí:kosiví

Vessel	Height (cm)	Rim Diameter (cm)	Height/Rim Ratio	Capacity (cc)	Painted	Maker/Decorator
145	22.4	35.0	.6	16000		Anne
M.N.A.E3123	27.5	21.3	1.3	20250		Betty

Poshímsiví

Vessel	Height (cm)	Rim Diameter (cm)	Height/Rim Ratio	Capacity (cc)	Painted	Maker/Decorator
94	12.6	5.6	2.2	416	*2	Terry
95	10.5	5.2	2.0	116	*2	Terry
98	10.0	10.0	1.0	750	*2	Terry
M.N.A.E5788	12.3	8.3	1.5	250		Anne
M.N.A. 6248	15.3	5.2	2.9	500	*2	Betty
P.M.248951	10.2	10.0	1.0	687	*2	Terry

Wikóro (unqualified)

Vessel	Height (cm)	Rim Diameter (cm)	Height/Rim Ratio	Capacity (cc)	Painted	Maker/Decorator
M.N.A.E6199	22.0	4.4	5.0	3375		Vera
P.M.248957	29.0	4.7	6.2	7000		Vera

Wikórohoya

Vessel	Height (cm)	Rim Diameter (cm)	Height/Rim Ratio	Capacity (cc)	Painted	Maker/Decorator
63	13.1	3.1	4.2	363		Vera
73	12.2	3.2	3.8	187		Anne

*Vessels marked with an asterisk are painted.
1. For a listing of decorator, design class, and motifs used, see Fig. 38, Appendix III.
2. For a listing of decorator, design class, and motifs used, see Fig. 39, Appendix III.

APPENDIX V

GLOSSARY

Artifact. An object that has been altered or made in accord with the norms of a given culture.

Attribute. Any distinctive physical feature of an artifact or design.

Background. *See* ground.

Band design. A single line of decoration, to which elements may or may not be attached, that is longer than it is wide and encircles the vessel.

Composition. The arrangement of design parts within the design area or field.

Design area. The total surface of an object.

Design field. The specific area of the entire surface that has been selected and/or defined as an area for decoration.

Design symmetry. The symmetrical arrangement of figures of equivalent size as these parts move along a line axis and/or about a point axis.

Design unit design. A design within a small, specific section of the design area that is totally surrounded by the background of the vessel surface.

Discriminant-function analysis. An analysis of group membership based on metric attributes.

Element. A simple geometric form that is often combined with other elements to construct a design.

Figure. Whatever is painted, carved, etc., within the design field.

Figure-ground reversal. This occurs when the background appears to be the figure of the design and the decorated area looks like background.

Framed-band design. A strip of decoration longer than it is wide, confined within bands that encircle a vessel.

Ground. The background of the design field.

Hanging discrete unit design. A discrete unit design that is attached to a single band.

Motif. A design which is termed and in Hopi thinking is considered to be a representation of an object or a sign for an event, place, or group of people.

Negative figure. *See* figure-ground reversal.

Sign. An explicitly conventional association in which there is a one-to-one correlation, e.g., bear's paw = Bear Clan; white flag = surrender.

Structure. The spatial relationship of decorated to undecorated areas.

Style. The observed attributes that are culturally determined.

Symbol. An object, act, event, quality, or relationship which serves as a vehicle for a concept. The concept is the symbol's "meaning."

Symbolic. When concepts, attitudes, values, or beliefs are communicated through the use of symbols.

World view. A given group's view of the world around them, including their views of self and of the natural and social order.

HOPI CERAMIC TERMS

ʔátkahapiʔala. A weight, which may be a ceramic dish or miniature, at the end of the prayer feathers worn by the Long-Haired Kachina.

Awátpicöqa. Clay from Awatovi.

Caqápta. Bowl, dish; a container that is wider than tall. A general reference for "pottery"?

Caqáphoya. Small bowl or dish.

Có:ŋo. A pipe with a reed (*Arundo dono*) stem.

Cöqa. Clay.

Homí caqaphoya. Cup or bowl with handles or lugs.

Kíkri (Kʷákʷspi). Vessel base.

Kitíksivi. Parched corn jar.

Kiyápi. Dipper, spoon.

Lóloqinsivi. A container, a pot, or jar in which the bride and groom wash their hair.

Masícöqa. Gray clay.

Móˀa. Rim, mouth of vessel.

Nahícaqapta. (Sacred) medicine bowl, dish.

Nöqkʷíscaqapta. Corn and meat stew bowl.

Oyâ:pi (óyoypi). Serving bowl or low walled container.

Palácöqa. Yellowish clay from Third Mesa that fires a brownish-red.

Pá:wikʷocaqapta (pá:wikcaqapta). Bowl in the shape of a duck.

Paqwíscaqapta. Batter bowl, for mixing batter; also called a "piki bowl."

Póno. Stomach or body of vessel.

Poshímsivi (poshímisivi). Seed corn jar.

Qahíncaqapta. A technically excellent bowl, dish, or container that is wider than tall.

Qahínsivi. A technically excellent pot, jar, or container that is usually taller than wide.

Sikácöqa. Yellow clay from Howell Mesa that fires red.

Sí·vi. A pot, jar, or container that is usually taller than wide.

Sivíhoya. Small jar, pot.

Tí:ma. White clay which is used as a slip or paint.

Tí·mi. Beeweed (*Cleome serrulata*) which is mixed with hematite to make black paint.

Wikóro. Canteen, bottle, olla.

Wikórohoya. Small canteen, bottle, olla.

Wí:kocaqapta. Large bowl.

Wí:kopaqwiscaqapta. A large bowl, vessel for batter mixing.

Wí:kosivi. Large pot, jar, or olla.

References Cited

ADAMS, MARIE JEANNE
1973   Structural Aspects of a Village Art.
        American Anthropologist 75(1): 265–79.

AMSDEN, CHARLES A.
1936   *An Analysis of Hohokam Pottery Design.*
        Medallion Papers 23, Globe.

ARNHEIM, RUDOLF
1954   *Art and Visual Perception.* University of
(1969) California Press, Berkeley and Los Angeles.
        Paperback ed. 1969.

ARNOLD, DEAN E.
1983   Design Structure and Community
        Organization in Quinua, Peru, in *Structure
        and Cognition in Art,* Dorothy K.
        Washburn, ed. *New Direction in Archaeology
        Series,* Cambridge University Press,
        Cambridge.

BANCROFT, HUBERT HOWE
1889   *History of Arizona and New Mexico, 1530–
        1888.* The History Company, San
        Francisco.

BANDELIER, A. F.
1890;   *Final Report of the Investigation among the
1892   Indians of the Southwestern United States,
        Carried on mainly in the years from 1880 to
        1885. Papers of the Archaeological Institute of
        America. American Series,* vols. 3, 4; 1890,
        1892. Boston.

BINFORD, LEWIS R.
1962   Archaeology as Anthropology. *American
        Antiquity* 28: 217–25.

BOOK OF MORMON
1830   The Church of Jesus Christ of Latter-day
(1963) Saints, Salt Lake City.

BOURKE, JOHN G.
1884   *The Snake Dance of the Moquis of Arizona.*
        Sampson, Low, Marston, Searle and
        Rivington, London.

BRADFIELD, RICHARD MAITLAND
1973   *A Natural History of Associations: A Study in
        the Meaning of Community,* vol. 2.
        Duckworth, London.

BREUNIG, ROBERT G.
1978   Museum Interpretation, *Plateau* 50(4): 8–
        11.

BREW, JOHN OTIS
1949a   The History of Awatovi. *Peabody Museum of
        Archaeology and Ethnology, Papers* 36.
        Harvard University, Cambridge.

BREW, JOHN OTIS
1949b   The Excavation of Franciscan Awatovi.
        *Peabody Museum of Archaeology and Ethnology,
        Papers* 36. Harvard University, Cambridge.

BROOKS, JUANITA (ed.)
1944   Journal of Thales Haskell. *Utah State
        Historical Quarterly* 12(1–2). Salt Lake City.

BUNZEL, RUTH L.
1929   *The Pueblo Pottery: A Study of Creative
(1972) Imagination in Primitive Art.* Columbia
        University Press, New York. Reprinted by
        Dover, 1972.

CARLSON, VADA F.
1964   *No Turning Back,* by Polingaysi Qoyawayma
        (Elizabeth Q. White). University of New
        Mexico Press, Albuquerque.

CHAPMAN, KENNETH M.
1953   *The Pottery of Santo Domingo Pueblo.*
        Laboratory of Anthropology, Memoirs 1. Santa
        Fe.

CLEMMER, RICHARD O.
1978   *Continuities of Hopi Culture Change.* Acoma
        Books, Ramona, CA.

CLEMMER, RICHARD O.
1979   Hopi History, 1940–1974. In *Handbook of
        North American Indians* 9. Smithsonian
        Institution, Washington, D.C.

COLTON, HAROLD S.
1939   Primitive Pottery Firing Methods. *Museum Notes* 11(10): 63–66. Flagstaff.

COLTON, HAROLD S.
1947   Hopi Deities. *Plateau,* 20(1): 10–16.

COLTON, MARY-RUSSELL
1939   The Arts and Crafts of the Hopi Indians: Their Historic Background, Processes and Methods of Manufacture and the Work of the Museum for the Maintenance of Hopi Arts. *Museum Notes* 11(3). Museum of Northern Arizona, Flagstaff.

COUES, ELLIOTT
1900   *On the Trail of a Spanish Pioneer. The Diary and Itinerary of Francisco Garcés in His Travels through Sonora, Arizona, and California, 1775–1776.* Francis P. Harper, New York.

CONNELLY, JOHN C.
1979   Hopi Social Organization. *Handbook of North American Indians* 9: 539–53. Smithsonian Institution, Washington, D.C.

CONSTITUTION AND BY-LAWS OF THE HOPI TRIBE
1936   Dec. 19, 1936. Amendments I and II
(1969) attached August 1, 1969. Washington, D.C.

COURLANDER, HAROLD
1971   *The Fourth World of the Hopis.* Crown, New York.

COURLANDER, HAROLD
1982   *Hopi Voices: Recollections, Traditions, and Narratives of the Hopi Indians.* University of New Mexico Press, Albuquerque.

CRANE, LEO
1925   *Indians of the Enchanted Desert.* Little, Brown, Boston.

CUMMINGS, BYRON
1953   *First Inhabitants of Arizona and the Southwest.* Cummings Publications Council, Tucson.

CUSHING, FRANK HAMILTON
1920   *Zuni Breadstuff. Indian Notes and*
(1974) *Monographs,* vol. VIII. Museum of the American Indian, Heye Foundation, New York. Reprint ed. 1974.

CUSHING, FRANK HAMILTON
1922   Oraibi in 1883. In *Contributions to Hopi History. American Anthropologist* 24(3): 253–68.

CUSHING, FRANK HAMILTON
1923   Origin Myth from Oraibi. *Journal of American Folk-Lore* 36: 163–70.

DEETZ, JAMES D. F.
1965   *The Dynamics of Stylistic Change in Arikara Ceramics.* Illinois Studies in Anthropology, 4. University of Illinois Press, Urbana.

DOCKSTADER, FREDERICK J.
1979   Hopi History, 1850–1940. In *Handbook of North American Indians* 9. Smithsonian Institution, Washington, D.C.

DONALDSON, THOMAS
1893   *Moqui Pueblo Indians of Arizona, and Pueblo Indians of New Mexico, Extra Census Bulletin. Eleventh Census of the United States.* National Archives, Washington, D.C.

DORSEY, GEORGE A., AND HENRY R. VOTH
1901   *The Oraibi Soyal Ceremony.* Publication 55, *Anthropological Series* 3(1). Field Columbian Museum, Chicago.

DORSEY, GEORGE A., and HENRY R. VOTH
1902   The Mishongnovi Ceremonies of the Snake and Antelope Fraternities. Publication 66, *Anthropological Series* 3(3). Field Columbian Museum, Chicago.

DOZIER, EDWARD P.
1966   *Hano: A Tewa Community in Arizona.* Holt, Rinehart and Winston, New York.

EGGAN, FRED
1934   Letter from Fred Eggan to Commissioner Collier, Jan. 11, 1934.

EGGAN, FRED
1950   *Social Organization of the Western Pueblos.* University of Chicago Press, Chicago.

EGGAN, FRED
1979   H. R. Voth, Ethnologist. In *Hopi Material Culture,* Barton Wright ed. Northland Press, Flagstaff.

EMMONS, GLENN L.
1955   Letter from Commissioner Glenn L. Emmons to Fredrick M. Haverland, Area Director, December 1, 1955. National Archives, Washington, D.C.

FERNANDEZ, JAMES W.
1966   Principles of Opposition and Vitality in

Fang Aesthetics. *Journal of Aesthetics and Art Criticism* 25(1): 53–64.

FEWKES, JESSE WALTER
1894   Snake Ceremonials at Walpi. *Journal of American Ethnology and Archaeology* 4. Washington, D.C.

FEWKES, JESSE WALTER
1898   *Archaeological Expedition to Arizona in 1895. Seventeenth Annual Report of the Bureau of American Ethnology.* Washington, D.C.

FEWKES, JESSE WALTER
1919   Designs on Prehistoric Hopi Pottery. *Thirty-Third Annual Report of the Bureau of American Ethnology.* Washington, D.C.

FEWKES, JESSE WALTER
1922   Oraibi in 1890. In "Contributions to Hopi History," *American Anthropologist* 24(3): 268–83.

FEWKES, JESSE WALTER
1927   The Katcina Altars in Hopi Worship. *Annual Report of the Smithsonian Institution,* 1926: 469–86. Washington, D.C.

FORDE, DARYLL C.
1931   Hopi Agriculture and Land Ownership. *Journal of the Royal Anthropological Institute of Great Britain and Ireland* 61: 357–411. London.

GEERTZ, CLIFFORD
1958   Ethos, World-View and the Analysis of Sacred Symbols. *Antioch Review* 17(4): 421–37.

GEERTZ, CLIFFORD
1966   Religion as a Cultural System. In *Anthropological Approaches to the Study of Religion,* Michael Banton ed. *Association of Social Anthropologist's Monographs* 3. Praeger, New York.

GEERTZ, CLIFFORD
1973   *The Interpretation of Cultures.* Basic Books, New York.

GRAVES, M. W.
1982   Breaking Down Ceramic Variation: Testing Models of White Mountain Redware Design Style Development. *Journal of Anthropological Archaeology* 1: 305–54.

HACK, JOHN T.
1942   *The Changing Physical Environment of the Hopi Indians of Arizona. Peabody Museum of*

Archaeology and Ethnology, Papers 35(1), Harvard University, Cambridge.

HACKETT, CHARLES WILSON
1937   *Historical Documents Relating to New Mexico, Nueva Vizcaya, and Approaches Thereto, to 1773.* Carnegie Institution of Washington, Publication 330, vol. 3, Washington, D.C.

HAMMOND, ERNEST H.
1934   Letter from Ernest H. Hammond, Superintendent of Indian Schools in Charge, to Commissioner John Collier, Feb. 15, 1934. National Archives, Washington, D.C.

HAMMOND, GEORGE PETERS, AND AGAPITO REY
1953   *Don Juan de Oñate, Colonizer of New Mexico, 1595–1628.* Coronado Historical Series, vols. V, VI. University of New Mexico, Albuquerque.

HAMMOND, GEORGE, AND AGAPITO REY
1966   *The Discovery of New Mexico 1580–1594.* Coronado Cuarto Centennial Publications, 1549–1940, vol. III. University of New Mexico Press, Albuquerque.

HANSON, F. ALLAN
1983   From Form to Content in the Structural Study of Aesthetic Systems. In *Structure and Cognition in Art,* Dorothy K. Washburn ed. New Directions in Archaeology Series. Cambridge University Press, Cambridge.

HARLOW, FRANCIS H.
1970   History of Painted Tewa Pottery. In *The Pottery of San Ildefonso Pueblo.* School of American Research Monograph Series, no. 28, Santa Fe.

HARWOOD, THOMAS
1910   *History of New Mexico Spanish and English Missions of the Methodist Episcopal Church from 1850 to 1910,* vols. I, II. E. Abogado Press, Albuquerque.

HIEB, LOUIS A.
1972   The Hopi Ritual Clown: Life As It Should Not Be. Ph.D. dissertation in Anthropology, Princeton University, Princeton.

HIEB, LOUIS A.
1979   Hopi World View. In *Handbook of North*

American Indians 9. Smithsonian Institution, Washington, D.C.

HILL, JAMES N.
1966   A Prehistoric Community in Eastern Arizona. *Southwestern Journal of Anthropology* 22: 9–30.

HILL, JAMES N.
1977   Individual Variability in Ceramics and the Study of Prehistoric Social Organization. In *The Individual in Prehistory: Studies in Variability in Style in Prehistoric Technologies*, James N. Hill and Joel Gunn eds. Academic Press, New York.

HODDER, IAN
1982   *Symbols in Action: Ethnoarchaeological Studies of Material Culture. New Studies in Archaeology*. Cambridge University Press, Cambridge.

HOLE, FRANK
1984   Analysis of Structure and Design in Prehistoric Ceramics. *World Archaeology* 15(3): 326–347.

HOPI HEARINGS
1955   Hopi Hearings July 15–30, 1955. Conducted by a team appointed by Mr. Glenn L. Emmons, Commissioner of Indian Affairs and composed of Mr. Thomas M. Reid, Assistant Commissioner, and Program Officers Joe Jennings and Graham Holmes. Bureau of Indian Affairs, Phoenix Area Office, Phoenix.

HOPI TRIBAL COUNCIL
1971   Minutes for July 1 and 2.

INDIAN LAW RESOURCE CENTER
1979   *Report to the Kikmongwis and Other Traditional Hopi Leaders on Docket 196 and the Continuing Threat to Hopi Land and Sovereignty*. Washington, D.C.

JACKA, JERRY, AND SPENCER GILL
1976   *Pottery Treasures*. Graphic Arts Center, Portland, OR.

JAMES, HARRY C.
1974   *Pages from Hopi History*. University of Arizona Press, Tucson.

JOHN, ELIZABETH A. H.
1975   *Storms Brewed in Other Men's Worlds*. Texas A and M University Press, College Station.

JORGENSEN, JOSEPH G., and RICHARD O. CLEMMER
1978   Review Essay: America in the Indians' Past. *Journal of Ethnic Studies* 6(2).

KALECTACA, MILO
1978   *Lessons in Hopi*. University of Arizona Press, Tucson.

KAUFMAN, EDMUND GEORGE
1931   *The Development of the Missionary and Philanthropic Interest among the Mennonites of North America*. Publication Board of General Conference of Mennonite Church of North America. Berne, IN.

KEAM, THOMAS V.
1886   Letter from Thomas V. Keam to Commissioner J. D. C. Atkins, Feb. 11, 1886. National Archives, Washington, D.C.

KENNARD, EDWARD A.
1979   Hopi Economy and Subsistence. In *Handbook of North American Indians* 9: 554–62. Smithsonian Institution, Washington, D.C.

KENT, KATE P.
1983   Temporal Shifts in the Structure of Traditional Southwestern Textile Design. In *Structure and Cognition in Art,* Dorothy K. Washburn ed. New Directions in Archaeology Series, Cambridge University Press, Cambridge.

KIKMONGWI OF SHONGOPAVI, KIKMONGWI OF HOTEVILLA, et al.
1949   Letter from Talaftewa, Kikmongwi of Shongapavi, James Pongayawyma, Kikmongwi of Hotevilla, and others, to President Truman, March 28, 1949. National Archives, Washington, D.C.

LAIRD, DAVID W.
1977   *Hopi Bibliography: Comprehensive and Annotated*. University of Arizona Press, Tucson.

LA FARGE, OLIVER
1936   *Constitution and By-Laws of the Hopi Tribe*. Washington, D.C.

LAMBERT, MARJORIE F.
1966   *Pueblo Indian Pottery: Materials, Tools and Techniques*. Museum of New Mexico Press, PSP 5, Santa Fe.

LANGER, SUZANNE K.
1957   *Philosophy in a New Key.* Harvard University Press, Cambridge (3d ed.)

LÉVI-STRAUSS, CLAUDE
1963   *Structural Anthropology.* Basic Books, New York.

LEZAÚN, FRAY JUAN SANZ DE
1760   An Account of Lamentable Happenings in
(1937) New Mexico, and of Losses Experienced Daily in Affairs Spiritual and Temporal. In *Historical Documents Relating to New Mexico, Nueva Vizcaya, and Approaches Thereto, to 1773. Carnegie Institution of Washington, Publication* 330, vol. 3. Washington, D.C.

LITTLE, JAMES A. (ed.)
1881   *Jacob Hamblin: A Narrative of His Personal Experiences as a Frontiersman, Missionary to the Indians and Explorer.* Juvenile Instructor Office. Salt Lake City.

LOMAHAFTEWA, VIETS
1934   Letter from Viets Lomahaftewa, Kikmongwi of Shongopavi, to Commissioner J. Collier, March 4, 1934. National Archives, Washington, D.C.

LONGACRE, WILLIAM A.
1964   Sociological Implications of the Ceramic Analysis. In *Chapters in the Prehistory of Eastern Arizona* 11, by P. S. Martin, J. Rinoldo, W. Longacre, L. Freeman, J. Brown, R. Hevly, and M. E. Cooley. *Fieldiana: Anthropology* 55: 155–70.

LONGACRE, WILLIAM A.
1970   Archaeology as Anthropology: A Case Study. *University of Arizona Anthropological Paper* 17. Tucson.

MacNEISH, R. S., F. A. PETERSON, and K. A. FLANNERY
1970   *The Prehistory of the Tehuacan Valley* 3: *Ceramics.* University of Texas Press, Austin.

MALLORY, GARRICK
1894   *Picture-Writing of the American Indians. Tenth Annual Report of the Bureau of American Ethnology.* Washington, D.C.

MALOTKI, EKKEHART, and MICHAEL LOMATUWAY'MA
1984   *Hopi Coyote Tales—Istutuwutsi.* American Tribal Religions, vol. 9. University of Nebraska Press, Lincoln.

MATEER, WILLIAM R.
1879   Letter from William R. Mateer to the Commissioner of Indian Affairs, May 1, 1879. National Archives, Washington, D.C.

McKENNA, KATHERINE L.
1983   Art, Business and the American Road. In *Hopis, Tewas and the American Road.* Willard Walker and Lydia L. Wyckoff eds. Wesleyan University, Middletown, CT.

McNITT, FRANK
1962   *The Indian Traders.* University of Oklahoma Press, Norman.

MEANS, FLORENCE C.
1960   *Sunlight on the Hopi Mesas.* Judson Press, Philadelphia.

MERA, HENRY P.
1937   *The "Rain Bird": A Study in Pueblo Design.*
(1970) Laboratory of Anthropology Memoir 2. Santa Fe. Reprinted by Dover Publications, 1970.

MONTGOMERY, ROSS GORDON, WATSON SMITH, and JOHN OTIS BREW
1949   Franciscan Awatovi. *Peabody Museum of Archaeology and Ethnology, Papers* 36. Harvard University, Cambridge.

MUNN, NANCY D.
1966   Visual Categories: An Approach to the Study of Representational Systems. *American Anthropologist* 68: 936–50.

MUNN, NANCY D.
1973   The Spatial Presentation of Cosmic Order in Walbiri Iconography. In *Primitive Art and Society,* Anthony Forge ed. Oxford University Press, London.

MURIOTT, ALICE L.
1942   Further Studies in Design Element Terminology. *Clearing House for Southwestern Museums, Newsletter* 44.

NAGATA, SHUICHI
1970   *Modern Transformations of Moenkopi Pueblo.* University of Illinois Press, Urbana.

NEQUATEWA, EDMUND
1936   *Truth of a Hopi.* Northland Press, Flagstaff
(1967) *Museum of Northern Arizona Bulletin,* 8.

NEQUATEWA, EDMUND
1943   Nampeyo, Famous Hopi Pottery. *Plateau* 15(3): 40–42.

NOBLES, A.
1978   "A Preliminary Analysis of Firing
        Temperatures and Selected Paints and Slips
        of Historic Hopi Pottery," Senior Honors
        Thesis, Harvard University, Cambridge.

OLSEN, STANLEY J., and RICHARD PAGE
WHEELER
1978   *Bones from Awatovi, Northern Arizona.*
        Peabody Museum of Archaeology and Ethnology,
        Papers 70, 1, 2. Harvard University,
        Cambridge.

OWEN, CHARLES L.
1911   Hopi Artifact Collection Procured in 1900
        and 1911. Field Museum Archives, A–4,
        box 1, 1911. Chicago.

PARSONS, ELSIE CLEWS
1939   *Pueblo Indian Religion.* University of
        Chicago Press, Chicago.

PEREA, FRAY ESTEVAN DE
1633   Second Report of the Great Conversation
(1945) (Sequnda Relacion). In *Fray Alonso de
        Benavides' Revised Memorial of 1634,* tr. and
        ed. by Frederick Webb Hodge, George P.
        Hammond, and Agapito Rey. *Coronado
        Cuarto Centennial Publications, 1540–1940,*
        vol. IV, Appendix XXV: 216–21.
        University of New Mexico Press,
        Albuquerque.

POWELL, JOHN WESLEY
1895   *Canyons of the Colorado.* Flood and Vincent,
        Meadville, PA.

QUA' TÖQTI
1979   September 13, Kykotsmovi (Oraibi).

RAYNOLDS, FRANCES R.
1939   Preliminary Report on Second Design
        Questionnaire. *Clearing House for
        Southwestern Museums,* Newsletter 31.

RENFREW, A. COLIN
1983   Divided We Stand: Aspects of Archaeology
        and Information. *American Antiquity* 48(1):
        3–16.

ROBBINS, W. W., J. P. HARRINGTON, and
BARBARA FREIRE-MARRECO
1916   *Ethnobotany of the Tewa Indians. Bureau of
        American Ethnology, Bulletin* 55.
        Washington, D.C.

SABIN, EDWIN L.
1935   *Kit Carson Days, 1809–1868.* Press of the
        Pioneers, New York.

SCHLEGEL, ALICE
1977   Male and Female in Hopi Thought and
        Action. In *Sexual Stratification: A Cross-
        Cultural View.* Alice Schlegel ed. Columbia
        University Press, New York.

SHEPARD, ANNA O.
1948   *The Symmetry of Abstract Design, with Special
        Reference to Ceramic Decoration. Carnegie
        Institution of Washington, Publication* 574.
        Washington, D.C.

SHEPARD, ANNA O.
1956   *Ceramics for the Archaeologist. Carnegie
        Institution of Washington, Publication* 609.
        Washington, D.C.

SIGÜENZA Y GÓNGORA, DON CARLOS DE
1693   *Mercurio Velente: An Account of the First
(1932) Expedition of Don Diego de Vargas into New
        Mexico in 1692.* Tr. by Irving Albert
        Leonard. *Quivera Society Publications* 3, Los
        Angeles.

SIKORSKI, KATHRYN A.
1968   *Modern Hopi Pottery.* Utah State University,
        Monograph series 15(2).

SIMMONS, LEO W.
1942   *Sun Chief: The Autobiography of a Hopi
        Indian.* Yale University Press, New Haven.

SMITH, WATSON
1949   Mural Decorations of San Bernardo de
        Aguatubi. *Peabody Museum of Archaeology
        and Ethnology, Papers* 36. Harvard
        University, Cambridge.

SMITH, WATSON
1952   *Kiva Mural Decorations at Awatovi and
        Kawaika-a. Peabody Museum of Archaeology
        and Ethnology, Papers* 37. Harvard
        University, Cambridge.

SMITH, WATSON
1971   *Painted Ceramics of the Western Mound at
        Awatovi. Peabody Museum of Archaeology and
        Ethnology, Papers* 38. Harvard University,
        Cambridge.

SPICER, EDWARD H.
1962   *Cycles of Conquest.* University of Arizona
        Press, Tucson.

STANISLAWSKI, MICHAEL B.
1969a   The Ethno-archaeology of Hopi Pottery
        Making. *Plateau* 42: 21–33.

STANISLAWSKI, MICHAEL B.
1969b   What Good Is a Broken Pot? *Southwestern Lore* 35: 11–18.

STANISLAWSKI, MICHAEL B.
1973   Review of Archaeology as Anthropology: A Case Study. *American Antiquity* 38: 117–21.

STANISLAWSKI, MICHAEL B.
1978   If Pots Were Mortal. In *Explorations in Ethnoarchaeology*. Richard A. Gould ed. University of New Mexico Press, Albuquerque.

STEPHEN, ALEXANDER M.
1929   Hopi Tales. *Journal of American Folk-Lore* 42: 1–72.

STEPHEN, ALEXANDER M.
1936   *Hopi Journal.* Ed. by Elsie Clews Parsons. Columbia University Press, New York.

STEVENSON, JAMES
1883   *Illustrated Catalogue of the Collections Obtained from the Indians of New Mexico and Arizona. Second Annual Report of the Bureau of American Ethnology*, Smithsonian Institution, Washington, D.C.

THOMAS, A. B.
1932   *Forgotten Frontiers.* Norman, Oklahoma.

THOMPSON, LAURA
1950   *Culture in Crisis: A Study of the Hopi Indians.* Harper, New York.

TITIEV, MISCHA
1944   *Old Oraibi: A Study of the Hopi Indians of Third Mesa. Peabody Museum of Archaeology and Ethnology, Papers* 22(1). Harvard University, Cambridge

TITIEV, MISCHA
1972   *The Hopi Indians of Old Oraibi: Change and Continuity.* University of Michigan Press, Ann Arbor.

TRAUX, W. B.
1876   Letter from W. B. Traux to the Commissioner of Indian Affairs, Sept. 25, 1876. National Archives, Washington, D.C.

UDALL, LOUISE
1969   *Me and Mine: The Life Story of Helen Sekaquaptewa.* University of Arizona Press, Tucson.

UNITED STATES DEPARTMENT OF COMMERCE, BUREAU OF THE CENSUS
1980   Summary Tape File, Tract /SNA: ED: 7001–7006, 7008–7010, 7012–7015, 7024, 7030, 7031, 7868–7871.

VALVERDE, FRAY JOSE NARVARES
1732   Notes upon Moqui and Other Recent Ones
(1937) upon New Mexico (written at Senecu, Oct. 7, 1732). In *Historical Documents Relating to New Mexico, Nueva Vizcaya, and Approaches Thereto, to 1773. Carnegie Institution of Washington, Publication* 330, vol. 3, Washington, D.C.

VOEGELIN, CHARLES F., and FLORENCE M. VOEGELIN
1957   *Hopi Domains. International Journal of American Linguistics, Memoir 14. Indiana University Publications in Anthropology and Linguistics.* Baltimore.

VOEGELIN, C. F., F. M. VOEGELIN, and JEANNE LAVERNE MASAYESAVE
1979   Hopi Semantics. In *Handbook of North American Indians* 9. Smithsonian Institution, Washington, D.C.

VOICE
1986   July 29, New York.

VOTH, HENRY R.
1901   *The Oráibi Pawamu Ceremony.* Publication 61, *Anthropological Series* 3(2). Field Columbian Museum, Chicago.

VOTH, HENRY R.
1903a   *The Oráibi Summer Snake Ceremony.* Publication 83, *Anthropological Series* 3(4). Field Columbian Museum, Chicago.

VOTH, HENRY R.
1903b   *The Oráibi Oáqöl Ceremony.* Publication 84, *Anthropological Series* 6(1). Field Columbian Museum, Chicago.

VOTH, HENRY R.
1905   *Traditions of the Hopi,* Publication 96, *Anthropological Series* 8. Field Columbian Museum, Chicago.

VOTH, HENRY R.
1912   *The Oráibi Marau Ceremony.* Publication 156, *Anthropological Series* 11(1). Field Columbian Museum, Chicago.

VOTH, HENRY R.
1967   *The Henry R. Voth Collection at Grand Canyon, Arizona,* Byron Harvey III ed. From a catalogue prepared for the Fred Harvey Company in 1912. Arequipa Press, Phoenix.

WADE, EDWIN LEWIS
1976   The History of the Southwest Indian Art
        Market. Ph.D. dissertation in
        Anthropology, University of Washington.
        University Microfilms, Ann Arbor.

WADE, EDWIN L.
1980   The Thomas Keam Collection of Hopi
        Pottery: A New Typology. *American Indian
        Art Magazine* 5(3).

WADE, EDWIN L., and DAVID EVANS
1973   The Kachina Sash: A Native Model of the
        Hopi World. *Western Folklore* 32(1).

WADE, EDWIN L. and LEA S. McCHESNEY
1980   *America's Great Lost Expedition: The Thomas
        Keam Collection of Hopi Pottery from the Second
        Hemenway Expedition, 1890–1894.* The
        Heard Museum, Phoenix.

WADE, EDWIN L., and LEA S. McCHESNEY
1981   *Historic Hopi Ceramics.* Peabody Museum
        Press, Cambridge.

WALKER, WILLARD, and LYDIA L. WYCKOFF
1983   *Hopis, Tewas and the American Road.*
        Wesleyan University, Middletown, CT.

WALLIS, W. D.
1936   Folk Tales from Shumopovi, Second Mesa,
        Journal of American Folk-Lore, vol. 49: 1–
        68.

WASHBURN, DOROTHY KOSTER
1977   *A Symmetry Analysis of Upper Gila Area
        Ceramic Design. Peabody Museum of Archeology
        and Ethnology, Papers* 68, Harvard
        University, Cambridge.

WASHBURN, DOROTHY K.
1983   Toward a Theory of Structural Style in Art.
        In *Structure and Cognition in Art,* Dorothy
        K. Washburn ed. *New Directions in
        Archaeology Series,* Cambridge University
        Press, Cambridge.

WASHINGTON POST
1974   July 21, Washington, D.C.

WATERS, FRANK
1963   *Book of the Hopi.* Penguin Books, New
        York.

WHALLON, ROBERT, JR.
1968   Investigations of Late Prehistoric Social
        Organization in New York State. In *New
        Perspectives in Archaeology,* Sally R. Binford
        and Lewis R. Binford eds. Aldine,
        Chicago.

WHITELEY, PETER M.
1988   *Deliberate Acts: Changing Hopi Culture
        Through the Oraibi Split.* University of
        Arizona Press, Tucson.

WHITING, ALFRED F.
1939   Ethnobotany of the Hopi. *Museum of
        Northern Arizona Bulletin* 15, Flagstaff.
        Second printing.

WHORF, BENJAMIN LEE
1936   Notes on the "Glossary" in *Hopi Journal,*
        Elsie Clews Parsons ed. Columbia
        University Press, New York.

WINSHIP, GEORGE PARKER
1896   The Coronado Expedition, 1540–1542.
        *Fourteenth Annual Report of the Bureau of
        American Ethnology,* part II. Smithsonian
        Institution, Washington, D.C.

WOBST, H. MARTIN
1977   Stylistic Behavior and Information
        Exchange. In *For the Directors: Research
        Essays in Honor of James B. Griffin,* Charles
        E. Cleland ed. *Anthropological Papers,
        Museum of Anthropology* 61. University of
        Michigan, Ann Arbor.

WRIGHT, BARTON
1973   *Kachinas: A Hopi Artist's Documentary.*
        Northland Press, Flagstaff.

WRIGHT, BARTON
1979   *Hopi Material Culture.* Northland Press,
        Flagstaff.

WRIGHT, MARGARET NICKELSON
1972   *Hopi Silver: The History and Hallmarks of
        Hopi Silversmithing.* Northland Press,
        Flagstaff.

WYCKOFF, LYDIA L.
1983   The Sikyatki Revival. In *Hopis, Tewas and
        the American Road.* Wesleyan University,
        Middletown, CT.

YAVA, ALBERT
1982   *Big Falling Snow: A Tewa-Hopi Indian's Life
        and Times and the History and Traditions of
        His People.* University of New Mexico Press,
        Albuquerque.

YRAETA, FRAY
1742   Letter to the Commissary General from
(1937) Pasa del Rio del Norte, Nov. 24, 1742. In
        *Historical Documents Relating to New Mexico,
        Nueva Vizcaya, and Approaches Thereto, to
        1773. Carnegie Institution of Washington,
        Publication* 330, vol. 3. Washington, D.C.

INDEX

Aesthetic judgment, 115, 122–26. *See also* Spatial concepts
Agriculture. *See* Subsistence
Alcholism, 65
American Indian Defense Association, 55
Amsden, Charles A., 93
Anglo-Americans: Hopi attitudes toward, 1–3, 27, 29, 42; mentioned, 7–8, 11, 15, 18, 23–24; trade and, 38; view of Native Americans of, 49–50, 53. *See also* Bahana; Cash economy; Market control; Museum of Northern Arizona; Spatial concepts; Tourists; Tribal Council
Ant Kiva, 18, 19
Antelope Society. *See* Snake-Antelope ceremony
Area painted/unpainted, 99–101
Arnheim, Rudolf, 5
Arts and Crafts Movement, 71
Ashtrays, 87–88

Bahana, 18, 36, 46, 69n1, 144
Bands, 93–98, 174–80. *See also* Decoration; Design analysis; Figure-ground reversal; Sixfold paradigm; Symmetry
Banyacya, Thomas, 60–61
Bear Paw motif, 107, 179
Bird motif, 83–84, 106–107, 113n8, 176, 180. *See also* Rain Bird design
Birth, 21–22
Boas, Franz, 53; mentioned, 55
Bottles, 91. *See also Wikóro*
Bourke, John G., 38–39
Bowls, 86–90. *See also Caqápta;* Duck bowls; *Nahíćaqapta;* Piki bowls; Serving bowls; Small bowls; Stew bowls
Boxes, 87–88, 162
Boyden, John S., 59–63

Buffalo Dance, 15–16
Bunzel, Ruth L., 103–104, 106, 108–109; mentioned, 110
Bureau of Indian Affairs (B.I.A.): land management programs of, 58–59; mentioned, 3, 8, 40, 50, 65, 67–68, 116. *See also* Indian Claims Commission; Navajo-Hopi Act
Burial rites, 14
Butterfly Dance, 15–16, 47, 107, 113n8, 117

Caqáphoya. See Small bowls
Caqápta, 161–67, 173–77. *See also* Bowls
Cardinal directions, 12, 17. *See also* Six-directional altar; Sixfold paradigm
Carson, Kit (Christopher), 37
Cash economy, 28–29; opposing attitudes toward, 65–69; pottery and, 71. *See also* Education; Market control; Production levels; Tourism; Tribal Council
Catholicism. *See* Spanish/Mexican administration
Ceramic collections, 25n2. *See also* Keam Collection; Melville Collection; Museum of Northern Arizona; Museum of the American Indian; Peabody Museum (Cambridge, MA); School of American Research; Smithsonian Institution
Ceramic domain, 2, 6. *See also* World view
Ceramic manufacture, 151–58. *See also* Vessel construction
Ceremonial bowls. *See Nahíćaqapta; Nahíkiypi*
Ceremonial cycle, 12–17. *See also* Initiation
Church of Jesus Christ of Latter-Day Saints. *See* Mormons

Clans. *See* Kinship
Classification, 85, 87, 161–72; vessels quantified by, 183–85. *See also* Aesthetic judgment
Clay, sources, collection, and preparation of, 151–53
Clemmer, Richard O., 56, 60, 64
Cloud people. *See* Kachinas
Code of Religious Offenses, 41, 43
Coe, Michael, 1
Coffee mugs, 90. *See also* Cups
Cognitive archaeology, 6
Collier, John, 55–59; mentioned, 140
Colton, Harold S., 17
Colton, Mary-Russell, 71, 80
Corn Clan. *See* Kinship
Corn plant motif, 83, 105, 107, 173–74, 179
Correspondence, 20
Crane, Leo, 48, 50
Creation myth, 17–18, 27. *See also* Factionalism
Cummings, Byron, *First Inhabitants of Arizona and the Southwest,* 125
Cups, 164. *See also* Coffee mugs
Cushing, Frank Hamilton, 41

Daniel, Robert E. L., 48–50; mentioned, 82
Dawes Act (1887), 40–42; land allotment under, 44; mentioned, 28, 43
Decoration, 154–55, 173–80. *See also* Paints; Raised Decoration
Design analysis, 91–112, 173–80. *See also* Aesthetic judgment; Individual variation in design; Spatial concepts
Design elements. *See* Motifs
Design structure, 92–93, 145. *See also* Decoration
Design units, 109–111
Discrete unit designs, 93–98, 173–80. *See also* Sixfold paradigm

Disks, 170
Domestic wares, 85, 87–91, 161–71. *See also* Classification; Style A; Traditionalist potters
Donaldson, Thomas, 43
Dozier, Edward P., 23, 42, 82
Duality, 18–20; names of months and, 26n6. *See also* Spatial concepts
Duck bowls, 88–89, 162, 173

Economics. *See* Cash economy
Education, 4, 28–29, 40–44. *See also* Third Mesa; Voth, Henry R.
Eggan, Fred, 7–8, 21–22, 56
Environment, 9–10. *See also* Subsistence
Ethnography, of Hopi, 7–8

Factionalism, 3–4, 24, 27, 149–50. *See also* Cash economy; Indian Reorganization Act; Third Mesa; Tribal Council
Feather motif, 83, 106–107, 113n8, 177
Fewkes, Jessie Walter, 38, 78, 80
Figure-ground reversal, 100–102. *See also* Spatial concepts
Firing, 157–58
First Mesa: ceramics, 1; Third Mesa ceramics sold as products of, 121. *See also* Environment; Keam Collection; Market control; Production levels; Sikyatki Revival; Style B
Fleming, J. H., 40–41
Flute ceremony, 15
Folk classification. *See* Classification
Forde, Daryll C., 11–12
Four Corners motif, 105–108, 142, 177
Framed bands. *See* Bands
Franciscans, 29–31, 33
"Friendlies." *See* Education; Lololoma; Third Mesa

Geertz, Clifford, 2, 5, 20, 92
Glazes. *See* Smudging and sealing

Hack, John T., 8, 11
Hamblin, Jacob, 34–37
Harwood, Thomas, 35
Hieb, Louis A., 14
Hill, James N., 181
Holder, Ian, 145, 147
Hópi, concept of, 25

Hopi Constitution, 54; election on, 56–57. *See also* Tribal Council
Hopi Cultural Center, 67
Hopi-Navajo Joint Use Area, 4, 150; conflict in, 63; mentioned, 69
"Hostiles." *See* Dawes Act; Education; Third Mesa
Household structure, 22. *See also* Matrilocal residence
Hoysícvi motif. *See* Four Corners motif
Humpbacked Flute Player motif, 84, 106–107, 112n6, 179

Indian Claims Commission, 59–60. *See also* Navajo-Hopi Act
Indian Reorganization Act (1934), 55–59; mentioned, 66
Individual variation in design, 181–82
Initiation, 22. *See also* Ceremonial cycle

Jacka, Jerry, and Spencer Gill, *Pottery Treasures,* 124
Jars, 90–91. *See also Sí·vi*
Jeddito Black-on-Orange, 73. *See also* Keam Collection
Jeddito Black-on-Yellow, 73. *See also* Keam Collection
Jorgenson, Joseph G., 56

Kachinas, 14–15, 17, 20, 25, 26n7; ceramic motifs and cult of, 104, 107, 109; ceremonies, 11; dolls, 10, 71; on ceramics, 77–78; reciprocal duality and costumes of, 144; societies, 22. *See also* Disks; Long-Haired Kachina; Sun Kachina
Katchongva, Dan, 61–62
Kaufman, Edmund George, 44
Kayenta Polychrome, 73
Keam, Thomas, 7, 28, 38–41, 43; impact of, on Hopi ceramics, 72; mentioned, 66, 71, 76, 82, 87. *See also* Keam Collection
Keam Collection, 77–80, 84
Kennard, Edward A., 7
Keres, 31; ceramics of the, 75–76
Kiet Siel Polychrome, 73
Kinship, 20–22, 26n8; pottery-making and, 115–17. *See also* White, Elizabeth
Kiva, ground plan of, 16, 141–43
Kogyengwuti. *See* Spider Woman

La Farge, Oliver. *See* Hopi Constitution
Lakon, 15, 20; society, 22
Land: opposing views of, 8–9; ownership of, 28–29. *See also* Dawes Act; Indian Claims Commission; Navajo-Hopi Act; Tribal Council
Lavayihoya, 18
Lightning motif, 107. *See also* Rain cloud motif
Line, 98–99. *See also* Figure-ground reversal
Lololoma, 41, 43, 46
Lomahongyoma, 46–47
Long-Haired Kachina, 90; motif, 98, 105, 112n5, 178–79. *See also* Disks

McNitt, Frank, 41
Maltese Cross, 109
Marau, 15, 20; society, 22
Market control, 81–82. *See also* Cash economy; Museum of Northern Arizona; Production levels
Masaw, 9, 13, 17–18; mentioned, 44, 108
Material culture, Spanish influence on, 32. *See also* Ceramic domain; World view
Matrilocal residence, effect of cash economy on, 66. *See also* Household structure
Melville Collection, Wesleyan University (Middletown, CT), 111
Mennonites, 44–45; mentioned, 7, 35, 46–48, 57. *See also* Voth, Henry R.; White, Elizabeth
Mera, Henry P., 109
Methodists, mentioned, 35
Mexican administration. *See* Spanish/ Mexican administration
Mineral development. *See* Navajo; Tribal Council
Miniatures, 87–90, 161–62, 164, 174, 180
Mormons, 34–40, 70n2; mentioned, 5, 42, 59, 63, 66, 69
Morris, William. *See* Arts and Crafts Movement
Motifs: as symbols, 103–105; identification and use of, 105–109; listed, 105
Muingwa, 14, 17, 111
Munn, Nancy D., 145
Museum of Northern Arizona